New Movements in the Study
and Teaching of English

In the series

NEW MOVEMENTS IN THE STUDY
AND TEACHING OF GEOGRAPHY
edited by Norman Graves

NEW MOVEMENTS IN THE STUDY
AND TEACHING OF HISTORY
edited by Martin Ballard

New Movements
in the Study and
Teaching of English

Edited by NICHOLAS BAGNALL

Temple Smith · London

First published in Great Britain 1973 by
Maurice Temple Smith Ltd
37 Great Russell Street, London WC1

© Copyright 1973 George Allen, Roger K. Applebee,
W. H. Auden, Myra Barrs, Edward Blishen, Garth Boomer,
James Britton, Anthony Burgess, W. Emrys Evans, Su Felton,
Noël Hardy, Andrew Macalpine, Michael Marland, John Mole,
W. A. Murray, Albert Rowe, Lewis Stedman Jones,
Frank Whitehead, Ken Worpole

ISBN 8511 7044 7

Printed in Great Britain by
Billing & Sons Limited, Guildford and London

Contents

Introduction

Introduction

NICHOLAS BAGNALL

We have come a long way since the teacher of English saw himself most of the time as an evangelist casting out original sin, with the great classics as his texts and draconian marking schemes his penances. At least some of us have. There are still teachers (and examiners) who set essays on a pseudo-Baconian model, exercises in uncreative writing starting with a generalisation and ending with an aphorism. There are still some whose systems of marking are purely subtractive, as in show jumping. (A beautifully clear round – no, there's a spelling mistake in the last paragraph. Two faults. Now let's have another look at that scoreboard. . . .)

The numbers of such teachers are dwindling. This book is not about them. It is about – and, to a large extent, written by – their successors. It is not, in other words, a collective jeremiad against the wicked old ways – although that would have been easy enough – but an account of what's happening now. The first two chapters show how we got here; they are essential to an understanding of our present position. The now generally accepted proposition that, in English, 'all the subject-matter is ultimately personal' was, I suppose, always true even in the old, unregenerate days: those set essays one used to write were personal confessions to one's English teacher if they meant anything at all. (It was only later that they became literary excursions, taking one's vocabulary for an airing.) And of course the best prose and poetry was that which one had discovered for oneself.

Today, all this is openly recognised. We see the absurdity of what James Britton calls 'unproductive busywork' in grammar or gobbets. To say that literature (whether the pupil merely consumes it, or actually produces it) must be for real, is almost to commit a truism. The logical implications of this discovery are another matter.

Once you regard English as primarily a function of personal growth rather than as a skill subject, you are in a new dimension. Making it 'relevant' to the child does not mean showing him how to pick things out from the 'Sits Vac' column and to write a nice letter of application for that job in the counting-house; nor does it mean 'switching him on' or 'getting him going' by appealing to what you hope (though you can't be sure) is his personal emotion. It may mean these things, but it means much more besides. It means looking at the function of the school and beyond that to the streets about it. So many of the ends which people thought were neatly tied become open again. No apology is needed for the fact that four whole chapters of this book are devoted to what I have labelled (I trust not too pompously) 'Social Contexts', including one from Myra Barrs, one of the instigators of Commission 7 at the York conference of the National Association for the Teaching of English, where the deeper social implications of 'personal' English were for the first time officially noted, as it were. And inevitably the theme spills over into the other sections.

There are those who would still argue that making English relevant to the pupil, or central to his own concerns, is not necessarily the same as educating him or doing him good: they would say not merely that the aims of the school are different from those of the home, but that they damned well ought to be different. Middle-class English may be a foreign tongue (or 'a stepmother tongue', as Edward Blishen calls it) to many children, but they must learn to be bilingual. Bernard Miles on radio successfully translated the Acts of the Apostles into Bernardese, a cosy, straw-chewing lingo, but you can't do that with Shakespeare. So the argument goes. And what about the dactyl, the choriamb and the anapaest, without knowledge of which, says, Auden, no young poet should be allowed to learn his craft? What is the 'model', as Emrys Evans asks in his chapter, which a teacher should offer his or her pupils? What, to use the jargon, is his role? It used to be (perhaps inexcusably) that of the scholar; now it is more likely to be that of the artist, journalist, or social worker. Particularly the last named. 'Every teacher is a teacher of English' was the old platitude. Now perhaps we ought to be saying that a teacher of English is a teacher of everything. In either case the subject blurs at the edges.

I hope that this symposium may help to bring a bit of focus. But not a single view. On two points at least there would seem to be some sort of agreement. The first is that 'personal' English need not, and should not, put 'cultural inheritance' English beyond the reach of anyone who wants or requires it. The second is that the present examination syllabuses, concerned as they are even today with such a narrow band of language, so hopelessly lacking in moral or emotional effect, are not the means of ensuring this. Now read on.

Bird's-eye views

How we got here

JAMES BRITTON

I began my teaching career in a storm of controversy about the teaching of English grammar. It was not at that time a question of *whether* to teach it, but *how*. The mast my colours were nailed to was that of 'the reform of grammar teaching'. And certainly the enemy was a real one – the best-selling English textbooks were mines of unproductive busywork. No doubt my own zeal was sharpened by the fact that my department head when I began teaching presented me with a first-form syllabus that consisted of an unbroken chain of exercise numbers in Morgan's *Junior English Grammar*, with counterparts in other courses for other years. My role in the mystique was clearly that of acolyte, hers (the department head's) that of priest. Long after Morgan was dead, teachers used to write to him *via* his publishers asking him to settle a point of dispute that had arisen between colleagues. The schoolchild, I need not add, was cast in the role of *catechumenist*.

My first act of insurrection, then, was to write my own grammar book and go off, armed with it, to another job. *English on the Anvil* was published in 1934, and was an attempt to contribute to the work being done by Dr Percival Gurrey, who had been my tutor during my professional training year at London Day Training College (now the University of London Institute of Education). Dr Gurrey's, influence on the teaching of English over the years I am considering has been enormous and invariably modest. If the study of grammar does not occupy today the place he saw for it in the English curriculum, it is in large part because other concerns he indicated to us have overtaken it.

English on the Anvil was available, to those who knew how to go about it, until a couple of years ago: as far as I was concerned, ship, mast and brave colours had sunk, almost without trace, long before that.

Things had not vastly changed by the time we started the London Association for the Teaching of English in 1947, and we could always

---

From a grammar school English syllabus, 1934

A English grammar is included in this syllabus as a means to
an end. It is intended to lead to a skilful and effective use of the
English language, spoken and written. Emphasis is therefore laid
on the grammar of function and on exercises in the uses of the
various parts of speech....

B ....The aim therefore is to give the pupil as much liberty *as
he can take:* to secure his co-operation and his interest; to develop
in him as strong a self-discipline as possible; to encourage him to
take as full responsibility for his own progress and his own future
as he can.

---

bet on the teaching of grammar as a topic to draw an audience of
English teachers when all else failed. By then, however, it was as much
a matter of whether to teach it as how. Professor Gurrey, the founding
father of LATE, was one frequent contributor, and his friend and
colleague, Professor Firth, was another – later to be joined by Dr John
Trim (before he left for Cambridge) and (as they successively arrived
in London) Professors Randolph Quirk and Michael Halliday.

By 1955, when we had a day conference on the topic, we called
it 'The Ancient and Wearisome Controversy on Grammar' and Mr
Hugh Sykes Davis opened the batting. But other issues had by then
moved into the centre of focus.

Today, if I try (as I must) to make a map representing 'what goes on
in English lessons', I need to begin by distinguishing sharply between
using the mother tongue and *studying* it. And efforts, however strenuous
and thought provoking, directed at coping with an utterance (whether
to make one or respond to somebody else's) I should categorise as
use and not *study*. Having made the distinction I should want to claim
that the main stream of activity in English lessons will be using the
mother tongue – using it to achieve some purpose on the part of the
user.

In the second place, however, there must always be the possibility
of moving out from an utterance into an *ad hoc* study of some feature
or aspect of the utterance or its context. Such an *ad hoc* study might be
grammatical, but it might likewise be phonological, lexical, semantic,
rhetorical, stylistic, historical, psycho-linguistic or socio-linguistic –
and I must even so have left out several possibilities. I shall know when

I move from use to study because, ignoring the purpose of the utterance I have in hand, I shall have some linguistic hypothesis in mind together with its exemplar from the utterance, and I shall be looking for parallel instances in other utterances: these 'observations' I shall then try to organise in such a way as to draw some inference. I believe such studies do deepen our understanding of language and may, as a kind of spin-off, improve our ability to use it. However, exactly in what circumstances it pays to make *explicit* what is known implicitly is a matter on which psychological evidence is scanty and inconclusive. Let me add that I value, both as worthwhile activities and for a possible spin-off, the kind of *ad hoc* studies that have been produced by Halliday's 'Linguistics and English Teaching Project' under the title *Language in Use*.[1]

Thirdly, there must always be the possibility in favourable circumstances of developing an *ad hoc* study into a systematic study. It seems to me that a systematic study of some aspect of language is an interesting and valuable undertaking provided the students are capable themselves of carrying out analyses of abstract data and providing they spend enough time on the study to reach the point where 'a system' begins to emerge. (So often in the past such courses have been all harrowing and no harvest.) I would regard such a study as what the Americans call 'an elective' – an alternative perhaps to economics in the sixth form or biology in the fifth form: and while clearly it builds upon all that goes on in English lessons I do not see it as essentially or necessarily within the domain of subject English.

What is important is to recognise that a 'map' of English activities is of no value without an accompanying key representing priorities. There are teaching situations where, in my view, any *ad hoc* grammatical studies would be a form of Nero's fiddling. And we need above all to be clear about what we do when Rome is in flames.

It was in my first job, I remember, that I came to the solemn conclusion that, if teaching were not demonstrably very inefficient (less than thirty per cent efficient it had been claimed), I would never dare to face the responsibility of taking it up as a profession. And viewing the statement in the terms in which I saw it then, my self today would say 'amen'. But I see it differently now. I have shared in a movement towards a conception of *learning* that gives quite a different meaning to *teaching* – reduces it in fact to an ancillary of learning. And from

---

Extract from lesson notes for a 'Matric' form at my teaching practice school, 1929

Aim   To get the class to appreciate the best qualities of Keats' and Shelley's work, and to realise where those qualities lie in each case.

Presentation   Golden Treasury No 285, *A Lament*
Singing quality of Shelley's verse.
Let them read the poem silently first. Ask for the meaning of 'spontaneity'.
Why do you like it? Expresses a mood: How?
A lyric: *a snapshot* . . . . . . (etc., etc)...

Blackboard:

Shelley:	Lyrical power (Spontaneity)	Keats:	Descriptive power (word weaving)
	Snapshot		Tapestry
	Men and world of today		A dead world
			Melancholy
	Belief in truth and knowledge		Belief in beauty

Application
Read as test St. 3, *Ode to Autumn* (Golden Treasury No 275)
Keats or Shelley? (Hands up)

---

this perspective we can make our teaching as efficient as may be without taking responsibility off the shoulders of the learner.

The counter-movement, however, is probably stronger and better formulated today than it has ever been. Skinner's model of learning, derived from experiments with animals but applied to human beings, assigns to the teacher the full responsibility for deciding what is to be learned and how. I am as likely to hear a writer of 'behavioural objectives' asking the student as to which responses to which stimuli are to be reinforced as I am to hear Skinner asking a pigeon. I cannot accept this emaciated view of the educational process; a view that marks school learning off from all that goes on outside school – the pursuit of curiosity, the random discovery, even the regime of asking and telling, giving and taking, by which in daily life we profit from each other's knowledge and wisdom. It is logical that Skinner should say, 'The school of experience is no school at all, not because there is no learning but because there is no teaching'.[2] It is surely nevertheless nonsense to speak as though teaching could be thus disjoined from learning. Psychologists, it seems to me, have usually tended to define learning too narrowly, to make it a special kind of human behaviour, tied to predetermined ends, associated with habit formation, and so on. I would prefer to recognise a learning aspect in a great variety of forms of human behaviour.

In fact, in recent years another American psychologist, George Kelly, has elaborated a theory that does just that. His ideas are active in this country, though they have barely begun to make inroads where they are most needed – in psychology as a contribution to teacher education. George Kelly takes the scientist as his model for man, and sees learning in man as behaviour at its most typically human. Like the scientist, every man generates hypotheses from past experience, submits them to the test of actuality, and modifies his predictions in the light of what happens. All this is heady stuff as theoretical backing for what as teachers we have been learning from life; meanwhile, in practice, we need to model school learning upon the processes by which every helpless infant becomes a more-or-less self-reliant individual by the time he reaches school at all.

One part of that transformation, of course, is of particular interest to us as English teachers. Moreover, it is on the grounds of this achievement – the way an infant learns to speak – that Noam Chomsky has launched the most formidable attack of all upon the Skinnerian model. Chomsky regards language as 'relatively stimulus-free behaviour' and as such a mark of man's creativity. 'The child who learns a language', he says, 'has in some sense constructed the grammar for himself on the basis of his observation of sentences and non-sentences.'[3] And John Lyons comments, 'Chomsky's criticisms of behaviourism are undoubtedly valid. . . . There can be little doubt . . . that the behaviourist account of the acquisition of language, as formulated at present, fails to come to grips with, let alone solve, the problem posed by what Chomsky calls "creativity".'[4]

The work of Chomsky and other linguists in recent years has certainly given strong support to a conviction on the part of English teachers that a child's own language is a precious means to his learning. To see how far this conviction has grown in the past forty years – despite Skinner and despite the opinions voiced in the Black Papers – one has only to compare, say, the Plowden Report with an official document issued in 1929, the year I began my teaching practice. Having recognised that 'learning takes place through a continuous process of interaction between the learner and his environment' and that 'each new experience reorganises, however slightly, the structure of the mind and contributes to the child's world picture', the Plowden Report goes on to consider the role that talking plays in this interaction, and finds 'every justification for the conversation which is a characteristic feature of the contemporary primary school'.[5]

From the report of Mr John Trim's talk to LATE, 1953:

'First, the dialect-speaking child should not be made to feel that his speech, which was to him after all an inherent part of his personality, is inherently bad, and that he consequently is inferior to someone else whose speech is not dialectal....He should be taught, simply, that his kind of speech is that which Londoners use when talking ordinarily to each other. It is very good for this. We understand each other, and feel that we have something in common....

'Mr Trim concluded by asking if this all seemed somewhat idealistic. It certainly made great demands on the teacher. It required of him knowledge, systematic knowledge about spoken English....But by restricting the use of standard spoken English to those situations where it was required, it offered the possibility of avoiding inner and outer conflicts which must beset any child who undertook a fundamental revision of his speech in all aspects of life, cutting himself off from his past, and from his whole speech environment, the whole community in which he had had his being. In this way, by promoting bi-lingualism (or multi-lingualism, since we had as many forms of speech as we had different personal relations) we made standard spoken English acceptable to a generation which was no longer afraid of being called working class.'

The 1929 document (*General Report on the Teaching of English in London Elementary Schools*, published by HMSO) takes a very different view of language. It is based on the belief that 'the use of English . . . is a fine art, and must be taught as a fine art'. While the *Report* stresses the importance of developing in children 'the power to express themselves in speech and writing', the only assessment of work in spoken English carried out by the inspectors was in fact a test in 'recitation' and a test in reading aloud – from which we can draw few conclusions. It is in the comments on written work that the report really shows its hand. It makes a distinction here between 'the language of the home and the street' on the one hand, and 'the language the school is trying to secure' on the other: and it drives the point home by urging teachers to avoid setting young children subjects for writing which 'deliberately throw them into the atmosphere of their out of school life'. Instead, 'the child's exercises in writing English should be based upon what he read and hears in school'.

The two policies represented by these documents are of course both alive in schools today. There are plenty of teachers whose energies are directed towards harnessing in the new situation the power of the language the children already possess – so legitimising, confirming and extending learning processes already in existence. And there are plenty of other teachers who, as far as language is concerned, attempt something of a fresh start. A 'fresh start policy', though they do not realise it, will inevitably tend to cut off a child's principal means of entry into the new worlds that schools and teachers can offer.

There is one respect in which, from the thirties to the seventies, the whole perspective has changed. In the thirties – despite warning shots fired in 1926 by the Hadow Report – the grammar school was seen as a spearhead of social reform in education. It was the bright hope of the public sector, year by year eating away at the areas of privilege of the public schools, the private sector. It stood as it were alone in this democratic role, and all that seemed necessary was for more and more money to be devoted to providing such an education for children whose parents could not afford to pay for it. It was the 1944 Act that, in practice, crystallised the 'dual system' (never more than nominally tripartite). The 1944 Act spelled out the planned provision at secondary level of a lower-grade education for lower-grade examinees. Even so, it was not till Floud and Halsey, Jackson and Marsden, and others in

---

An LATE report reflects a view taken of literature and the sixth form in 1952:

'The study of literature gives the moral training once given by the classics to all, but which now only a few continue into the sixth form. Literature helps to define right and wrong, and relates them to real life. It offers an experience of life and of human nature to the inexperienced; to the boys and girls we expect to be the future leaders, but whose sheltered studies at school and university seldom include those rough experiences they will not only meet, but be expected to control when they go out to work.'

their wake, had demonstrated that the dual system, far from opening up new opportunities, was likely to have the effect of preserving the *status quo* in a (roughly) dual society, that the grammar school as democratic vision – if visions can do so – really turned sour. As in 1930 I looked for my first job in a state grammar school, so today I would look for it in a comprehensive school and for essentially the same reasons.

Reasons, too, no less fallible: something has certainly been achieved – the dual system has been recognised for what it is – but the problems indicated by Floud and Halsey, and Jackson and Marsden seem as far away as ever from solution. It is likely, as it has often been before, that English teachers will be the first to feel the increasing pressures, and the first who are constrained to look for alternative approaches: and this by reason of the kind of preoccupations they share with the children they teach – their concern, among other things, with the quality and configuration of everyday experience.

Another view of the grammar school, twenty years earlier.

From a prize day report, 1932:

' "Take a little boy," said Sir Percy Nunn, "put him in a test-tube, pour in a little algebra, a little French, a little handwork and so on, in the hope that the final product will be an educated man. It is a strange process, the chemistry of education, but it works." '

The membership list for LATE as it was first established looked, with a few exceptions, like a select gazetteer of London grammar schools. However, one of the first reports to be produced by a study group was on 'English in the Secondary Modern School', and by 1957 there was in existence a comprehensive school discussion group within LATE, holding regular meetings under the chairmanship of Guy Rogers, then headmaster of Walworth School. It represented a power-ful extension of LATE's activities and brought into its membership such people as John Dixon, whose book *Growth through English*,[6] written some ten years later, must surely be the most widely influential book on the topic we are considering to be written within the period I have under review.

The story continues with the vastly enlarged opportunities that came with the formation of NATE, the National Association for the

Teaching of English. As I remember it, it was a word dropped by Professor George Allen that sowed the first seed. Her Majesty's Inspector at the time, and chairman of the Secondary School Examinations Council's English panel, George Allen took the opportunity of a panel meeting to remark that it was high time English teachers got together to form a national association: one panel member present was Denys Thompson – whose editorship of *The Use of English* dated back at least into the forties.

To tell the whole story, LATE had several times been urged by groups of teachers in other parts of the country to set up a national association. Each time, after careful consideration, the committee had recommended that resources of time and energy were insufficient to allow them to take up the challenge. Each time they had, instead, encouraged the formation of a sister association and given what help they could to get it going. The first such group was the Forest ATE, formed in Essex in 1954; others followed in Fleet (Lancashire), and Leicester, and finally in 1962, in Bristol.

At all events, Denys Thompson called together representatives of LATE and the other ATE's, and of the 'Use of English Groups' that were by this time scattered about the country. They met, about twenty of them, on 4 April 1963, and as a result NATE was born, with Professor Boris Ford as its first chairman.

Some of the most original and valuable work NATE did in its early years concerned teaching in the primary school – the subject of its evidence to the Plowden Committee, and at the same time the object of a grant from the Calouste Gulbenkian Foundation, for the purposes of follow-up.[7] But my topic at the moment is the changing context of secondary school English – NATE and the growth of comprehensive education.

That English panel meeting of the SSEC was one of the last to be held; it heralded, and not by coincidence, both the death of that body and the birth of the Certificate of Secondary Education, and NATE's early years were considerably taken up in the general hum of activity that brought teachers out of their classrooms and administrators out of their offices to get the CSE Boards floated. NATE made its voice effectively heard, publishing scrutinies both of the blueprints and of the early achievements of the Boards, and turning some of its attention in a similar way to the GCE machinery. No doubt it was the course of events that determined this focus upon examinations; yet, as we realised when we began to exchange ideas with English teachers in

America, the role of public examinations in the secondary school system of this country is in subtle ways a key one.

Then came the Dartmouth Seminar, in the summer of 1966, and the transatlantic dialogue in our sphere began in earnest. Twenty representatives of English teaching in England were invited by NATE to meet a similar number of American representatives in New England and spend a strenuous month together. The whole affair was the brain-child of Dr James Squire, then Executive Secretary of the National Council of Teachers of English. The Americans were our hosts, thanks to a grant from the Carnegie Foundation, and NCTE were joined in their sponsorship by the Modern Language Association of America. Frank Whitehead, NATE chairman, led the British contingent. The following year, largely as a result of the efforts of Merron Chorny of Calgary (who had also attended the Dartmouth Seminar), a Canadian Council of Teachers of English was formed. Then in 1971 members of NCTE, MLA, NATE and CCTE met for a week's conference, 550 strong, at the University of York. Of the six 'commissions' planned for that conference, two were exclusively concerned with the secondary school and three more were concerned in part.

The transatlantic dialogue, highlighted by Dartmouth and York, has been an important source of new thinking about English teaching. We can look to America for the fruits of long experience of comprehensive education; from Britain we can contribute something of the dialectic of autonomous classrooms – disorganised often enough and sometimes ingenuous, but practical and comparatively free from dogma. Above all I think a ferment of ideas is likely to arise whenever diverse people experienced in widely different situations come together and discover common problems. (That is easy to say: but it takes genuine concern, commitment and sympathy to penetrate beyond alienating differences and find, from a common viewpoint, common problems.)

The dialogue at York, it appears to me, came to concentrate on two problems: that of 're-defining our subject *in the light of the needs of all children*'; and that of the relation between our conception of English teaching and the context – the educational system and beyond that the society – in which we tried to realise that conception.

Of the first it must be said that NATE had already amply demonstrated its commitment to the task. In 1968 it had organised, as a follow-up to Dartmouth, an Anglo–American seminar on 'The Language of

Failure'; forty teachers, inspectors and administrators from both sides of the Atlantic spent twelve days at Walsall studying the relation between language and failure in school. Patrick Creber's recent book, *Lost for Words*,[8] is an important outcome of that seminar. The controversy now raging as to what is meant by 'language deficit' and 'cultural deficit' and what implications lie here for the re-definition, not of English alone but of the whole educational process – this is a far cry from the debate about grammar teaching:[9] the walls are down and we're facing some real weather – I hope.

The second problem from York is intimately related to the first and turns out no more comfortably. But I must make my own way towards it.

We have, I believe, made some real progress in recent years in this business of re-defining our subject. A kind of consensus is beginning to emerge and ideas and experience and research findings have seemed to fall in place behind it. It grows out of a concern for what language is and the many purposes for which we use it. Clearly we use it, in the first place, for all sorts of practical purposes: to inform or instruct or persuade people, and likewise to get information, to acquire knowledge or expertise, to consider the arguments and blandishments that others offer us. And these 'practical' purposes are not always so practical – they evolve into what we should probably call 'intellectual purposes': thus we may use language in an attempt to explain things to ourselves – to draw inferences, to construct theories, to speculate. The practical and the intellectual purposes share what I might call a common structure, a common mode of organisation. Psychologists,

---

From a US participant in York 71:

'I have been looking for an over-riding structural principle for my English program. At the York Conference I was exposed to the British concept of "language" and the work being done to use growth and communication models and language theories to understand and organize the sequence and type of language experiences students have. It will now be possible for me to create beneficial and appropriate language environments and situations for my students, recognizing that the previously fragmented aspects of the English program are related by their common denominator — language.'

who have for generations been primarily interested in this kind of organisation, describe it as 'cognitive'. In using language in these ways, we take on responsibility for abiding by that organisation, obeying its rules. We take responsibility, for example, for the existence of the things we refer to in the real world, for the reasonableness of our generalisations, for the logic of our arguments.

But quite other rules seem to reflect quite a different kind of organisation when, let us say, we write (or read) poems, novels and plays. That these utterances are highly organised is something we feel certain about – in fact we might even feel that such writings primarily exist as an expression or experience *of order*. But it is a very difficult and perhaps impossible task at present, to describe by what principle the order is achieved.[10] Perhaps the clearest thing about such writings is that they are *not* practical, they are not concerned to keep the world's affairs on the move. In fact they reflect above all our involvement in *what is not going on now*. For this reason we might say that when we use language in this way we are using it 'in the role of *spectator*' – and when we use it to keep the world's affairs moving, we use it in the role of *participant*.[11]

Then again we very frequently use language in ways where there seem to be very few rules applying of either kind, and where the 'organisation' seems loose or undemanding. When we chat with other people simply to enjoy their company, or to satisfy an interest in what they have been doing, or for the pleasure of recalling shared experiences, or to let off steam about things that have annoyed us or gloat over things that have pleased us – gossip or chat of this kind seems free to follow the personal whims and fancies of those taking part in it and to lay very few responsibilities upon them as speakers.

Such language has been called 'expressive'. To say that it is comparatively free of rules is to suggest that it is not very different from the kind of language we might use silently in speaking to ourselves. I would see it as a kind of 'matrix', a starting-point from which the two other kinds develop. When the demands of a participant role – the need to get something done in the world – reach a certain point (and are met), I would call the resulting use of language *transactional*; where the demands are of the other kind – those of spectator role – I would call the use that satisfies those demands *poetic*.[12] (As you might suppose, expressive language, loosely structured, is free to move at will from participant role to spectator or *vice versa*: it straddles, as it were, that dividing line.)

As English teachers we have more and more come to see our responsibilities as focusing upon the spectrum of language usage from the expressive to the poetic – language, in other words, in the role of spectator. Yes, we still recognise the difference between what Shakespeare wrote and what will come from the pen of a fourteen-year-old – in fact we are learning a little about the *nature* of those differences, the nature of the organisation that gives Shakespeare's writing so much power as *an experience of order*. Yet we value the ordering process the fourteen-year-old achieves in his writing as of the same *kind*. It follows that we see as essentially similar processes, directed towards a similar end, his response to Shakespeare's words and his shaping of his own experience in his own words. He can go further when he has Shakespeare at his elbow. Both his writing and his response are educationally important because they are assimilative processes – they reflect an individual's concern for the unity, coherence and order of his accumulated representation of the world he has lived in.

Of course this reflects a great deal that we have known for a long time about the importance of literature in a child's education. But it reflects it in a new way, relating it directly to the child's own use of language upon his own experience.

At this point we rub our eyes and realise that the other half of the spectrum of language uses – from expressive to transactional – is primarily the concern of those teachers who already call upon its use in all the talking, reading and writing upon which the learning of their subjects relies. In fact, this conviction marked another milestone in the history of LATE. In a series of conferences and study groups beginning in 1966 LATE worked up to a conference in 1968 on 'Language across the curriculum'. The ideas of Douglas Barnes, who had been looking at the language of teacher/pupil exchanges in the classroom, and of the Schools Council Writing Research Unit, were important contributions, but a principal outcome took a very practical form – an attempt to persuade school staffs to get together and thrash out 'a language policy' for work in their school throughout the curriculum. All this, and the thinking that led up to it, will be found set out in Harold Rosen's contribution to *Language, the Learner and the School*.[13]

In 1971 NATE devoted its annual conference to 'Language across the Curriculum'[14] and was able to secure the co-operation of teachers of other subjects and make valuable links with other subject associations. And the Schools Council Project, 'Writing across the Curri-

culum, 11 to 13', set up that same year under Nancy Martin's direction, is actively exploring the implications of many of the ideas we have
touched on here – working with teachers in a variety of classroom
situations over a range of subjects and integrated programmes.[15]

Expressive speech, as we have seen, is the mode of language in
which we develop 'togetherness' – get to know people and enjoy
the company of those we know already. The expressive writing of
personal letters satisfies both writer and reader by using language
as though in each other's company, creating a virtual presence in absence.
But expressive speech and writing embrace other purposes too: it is
the form of language in which we 'first-draft' our tentative or specula-
tive ideas. In other words, it is an essential mode for *learning* – for the
tentative exploration of new areas of knowledge. And it serves this
purpose precisely because it is free from constraints and uninhibiting.
It bespeaks a relationship of mutual trust between the parties, and
it cannot function adequately where that relationship does not exist.
Thus, it is not to be had simply on demand – any more than an angry
call of 'Relax, will you!' can have the desired effect.

Of course, learning can take place wherever there is a motivated
learner and a teacher who knows. It has even been suggested that *conflict* between the two may be helpful to the learning.[16] But all that is
no model for education in the broad sense. As school teachers we are
concerned with processes far more complex and more fundamental
than, for example, what passes between a learner-driver and his
driving instructor. The achievement of a greater willingness to learn,
the achievement of a livelier curiosity – these are a part of the growth
we are trying to foster. Yet, as John Holt[17] and others have shown,
what comes through to the child is often the very reverse.

In general, teachers do not yet recognise the importance of language
to the learning they are trying to secure, and this being so they do not
allow sufficient opportunities for the use of expressive speech and
writing. Central to the kind of understanding we need to promote
among all teachers will be the recognition that young children need to
use language almost wholly within the expressive band if they are
to build firm foundations; and that thereafter there should be a constant returning to the expressive as exploratory stages on the way to a
confident and efficient use of transactional language – the language of
recording, reporting, arguing, theorising, speculating and any other
transaction required of scientists, geographers, historians and so on.
Then, having said that for all teachers, we need to add for the English

teacher that a similar relationship exists between the expressive and poetic ends of that spectrum. The expressive is the natural medium for talking or writing about our own experiences: its shaping, ordering effect will be sharper as it moves towards and into the poetic; and the expressive (both in spectator and participant roles) will be a principal means by which students will enter into and interpret the stories, poems and plays that they read.

Clearly, what we have been looking at at some length is no more than the formulation from a limited linguistic point of view of a massive truth about the nature of the teaching/learning relationship. We have learnt from bitter experience that there is in the long run no means of enforcing learning. We have come to recognise that the most precious means to a child's progress in learning is his own acknowledged responsibility for it: and, complementary to that, that we have no diviner's powers or rights by which we could so predict the society he will live in that we dare take on that responsibility ourselves. We have come to accept that learning in school should be an extension and intensification of out-of-school learning, and as a consequence we both seek to encourage students to learn from each other and recognise that we are constantly, as teachers, committed to reaping harvests we have not sown. And we know also that the kind of talk, writing and reading that best serves learning can flourish only in a situation of genuine trust.

(A massive 'truth', I have called it. Is it a truth? Is it a fallacy? What evidence am I offering? I can only, in the first place, state it as a growing conviction born of the experience of a growing number of teachers; and, in the second place, suggest that some of the evidence seems to

---

From the recommendations made at the final plenary session of the York Conference in 1971:

'We look for the opportunity to enquire further into such matters as the following:
    the full implications of the non-authoritarian teacher role we are committed to, and how it relates to methods of control, school organisation and the form of the curriculum;
    the re-defining of our subject in the light of the language needs of all children and their probable needs in a kind of society we cannot predict.

support these ways of looking. Finally, I suppose, we have to live with a conception of our task that can satisfy us.)

What came forcibly home to us at York in 1971 was the fact that *teachers are where these things are to be learned*: where the experience of failure has often enough prepared the way for a revaluation, and the experience of individual successes – indeed experience in general in close contact with the learners – has suggested lines along which a revaluation must be made. Heads and administrators, however, have not that advantage. As a result, the system in which teachers work grows less and less appropriate to what they are trying to do. It seemed clear to us at York that part of our efforts as associations must be directed towards influencing, not more teachers, but those who keep the educational system running.

Groups within the conference commissions were already concerned with such matters, but the conference's concern broke these bounds. As a result of action by individual members, the issue was raised for discussion in an open session, and following that a seventh unplanned commission was formed to devote itself wholly to the problem and its broader social implications. The work of 'Commission 7' goes on, and must do so. It may have a James Bondish ring to it, but there is nothing secret or sinister about it. It may run the danger of descending at times to pointless grumbling and destructive approaches. On the other hand I know we have allies at all levels of the system: and we shall need them.

One thing is quite clear: there is no going back. The generation gap, teddy boys, the teenage cult, hippydom, the pill, the drug scene, the welfare state, student protest and student participation, earth-shrinking, electronic aids, and pigeons who play table-tennis – good and ill, they have all happened, or are happening. Get down to where it is all taking place and you will know that there is absolutely no future in trying to go back to the educational manners and methods that worked forty years ago.

References

1 Doughty, Pearce and Thornton, *Language in Use*, Edward Arnold, 1971.
2 Quoted (without source) on the title page of R. Peters *et al.*, *Perspectives on Plowden*, Routledge, 1969.
3 Review by Noam Chomsky of *Verbal Behaviour*, by B. F. Skinner, *Language*, Vol. 35, January–March 1959, p. 57.
4 J. Lyons, *Chomsky*, Fontana Modern Masters Series, 1970, p. 85.
5 *Children and their Primary Schools* (Plowden Report), HMSO, 1967, pp. 521 and 535.
6 J. Dixon, *Growth through English*, OUP, 1967, was a direct outcome of the Dartmouth Seminar I refer to later.
7 The publication produced by NATE as part of this follow-up was *Children Using Language*, edited by A. Jones and J. Mulford, OUP, 1971.
8 J. W. P. Creber, *Lost for Words*, Penguin, 1972.
9 See in this connection H. Rosen, *Language and Class*, Falling Wall Press, 1972.
10 Susanne Langer is concerned to explore this alternative form of organisation to the cognitive. See her *Philosophical Sketches*, Mentor Books, 1962; and *Mind: An essay on Human Feeling*, Johns Hopkins Press, 1967.
11 For a fuller account see D. W. Harding, 'The role of the onlooker', *Scrutiny*, VI (3), 1937; and my *Language and Learning*, Penguin, 1972.
12 This description of language uses is drawn from the work of the Schools Council Writing Research Unit at the University of London Institute of Education, and I acknowledge my indebtedness to my colleagues in the unit, Miss Nancy Martin, Dr Harold Rosen and Messrs Tony Burgess, Dennis Griffiths, Alex McLeod and Bernard Newsome.
13 D. Barnes, J. Britton and H. Rosen, *Language, the learner and the school*, Penguin Books, revised edition, 1971. This also contains Douglas Barnes's contribution to the original conference.
14 For a full report see *English in Education*, vol. 5, no. 2, 1971. OUP for NATE.
15 Teachers are invited to write for further information to Writing Across the Curriculum Project, University of London Institute of Education, Malet Street, London WC1E 7HS.
16 See Blanche Geer, 'Teaching', *School and Society*, Open University Reader, Routledge, 1971.
17 J. Holt, *How Children Fail*, Penguin, 1969.

2 English past, present and future

GEORGE ALLEN

As recently as 1960 English as a school subject was in a state of suspended animation which had hardly changed over forty years. The trouble was not lack of good example; some schools were outstanding, ahead of their time in English and much else; many reached a decent average. And yet English remained what it always had been, a very odd kind of subject anyhow.

In practice it embraced two main areas somewhat uneasily, the communication arts or skills on the one hand, and literature on the other. The tradition also included a great deal of language study, usually rather obsolete in form and discontinued just at the stage when many pupils might have been ready to begin a serious study of language; until very recently any serious study of the spoken word was excluded. All this probably reflects the slow evolution of English as a respectable academic subject along lines described by Stephen Potter in *The Muse in Chains*.[1] There were perpetual analogies with Latin, a language no longer spoken; and within the universities English acquired a semi-classical, semi-respectability through the study of Old and Middle English. Many graduate teachers of English entered their first schools well versed in West Midland dialect forms or Chaucer's way with strong preterites, yet almost ignorant of the living language. No wonder that much of what was studied in English was seldom applied; what else could one expect of a subject so treated?

If there were wide areas of English which specialist teachers did not know, we should not forget that much English, often most, was and often still is taught by teachers whose own specialist studies lay elsewhere; all too often they knew very little about English generally.[2] One cannot teach English in the light of nature, without any awareness of what English teaching means. Of course we all speak English: but if George Sampson's memorable phrase 'Every teacher is a teacher of English' is allowed to mean in practice that 'Anyone can teach English whether or not he has any real idea of what is needed' the result is bound to be disappointing. Nor were the lacks, gaps and lags even recognised; in spite of steady prodding from a surprising number of individuals such things were regarded as normal by most people in this best of all possible worlds. The whole problem is still very much with us; what makes it much harder to solve is that so little has been done to equip or help either specialist or non-specialist teachers of English, whether in the initial stages of their professional education or subsequently; in-service training until recently was provided on a very small scale. Add to this the general lack of resources: how many schools today possess or may look forward to eventually enjoying an English workshop? For that matter, how many schools are adequately supplied with books and other teaching material? Traditionally each economy wave has meant cutting down on the book supply. All too often the English teacher has been left without adequate professional briefing to function as best he could with tatty and obsolete material in a room unsuited for the job – and not least in schools which have quite new buildings.[3]

One consequence of this haphazard and amateur situation has been a profuse supply of course books, designed by publishers to provide courses for non-specialist teachers. A school would choose one or more of these books, which had the merit of keeping the pupils occupied, and follow it through successive parts for several years. Very often such books led towards an examination upon which much depended. David Shayer[4] traces very skilfully the proliferation of these books in recent times. They varied in quality and some included good material. None the less, such books tended to perpetuate traditional and curiously abstract unapplied patterns of language study, and they combined with the examination to produce a singularly formal, even penal, approach hardly conducive to real communication: 'candidates are warned that Marks will be deducted for bad handwriting, spelling or punctuation'. Small wonder that many a pupil, whether gifted or not, found little in English to interest him and too often emerged with his reading 'done' for life; one 'did Eng Lang' or 'Eng Lit' at fifteen or sixteen and then gratefully dropped it. After that the subject virtually disappeared for most sixth formers, except for the English specialists; their progress and problems have been skilfully charted by Frances Stevens[5] who shows very clearly what many university teachers have suspected, that the influence of advanced levels upon many pupils is often by no means good. As for those who had dropped English to specialise in history, modern languages and so on, they were all usually too preoccupied with subject content to have much time for the quality of written expression. So it just languished: critic after critic, report after report lamented the poor standards achieved. Soon after the Crowther Report,[6] which more than once deplored the state of English, a spate of correspondence swelled the clamour for reform.

What happens when curriculum and teaching are clearly showing signs of strain? In these circumstances the English usually think of yet another examination, hoping to treat the symptoms even if the disease is incurable. So in came an examination called 'Use of English' (a title possibly cribbed from the outstanding journal of that name for long edited by Denys Thompson and now by Frank Whitehead) which was apparently designed to compel the candidates to take a little trouble over their written English. Whether this produced results or helped the schools is a matter of opinion. To me at the time it seemed a trivial last straw. In no other country do examinations bulk so large or so often dictate the teaching syllabus. And so much depends on them; I do not say that examinations generally, or these examinations in particular, are necessarily or entirely evil and there is something to be said for this comment by James Squire and Roger Applebee:

But it is also possible that much of the freedom allowed to earlier forms may be due to the system of external examinations. Society will always demand some assurance of quality in education. In America this assurance is attempted, perhaps hopelessly, through the creation of detailed, sequential courses of study which tell the teacher what and sometimes even how to teach. In the United Kingdom, teachers are free to plan any instruction they choose in the lower forms, providing only that students secure a sufficiently large number of passes on the O and A level exams.[7]

Nevertheless, in their present form examinations bulk too large and sometimes seem to be vitiating motive and obstructing progress.

Somewhere about 1960 the subject appeared to touch rock bottom. This was not for lack of effort, good teaching or pungent criticism over many years, and indeed the Ministry of Education's 1954 pamphlet on *Language*[8] considered that: 'Probably a slow general improvement is taking place the whole time; but this is scarcely perceptible in one teacher's lifetime and the improvement would be difficult to demonstrate conclusively to a sceptic.' For this state of affairs there could be several reasons: one reason has been the lack of effective means for disseminating good ideas and practice on a sufficiently large scale, so that the exception might by degrees modify and even inspire everyday routine elsewhere. Only examinations appeared to qualify for official attention from such bodies as the Secondary School Examinations Council; when asked about the curriculum the Ministry of Education (as it still was) replied blandly that the curriculum was free, overlooking the point that a nominally free curriculum can starve for lack of nourishment. As William Blake (who, fortunately for us, did not go to school) wrote before he was fourteen:

> The languid strings do scarcely move!
> The sound is forc'd, the notes are few!

But somewhere about the year 1960 something began to stir; or, rather, what had long been stirring began to gather momentum. I have already noted the Crowther Report. In 1963 the Newsom Report considered the unacademic half of our children and had much to say about the weakness of so much English teaching in the unselective schools. The year 1961 saw David Holbrook's *English for Maturity*,[9] 1963 Sybil Marshall's *Experiment in Education*.[10] But 1964 was to stand out for the magnitude of its achievement, or at least its beginnings. That year produced two more seminal books: Sir Alec Clegg's *The Excitement of Writing*,[11] and David Holbrook's *English for the Rejected*.[12] 1964 also saw the forming of the Schools Council for the Curriculum and Examinations, the institution of the examination for the Certificate of Secondary Education, the founding of the National Association for the Teaching of English and the Lockwood Report on the examining of English language at ordinary level. The Schools Council lost little time in making English one of its priorities; NATE, though not yet the powerful equivalent of its American opposite number, the National Council of Teachers of English, has made a good start and does represent a major advance in professional involvement – probably its future does not lie in too large a scale of development. The Certificate of Secondary Education is immensely significant. Here at last is an examination which is designed to follow the curriculum, instead of leading it; CSE has made possible a whole range of developments which include Mode III,[13] an examination set by the school on its own syllabus and externally moderated; other experiments include multiple marking, in which, say, three examiners each

B

assess a piece of work by impression and an average is taken,[14] and the assessing of oral expression and comprehension.

Behind these events, and helping to inspire them, there has been a profound change in the whole approach to the teaching and learning of English. Dullness and deadwood are still quite often associated with the now obsolete tradition which I have been describing; at the same time, new approaches to English are here already, working like yeast in the dough and clearly spreading. One impression of the changes at work exists in the splendid book by two sympathetic but not uncritical American observers from which I have already quoted.[15] They studied a sample of forty-two schools that could be regarded as 'pace-makers' throughout the United Kingdom, and wrote that 'The revolution in British state-supported education now sweeping through the schools appears directly related to egalitarian pressures emanating from changes in the British social structure'. In English the main influence making for change comes from the work of ardent teachers within the schools themselves. These teachers are profoundly concerned with the social and creative development of individual children in a rapidly changing society, and with all that English can do to promote their development. This means relatively less emphasis upon sequentially planned curricula; indeed, a major weakness of contemporary English teaching is said to be its haphazardness and lack of continuity. Some aspects of literature are relatively neglected by comparison with United States practice. At the same time, English as a whole is seen as very much alive, with a strong emphasis on oral expressive work, creative writing and drama, and on the learner's response in reading. The observers found much from which American schools could learn, in the whole approach to slow learners, for example, and in the approach to oral work and not least in writing: 'In classroom after classroom, students were eagerly putting pen to paper.' It may be that too much has been inferred from a comparatively small group of schools; but when so much criticism is flying about it is interesting to see American observers paying serious attention to what is happening here.

Thus there seems a good deal in the contemporary picture that is by no means discouraging, even allowing for all that still needs to be done. Is there then any general sense of encouragement and progress at long last which might at least be set against the dark side of our picture? Far from it. There is more confusion, criticism and real dissatisfaction than ever, and as I write Sir Alan Bullock and his colleagues are investigating 'all aspects of teaching English including reading, writing and speech; and how teaching methods might be improved'. Their terms of reference have a faintly ominous ring: such phrases as 'teaching methods' need to be taken seriously in their proper context. But the Bullock remit, which, after a brief initial reference to 'all aspects of teaching English', then specifies the main communication skills and ends abruptly with teaching methods, conveys to at least one student of 'tone' the suggestion that what is wanted is result without process, communication skills without real experience, particularly of literature, with the effect of prescribing for such symptoms as poor reading without really considering what may lie behind them. Some of those who make much of lowered standards of reading probably disapprove of the social concern and emphasis upon creativity whose influence upon contemporary English teaching I have already noted. There are certainly dangers, as the history of the American progressive school will show; of course, there are schools in England and Wales in which new ideas are being enthusiastically taken up with a fine disregard for precision or clarity of statement. And yet precision in reading and writing are fully compatible with the new approach to English; it is not likely to be achieved by most pupils through any other approach.

Certainly there are not likely to be any simple or easy solutions for complicated issues. And the issues are complicated. To begin with, the English that is taught and learned in schools does not happen in a vacuum. The school and everything that goes on in it is affected by all that is happening outside: examples gross as earth are all around us. In a world of telephone, tape recorder and television (and who knows what tomorrow?) the rising importance of speech speaks for itself, though in how many schools can teachers even now use tape recorders or record players freely and selectively whenever they want to?

Meanwhile an increased concern with speech may have implications for reading and writing. In a remarkable book[16] Eric Havelock comments on the amount of psychic effort which now goes into the contemporary effort to achieve literacy. A great and on the whole very successful attempt is made to enable every child to 'learn to read'; a number of children may be held up by various frustrations and blockages, but some of the trouble comes after the normal stage of 'learning to read' is passed and at this point competence in reading techniques, though important (and certainly needing attention), is not enough; the teacher is wrestling with the learner's inner motivation or lack of it and often also with the world outside, in which to the pupil there may seem little point in reading. As for the school itself, does it have enough of the right books? Is there something that even the slow learner can enjoy as he does come to understand printed words and sentences? Above all, how can his probably deep-seated sense of failure be turned into success? Remedies are not going to be easy. And yet already, in many schools and often against odds, children of all ages and over a wide range of ability *are* finding out for themselves something of the pleasure and excitement of reading, enlarging and deepening personal experience. So in writing; one of the remarkable developments of our time has been the way in which so many quite young children have learned how to write not so much in a formal impersonal way, but in a simple personal style which is often astonishingly precise – they write because they want to and because they have plenty to write about. This personal approach to writing forms the best possible basis for a gradual approach to more impersonal forms of writing later on, though the transition depends very much on the individual child, must not be hurried and needs generally sensitive handling and concern for continuity. Here too, of course, the attitude of the world outside is important; is it one which really cares about writing, and will the children go on writing as they grow older? The start is sometimes better than the sequel.

School has its responsibilities, which may not be shirked, but cannot work in splendid isolation from the surrounding culture. The very word 'culture' is enough to make Dr Goebbels turn in his grave, not to mention some of those still alive, who will reach for their revolvers. I do not myself particularly care for a word which is ambiguous and often, in English at least, portentous and humourless; a diet of unrelieved traditional masterpieces may not satisfy either childhood or maturity. But the issues behind the word are important.

Some see the great works of literature as socially divisive, because not everyone can read or enjoy them. Some are troubled because the gap between school and the outside world is so dangerously wide. One can sympathise; the gap *is* often dangerously wide though that is not necessarily the school's fault.

How closely should the school's cultural standards relate to those prevalent in the surrounding world? Perhaps many parents would be the first to be shocked if school and the outer world were identical. Perhaps the central point is that teachers, and particularly English teachers, should know something of adolescent subcultures generally, be aware of their pupils' environment, and be in human touch with them as individuals: without this nothing is possible, and with it most other things will follow. And at the far end of what school can offer (and home often cannot) it remains vital to remember that most of our pupils, like most of us, have a capacity for experience which goes well beyond their capacity for explanation. Many a boy or girl who has been fascinated by Romeo and Juliet could not, at speed, have answered prosaic questions concerning Tybalt, Queen Mab, or apothecaries, and for some the experience has been ruined by just this. Too many schools in the past have made literature a field in which no flower is really fragrant; all the pleasure goes out of reading because of excessive explanation which, as I. A. Richards and L. C. Knights long ago realised, can itself militate against effective reading of an original. Examinations made matters worse: L. C. Knights in *Scrutiny* (September 1933) urged that literature texts should no longer be set for examination; in 1938 the Spens Report actually made a similar recommendation.

It might be asked whether literature would be read but for the examination by those who take it, but is this the real question? Do they in fact *read* the texts at all, or do they 'get them up' well enough to answer the questions? A diet of notes, contexts and short pieces of written work does not necessarily lead to proper reading and may surfeit instead of satisfying; there is no 'vision of greatness' here. Real reading is something different and, without embarking on a discussion of literary masterpieces versus the rest, I should like to see the choice of books widened. What is read should reach the mind and sometimes the heart of the individual reader; but that is not likely to happen if the whole class is continually put through the same hoop. As Blake put it, 'One law for the lion and ox is oppression', not least in the comprehensive school. Reading is ultimately a personal experience, even though in many of its aspects it can be shared. It means a great deal that in many schools many books *are* being enjoyed and seriously studied; but too often the books are neither *read* nor enjoyed.

What about the future? Everything is in a state of flux, not only English but also the school as a community or institution, the curriculum which it offers and the children who may follow that curriculum, the teachers who teach in it and their professional education, and even the local government area in which a school finds itself; in the outside world there have been profound changes in the cultural pattern within which reading, writing, and other English accomplishments find their place.

The trouble with prophecy lies not so much in imagining what is still to come, as in assessing the present in which we ourselves are working. As for English itself I would expect in ten years' time to find much that is associated with English teaching of the recent past and present day still persisting: speaking, listening, reading and writing will not die out while human beings survive, even though emphasis may change. Literature will still be speaking out of the dead past into the living present; poetry will still make its demands and offer its rewards. The new developments within English over recent years hardly suggest a dying subject; as we have seen, new approaches to grammar, speech, reading and generally to the creative use of language are still developing. The implications of recent developments in linguistics and the light they throw on the different ways in which children use language in different environments or situations; the implications of a command of certain kinds of English – or the lack of such command – for the whole of a child's life and school work; new conceptions of resources and how to use them; and new thinking about what for short is called creativity: all these are only now really beginning to make an impact upon the teaching of English.

But the teaching exists only for learning, and it is the discovery of the full implications of the shift in emphasis towards the learner learning that will, I hope, do most to transform the English scene in the next ten years. I expect many more boys and girls to find school a place in which they are encouraged to work steadily and systematically, on their own or in groups, with the right kind of rooms, the right materials and the right atmosphere to work in. The present-day schools and teachers are still so often not really interested in what children have to say, and discussion, learning and expression will only flourish where the atmosphere is encouraging, not restrictive. When will all teachers discover that the real discipline of English begins once interest, involvement and perhaps delight are there?

In this picture I doubt whether there is much room for the traditional 'Eng Lang' or 'Eng Lit', even for able boys and girls. Language and literature will indeed continue to command their own disciplines but too often the students have experienced not so much these as an abstract parade of meaningless requirements deriving from obsolete theory and boring practice. Far from producing results, they only serve to obstruct the real problems of communication, when there is really something to be said or written. 'Language is learnt in operation, not by dummy runs. In English, pupils meet to share their encounters with life, and to do this effectively they move freely between dialogue and monologue – between talk, drama and writing; and literature, by bringing new voices into the classroom, adds to the store of shared experience.'[17]

Too much traditional English failed just because it was a dummy run; students expert in ritual précis often fail dismally when they have to set down their own notes; and there is insufficient transfer from English to other fields of study. I was once allowed to ask successive groups of examiners whether in an external examination in history, geography and so on, any account was taken of the quality of the written work. The invariable answer was no, unless the writing was so disjointed that the examiners could not divine what the candidate was trying to say. I remember, more happily, a lecture by Dr G. B. Jeffrey, Director of the London Institute of Education, not long before he died: 'The development of expression cannot be separated from the development of what is expressed.' As for traditional 'Eng Lit', it encouraged boys and girls to write three or four skilful answers against the clock and give settings, contexts, character studies, historical notes and nice assessments of style, often without ever really reading the original. English has a future but this is not it.

The ultimate question is not what *is* English as a subject, but what is it aiming at? What is the English teacher trying to do? Looking back at the apparent aims of English teaching half a century ago the observer finds much that is still relevant: clarity of thought and expression, a command of spoken and written words, and awareness of literature were and still are, for most of us, achievements to be respected. But to-day the ambiguities and curious assumptions of the traditional approach are perhaps more obvious. What do such terms as clarity of thought or a command of the spoken and written word or awareness of literature really mean? What is meant by correctness or by such a term as standard English? As for assumptions, does it really follow that rules learned in abstraction can be readily applied in a context, or that the language used for teaching and learning in school should as far as possible be of formal and adult pattern, or that exposure to literary masterpieces is invariably productive of the results sought? I recall that school whose syllabus proposed to 'inculcate [root meaning "to grind in with the heel"] a love of literature'. And what of priorities? Does one aim at everything all the time, or, if not, then what and for whom, in what order and how? In the past fifty years a good deal has been discovered about the nature of language and its acquisition, and also about the ways in which children learn or do not learn. Many of the aims and assumptions behind English as it then was deserve respect and did produce results, but the mummified aims of fifty years ago will not necessarily meet the needs of today, and for many perfectly normal and responsible students the whole traditional approach would be – and quite often still is – unproductive. A complete rethinking is needed, and is under way.

For what, more than anything else, differentiates today's English teaching from that of fifty or even twenty-five years ago is the amount and intensity of the thought that is now being given to its main aims. Above all, there is a deep concern for the development of each individual child and the part which English can play in this development. John Dixon's account of the 1966 Dartmouth English Seminar puts the whole issue well:

In the map that emerges from the Dartmouth Seminar, one dimension is historical. Among the models or images of English that have been widely accepted in schools on both sides of the Atlantic, three were singled out. The first centred on *skills:* it fitted an era when *initial* literacy was the prime demand. The second stressed the *cultural heritage*, the need for a civilizing and socially unifying content. The third (and current) model focuses on *personal growth:* on the need to re-examine the learning processes and the meaning to the individual of what he is doing in English lessons. Looking back over the history of our subject, we see the limitations in the earlier models and thus the need to reinterpret our conception of 'skills' and 'heritage'.[18]

This speaks for itself, though some would like more reference to language as a means of communication or to language in relation to social change. Language is essential, and central, to human development; and the child will never grow up to be a mature man without it: language makyth man! In the course of growing up every child has a long linguistic journey to make and much to learn, but only if the language of school makes sense to all who use it, both taught and teacher. Rigmarole is only a pale shadow of language; if the school's approach to language is meaningless for the learning child then school will only hinder.

However, we now know more than we did about the views on such matters of our pupils and parents, and there is a marked and disquieting divergence between these views and those of their teachers.

This comes out very clearly in the Schools Council *Enquiry into Young School leavers*.[19] According to this, boys and girls alike tend to rate English as useful, though only about half the boys and just over two-thirds of the girls find it interesting. Most wish they had been better at English, putting first the practical and vocational aspects of language, speaking well and easily (particularly girls), and being able to put things easily into writing (both boys and girls). Parents too put the vocational aspect first. Teachers, by contrast, are more concerned with 'the development of pupils' characters and personalities', and much less concerned with the vocational. The enquiry was, of course, concerned only with early school leavers; but the same conclusions would probably apply to many other children and their parents. Both points of view seem reasonable as far as they go. Of course, as teachers claim, a programme actively concerned with the whole human experience is more likely to be effective even in terms of vocational preparation than anything narrower; nothing less will do. But parents and children have some legitimate grounds for complaint: too many schools do too little to prepare their pupils for working in the outside world and are often somewhat remote from that world. As for parents, they are too seldom consulted, so they naturally think in terms of English as they had to learn it when at school. What are schools doing to liaise with their parents?

In the past there has been too much concern with pushing children prematurely from the more personal and expressive forms of language towards the more impersonal language of formal communication. Here, of course, the schools are ultimately influenced by the personal and intense demands of the outside world; so great has been the stress upon formal communication that many other aspects of English have been allowed a very subordinate place by comparison. And yet the language of formal communication represents only one register among others; it is most important but has little to do with the language which children or for that matter adults employ while they are learning for themselves – that is in a far more colloquial register.[20] Professor Britton has shown in a recent and important study[21] (and in the preceding chapter in this book) how the expressive language of young children leads as they mature in one direction towards 'transactional' language, concerned 'to get something done in the world', and in the other direction towards more personal expression and poetry. The imaginative and expressive uses of language provide the best possible springboard for more prosaic and everyday kinds of English, which probably develop later than is often realised. The newer approaches to English teaching which have developed in recent years can certainly fail to do justice to the more mundane aspects of language: where this is the case, the remedy lies not in the kind of latter-day philistinism that would revert to 'inculcating' outworn grammar or atavistic exercises in the name of discipline; discipline (once again) cannot begin in any worthwhile form till the learner has something to say which seems worth saying. The remedy lies in a better general understanding of language and how it is learned, and in better communications between teachers and their opposite numbers in the outside world, including parents.

A further source of possible confusion for the learner may lie in the difference between the language which comes naturally to him and that used by teachers generally (not merely in teaching English). I am not suggesting that teachers should speak like their pupils. But too many abstractions or complicated sentence constructions will only confuse pupils who cannot grasp what is being said, and the less able and socially deprived will suffer most. Respect for the learner should be incompatible with either talking down to him or talking over his head.

The solution to such problems and the achievement of generally higher standards (including increased competence in reading and writing) will be a slow, painstaking business. Everything depends in the long run on the quality of teacher education, both initial and in-service; and the chief difficulty will be to keep in mind attitudes on the one hand and skills and knowledge on the other; neither good will alone nor competence alone is enough. There are no short cuts along this difficult road. The competences may need more attention than they have sometimes been getting; but they will not be achieved in isolation.

In what space is left I propose to explore one or two areas which are important both for English and for the way in which teachers are prepared to teach English; these areas are not less important because they are so often either overlooked or dealt with in partisan fashion by both sides.

My first concern is with the relation in teacher education between the subject aspect and the interdisciplinary aspect. Many of us have fought on this battleground 'where ignorant armies clash by night'. I have already suggested that English is likely to survive in the coming curriculum, but not necessarily in its traditional form; its interdisciplinary aspects need much more attention. This is particularly the case if justice is to be done to the plain-prose transactional aspects of language. While language will always need its focusing points, which 'English' can provide, it is best learned on the job. James Britton comments on

the conditions necessary in school for the development of transactional writing, speaking and reading. The point is this: these uses of language are the joint responsibility of all subjects in the curriculum. Children will learn to master transactional language by using it and they will need to learn it in every kind of lesson. It seems to me urgently necessary that this responsibility should be faced, and the first necessary step is that secondary school staffs should by consultation arrive at an agreed policy for language across the curriculum in the school in which they work.[22]

The effort now going on in many schools to replace streaming by mixed ability groups makes such a policy even more important, since with such groups the traditional subject-based curriculum is unlikely to work. Not that the subject is in essentials obsolete;[23] it is rather that subjects are more complex than we realise and need thinking about more in terms of objectives than of territory.

There is sometimes a tendency for schools preoccupied with interdisciplinary possibilities to regard fully qualified teachers of English as potentially dangerous (which indeed they can be) 'because we don't want narrow specialists'. Nothing could be sillier than such a point of view, however understandable. It is not as a rule the qualified specialist teacher of English who takes too narrow a view of his job in a school which gives him an intelligent brief and a fair chance. Such a teacher will need to know a good deal (in theory as well as practice) that seldom enters into the average university English honours course as it exists today, particularly in respect of language, how children use it and how language in all its aspects bears on their development as human beings. He will still need to make full use of what he learned as an undergraduate but in a very different context. To provide this kind of specialist is one important branch of teacher education, though initial training can only offer a start.

There is not likely in the foreseeable future to be a very large number of these teachers, and, as John Blackie says of secondary schools, 'a considerable proportion of the English teaching will fall upon teachers who are specialists in other disciplines'.[24] In theory this is clearly as it should be; not every secondary school teacher, particularly in the earlier years, needs to be a traditional 'specialist', any more than in the primary school. In practice, there are difficulties, as Squire and Applebee remark:

Excellent teachers of English were found among the group of non-specialists, to be sure, but their excellence was the exception rather than the rule . . . lacking any real instinct for the nature of language and literature, they frequently planned mundane lessons, relied completely on textbooks, or slavishly followed the form of the school syllabus. . . . (In England, as in America, qualified teachers of English are in short supply.)[25]

One can only sympathise with the non-specialist. Many can contribute to the earlier stages of music or science without elaborate specialist preparation as we know from primary schools; and so in English; but such teachers probably acquire a better understanding of some vital subject elements than the experts realise. Certainly a teacher cannot teach English in the light of nature without initial understanding or thought, particularly if the need is not even perceived. And it is all the harder for him that, as Anthony Adams puts it,

Just when the new developments in organisation have put a particular strain on schools and teachers, the new ideas in English teaching have taken away some of the supports upon which the inexperienced teacher might have relied. In particular, they have taken away the traditional course book, which at least answered for the bewildered teacher that most fundamental of all questions: what do English teachers teach, or, more baldly, what am I going to do next time I walk into that classroom?[26]

The answer to such a question, particularly where streaming is replaced by mixed ability groups, lies for all concerned with either teaching or teacher education in the interdisciplinary aspects of subject teaching. As Anthony Adams says, 'it is incapable of solution so long as we continue to think of the traditional teacher in a classroom'.[27] His book gives a vivid and well-documented picture of what can be achieved by a policy of team teaching to bring in and develop the combined contribution of student, new teacher, non-specialist and experienced specialist, in a way that does justice both to English and to the needs of the school, 'the department becoming a continuous training ground'. Of course, the development of team work within any one school is likely to vary with local circumstances, which include the interests and point of view of individual teachers; there is no single recipe for success. But that such a development is needed and will come I have little doubt. Planning, preparing, teaching, recording and assessing all form part of a single process, a *Gestalt* involving not one but a number of individuals who can work with each other and not merely in unsplendid isolation. And it is only in ways such as this that English can hope to retain its essential integrity and yet link up with all the other areas in which English is practised.

My second main area of preoccupation follows from the first. Matthew Arnold, HMI, in his oddly contemporary *Culture and Anarchy* expressed his concern at the current obsession with what he called 'machinery'. He would be concerned today. Too often those who make plans for education are primarily concerned, in the name of planning, with an endless sequence of organisational changes, each probably inevitable in itself and desirable, but all combining to make it harder rather than easier to concentrate upon the slow and steady progress in human terms of boys and girls as they go through school. Central government, local authorities, schools and teachers have only time for so much; too many melting pots will spoil the mix. I am arguing not against change but for a more sensitive recognition of what is at stake. Merely to call a school comprehensive will no more bring about what is needed than calling it secondary modern did after the 1944 Act; one cannot assume that with a new organisation on paper the rest will somehow follow.

The 1972 White Paper[28] appeared to envisage teacher education as something which must be run efficiently as a routine servicing operation, much of it cut off from universities and in the main divorced from real experiment and questioning. I hope that time and experience may dispel this first not very happy impression; but if it should prove correct, the implications for English are profound. For English needs all the intangibles which in theory good administration exists to promote. In the present and coming scene I see continuing the old debate between efficiency on the one hand and the things of the spirit on the other. Unimaginative administration seems to me a greater potential threat to English than technology, which properly interpreted and used is concerned with ends and means. At that end of the spectrum which is concerned with resources technology has much to offer teachers of English, who should, but seldom can, be making lively and frequent use of a large variety of tapes, records, slides, films and much more; the future of the learning-oriented curriculum and certainly of English within this demands no less. At the other end of the spectrum is the whole question of selectivity in respect of the use of such resources; to what end are they likely to be used? Here technology can be most helpful too – though teachers cannot hope to use selectively resources which simply are not there.

Nevertheless technology has aroused some suspicion, in part because of past history. In the United States technology appeared to come into the English field in the fifties and early sixties to some extent as a result of developments elsewhere, particularly in science and modern-language teaching; a poem of Robert Frost's, for example, was reduced to innumerable little questions in the name of programmed learning, and there was also a period when some very influential administrators hoped that television might take over some of the teaching and make major economies in staffing possible. Much new and often valuable thinking also developed which in such books as Bloom's *Taxonomy of Educational Objectives*[29] has become perhaps the single strongest influence upon contemporary thinking about the curriculum in the English-speaking world. The impact, however, of Handbook 1 (*The Cognitive Domain*) has so far proved greater than that of Handbook 2 (*The Affective Domain*); and the factorising treatment (dividing up what is complex into a sequence of constituent parts or aspects), while perfectly legitimate for a number of purposes, may not always inspire its readers to put the parts together again – with serious consequences for English, which involves so much more than the cognitive aspect and needs ultimately to be seen in terms of wholes not bits. Another book of the period, Jerome Bruner's *The Process of Education*,[30] has also been influential ever since, though the circumstances which led to its production have by now passed.

The quest for more systematic teaching and teaching material led in America to the emergence in 1962 of the federally financed US 'Project English', which began to sponsor a number of sequential English syllabuses worked out with teacher co-operation, but ultimately academic in their strong and weak points alike. However, this appears in retrospect to have been supplanted by quite different concerns arising out of new developments in the social sciences and placing much stress upon the problems of coloured, immigrant, and generally disadvantaged children. By comparison the teaching of English in the United Kingdom has been less buffeted about, though not uninfluenced by American thinking. One main difference is that our changes (even allowing for the influence of such university teachers as Professor Leavis) have often tended to well up from below, and particularly from the primary school; whereas in the United States the influences making for change have traditionally emerged at the top and worked downwards. And perhaps the polarisation between new and old, between organisation and the spirit, has never been quite so sharp in the United Kingdom.

A particularly lively and significant encounter was the Dartmouth Seminar of 1966, which brought Americans and British together for a whole month. There were times when the British seemed to be thinking in terms of the creative imagination, where the Americans were thinking of a more systematic course, and yet discussion nearly always seemed to go well over any national boundaries, real or imaginary, and was certainly not just a straightforward confrontation between organisation and creativity.[31] The result was not a compromise and since Dartmouth there has been a continuing interaction between the United States, the United Kingdom and Canada, which I hope will put an end to the isolation in which we all used to work. In America, beset as it is by many urgent and wounding realities, and here there has been a good deal of rethinking in English even over the past five years. I have already mentioned the developing awareness of language problems of deprived children, particularly in depressed areas.

Some would go as far as rejecting both 'school' and 'English' as a school subject; 'at least let us get rid of compulsion, and why insist on literacy in the age of mass media?' I can understand how such things come to be said; but here and now the consequence of any such policy could be socially most divisive, creating or at least conniving at a new helotry from which it would be difficult for the illiterates to escape. As things are today, men and women in a country such as ours cannot hope to take much part in what is going on if they cannot read. This calls for a more systematic concern particularly in secondary schools to help readers first to learn to read and then to read! Methods need to be carefully considered, the teaching competently organised. At the same time there has been a marked reaction among thoughtful English teachers everywhere against over-organisation. As an American said at Dartmouth, 'you wanted us to come up with something less specific than a curriculum and more ordered than chaos'; and a recent American comment[32] which could be parallelled here puts its point of view clearly: 'Teachers tend to disregard the curriculum and teach what they want to teach anyway. . . . Most curriculum guides are useless. . . .

The word curriculum is all wrong for a subject like English. . . . If we would cultivate the horizon, we are not concerned about young peoples' conforming to a preconceived mould, but we are concerned with what literature and language can do for them'.

Such a point of view implies no disrespect for competence or attention to detail; but over-organised teaching will not necessarily display either. A clear understanding of general objectives is essential, and these need to be spelled out; once that is done the day's work should not be too rigidly defined. There seem to me dangers in behavioural objectives which expect a daily dose of self-questioning. Again, this implies no criticism of real technology. A symbol for the central problem I have in mind will be found in Arthur Koestler's vision of the Yogi,[33] representing change from within, and the Commissar, change from without; and how difficult it is to effect a genuine interaction: 'It is easy to say that all that is wanted is a synthesis . . . but so far this has never been achieved. What has been achieved are various motley forms of compromise.' Is that the best that can be expected for English? Or is the future which we are making for ourselves (in the White Paper and elsewhere) one in which such problems can be resolved, at least in part?

It is better not to look too far into the future, which will in any case pursue its own way and not ours. From apparent stagnation we have come to a sudden period of great change. The next stage in English is still obscure, and will depend only in part upon the English teacher. He in turn must depend in the long run on the care and concern for English of all for whom it is the mother tongue. The comment in the Ministry of Education pamphlet on *Langauge*[34] remains significant in an age in which there is more than a hint that precision in language is seen by some as an obsolescent virtue, perhaps even as a picturesque relic of 'upper-class elitism'.

No substantial and permanent progress is likely to take place until 'English', literature as well as language, is regarded by all in authority as the central expression of English life and culture and as the central subject in the education of every English child of every age and every grade of intelligence. The French, the Welsh and the Scandinavians are not afraid to exalt their national cultures and to honour their national languages accordingly. The English have at least an equal need to recognize their own most priceless inheritance before it is seriously debased.

Perhaps we can learn from our neighbours. Meanwhile, the teacher of English has his work cut out if he is to help his pupils to discover for themselves something of the delight which can come of language learned well. All of us can help him.

References

1 Cape, 1937.
2 See J. R. Squire and R. K. Applebee, *Teaching English in the United Kingdom*, NCTE, Champaign, Illinois, 1969, p. 49.
3 Ibid., pp. 80 and 113.
4 In *The Teaching of English in Schools 1900–1970*, Routledge, 1972.
5 In *English and Examinations . . . with special reference to examinations at 11 and 18*, Hutchinson, 1970.
6 HMSO, 1960.
7 *Teaching English in the United Kingdom*, op. cit., p. 53.
8 HMSO, 1954, p. 49.
9 Cambridge University Press.
10 Cambridge University Press.
11 Chatto & Windus.
12 Cambridge University Press.
13 Schools Council, *Examinations Bulletin No. 1, CSE*, HMSO, 1963, p. 18.
14 Schools Council, *Examinations Bulletin No. 12*, HMSO, 1966.
15 *Teaching English in the United Kingdom*, op. cit.
16 Preface to *Plato*, Blackwell, 1963. Marshall McLuhan made use of it.
17 J. Dixon, *Growth through English*, OUP for NATE (1967) 2nd ed. 1969.
18 In *Growth through English*, p. 13.
19 HMSO, 1968.
20 A good definition of register is in the index to A. Wilkinson, *The Foundations of Language*, OUP, 1971: 'the kind of English appropriate for a particular purpose in a particular situation'. See also pp. 39–46.
21 *Language and Learning*, Allen Lane, 1970.
22 Ibid., p. 263. See also Part III of *Language, the learner and the school*, Penguin, 1969.
23 See P. H. Hirst and R. S. Peters, *The Logic of Education*, Routledge, 1970, chap. 4, 'The Curriculum', especially pp. 68–70.
24 *English Teaching for Non-Specialists*, Faber, 1969, p. 13.
25 *Teaching English in the United Kingdom*, op. cit., pp. 50 and 214.
26 *Team Teaching and the Teaching of English*, Pergamon, 1970, p, 5.
27 Ibid., p. 8.
28 *Education: A Framework for Expansion*, HMSO, 1972.

29 Longman, 1956 and 1964, 2 vols.

30 OUP, 1961. This book has also considerable implications for English. It is the record of a conference at Woods Hole, Massachusetts, held in 1958. See also *English in Education*, NATE, Summer 1972, especially Wallace W. Douglas, 'An American view of the failure of curriculum reform and the way ahead'.

31 See J. Dixon, *Growth through English*, op. cit., for the professional reader. H. Muller, *The Uses of English*, Holt, Rinehart & Winston, 1967, was written for the more general reader.

32 G. Robert Carlsen, 'Some random observations – about the English curriculum', paper presented to the NCTE Convention, November 1971; reprinted in *The English Journal*, NCTE, October 1972.

33 *The Yogi and the Commissar*, Cape, 1945. It is hard to realise that the essay which gives the book its name first appeared in *Horizon* thirty years ago, in 1942.

34 HMSO, 1954, p. 49.

3 The transatlantic dialogue

ROGER K. APPLEBEE

Fifteen years after Sputnik the American educational cauldron still simmers with some intensity, but some new ingredients have been added since that electrifying event. In spite of the more humane attitude towards teaching and learning espoused by Charles Silberman, Herbert Kohl, and Jonathan Kozol, the most constant instrumental force in American secondary education today comes from the behaviourists as represented by Professor B. F. Skinner and his associates. It suits the American temperament to think of education as a single construct whose parts are different only in degree and whose single purpose is to add skills or bits of knowledge until the student has reached the educational level that his abilities will allow. Such a view, suggesting that any properly motivated student can reach any step he desires, seems eminently democratic in principle and therefore appealing to our collective conscience and sense of fair play.

Some Americans consider it a strange paradox that the British can venerate a queen even as they claim to enjoy the virtues of democracy. But another kind of contradiction prevails in the United States that has also had a continuing effect on education, particularly in English. It is a common impression that the 'typical' American is individualistic, highly inventive, and under suitable conditions, hard working and economically enterprising. Literary folk heroes such as Huckleberry Finn, Holden Caulfield and Horatio Alger share a dearth of schooling and at least two of them a complete disdain for formal education. Against this general backdrop it is scarcely necessary to provide an educational programme to draw out one's individuality or to spark one's imaginative spirit; what is needed apparently is pragmatic purpose and, if possible, a touch of civilisation. This melting-pot philosophy has tended to bring everyone to some common ground, wherever that might be found in our brief history. At first it was religious morality; much later, as successive waves of immigrants came to the country, it was political and linguistic uniformity; now it is the preservation of a common culture in a society which grows ever more diverse. The levelling effect of these principles has been particularly felt on the English curriculum, where they have worked towards an orthodoxy that has recently been challenged in a number of ways within the profession but none with more influence than that of our colleagues in the United Kingdom.

When a small group of British and Canadian English specialists came to Boston for a conference during the convention of the National Council of Teachers of English in 1965, the mood was one of congeniality and amiable anticipation, as though long-separated cousins had been brought together to find mutual interests and pleasant coincidences. Papers were prepared; other papers written in response. Discussions probed the unfamiliar areas of common ground, and what was to become the first of a series of transatlantic collaborations took on the air of a family reunion.

There was nevertheless a certain formality that belied the occasional shocked response – the lifted eyebrow resulting from a challenge to a firm and long-held view about the teaching of English. American participants spoke of bringing their students to a 'mature criticism', of pressing for 'understanding and enjoyment . . . of our literary heritage', 'the four basic functions [of English] – listening, speaking, reading, and writing', 'developmental reading programme', and cited as an aim of English 'to help the student absorb a knowledge of the language elements which provide a basis for speaking and writing'! British colleagues appeared to be talking about the substance of English in another key. They spoke of literature: 'An education which does not try to develop a response to imaginative literature, including poetry, does not deserve the name of education.' 'It [literature] enables us to see into the heart of things.' 'The experience of literature should be central to education.' And writing: 'It is much more important, surely, to be bursting with things to write about and not know precisely how to write them, than to know all the rules and not have anything to write.' But either because of the formality of the meetings or the camaraderie that accompanies first reunions, the report of this first conference, aptly titled A Common Purpose,[1] stresses the similarity of problems and purposes on either side of the Atlantic rather than their differences. In the final discussion session on 'Problems and Possibilities of International Co-operation', the most divisive point seems to have been whether or not it is justified to abridge works of literature for teaching purposes.

Less than a year later, in a longer, more informal reunion at Dartmouth, New Hampshire, the fragile formality gave way; family differences erupted into quarrels; rhetoric became sharp; some participants became intractable. Although papers had been prepared and positions had been formally taken, the essence of Dartmouth is in the differences in viewpoints towards the profession of English, differences that were best revealed in the heat of discussion and debate. In general American participants pressed for structure, sequence and system (in English) while British participants held out for self-discovery, spontaneity and growth. There were renegades from both sides, but there was little consensus evident at the conclusion of the Seminar in August 1966, although subsequent gatherings and reports suggest that this meeting was of paramount importance to the professional thinking in both countries. In retrospect it is fair to say that each country borrowed some insights from the other, but the balance of trade favoured the Americans who found more glittering and saleable merchandise than did their British cousins. These differences may be seen clearly in the two candid reports of the Dartmouth conference: *Growth through English*[2] and *The Uses of English*.[3]

In fact the leading edge of English education in Britain had little in common with developments in the United States at this time. In some ways, the contradictions were manifestations of social and cultural differences; in others the distinctions were simply reflections of institutional uniqueness. It has been thought by some that the more developmental view of English teaching to be found in Britain is simply a latter-day progressive movement experienced in the United States some generations earlier. In my view this interpretation is not altogether valid; the two 'systems' are themselves historically different although they are growing more like one another as time passes. The social and cultural differences remain, and these are less likely to change so quickly as overt institutional variations.

To an American teacher visiting a number of secondary British schools (as I did five years ago) a host of institutional differences would appear – some peripheral, others substantial, and some which may be seen as indices of larger cultural differences. He is struck at once with the pervasive influence of examinations in Britain; he is much less conscious of the fact that English programmes across the United States are controlled by external pressures which can be even more pervasive. Apart from the few schools which are honestly (and sometimes foolishly) experimental, the majority of American English programmes have tended to be stereotyped by the availability of commercial textbooks and by the practice of developing common curriculum guides for schools and school districts.

In contrast to the examination schemes in Great Britain, schools in the United States depend on various patterns of continuous assessment – which often means that students and teachers spend an inordinate time in contemplating grades. In this context healthy competition (surely an American axiom) leads to anxiety or worse – a false sense of success or failure. The tasks of learning and the processes of discovery become less important than do the rewards or punishments represented by grades.

In spite of the lack of an examination system comparable to the GCE, standardised and nationalised testing patterns are everywhere. College Board tests, ACT tests, SATs, STEPs, GREs, LSATs, MCATs, CLEPs and many others swell an ever-expanding catalogue of testing programmes that have somehow become a part of the educational fabric in the United States. Unlike the General Certificate of Education tests (or our own Advanced Placement tests), the common element in all of the above-named programmes is that they are 'objective' – which is to say that they depend entirely on short answers, usually in response to multiple-choice questions, and they are standardised so that comparisons may readily be made against a mythical average pupil at any point in the academic calendar. While these testing programmes do not have the immediate effect on a school programme as do the O or A level examinations, the indirect effect is considerable. For example, although recent practice tends in another direction (thanks in part to the influence of British programmes), the common practice in American secondary schools has been tracking (or streaming) and the tests of achievement or ability have usually been the arbiters.

Towards the end of a pupil's high school the technology of testing is applied to determine not so much whether he can continue on to college or university but rather to see which institutions might accept him. Students are also subjected to a variety of diagnostic tests throughout their four years. Thus, if a high-school pupil is found to need additional work in reading as a consequence of one of these tests, he may be required to take part in a special reading class. The British teacher of English is ideally concerned with developing the full potential of the children; his counterpart in the United States is constantly assessing or 'diagnosing' his charges in an attempt to discover deficiencies or shortcomings. The analytic emphasis is what makes the process of education so distinctly different from that to be found in the better programmes in Great Britain. Whereas the British teacher is apt to consider his student as a unique being whose imagination and intellect are personal gifts to be nurtured and brought out, the American teacher is more likely to see his student as one who needs a bit of this and that to make him whole – the bits being the extrinsic pieces of the English curriculum.

The images of teaching English described by John Dixon in *Growth through English* are very useful in describing these differences. An interesting and contradictory point is that they can all be found on both sides of the Atlantic although it is clear that English (USA) has tended toward the *skills* and *heritage* models far more than that of *personal growth*. From what I have seen of English (UK), and from my talks with British colleagues, it is clear that the British ideal is the personal growth model.

In the United States the most commonplace notion about high school English is that the subject is concerned primarily with language skills, especially the skills of writing. To the layman the English teacher's function is to instil proper habits of mind, particularly those habits which induce correct spelling and sentence construction, but also those that enable one to speak grammatically if not fluently.

But pressed by the need to establish a more respectable and rigorous discipline fifteen years ago, the profession turned obliquely towards the kind of literary studies which had previously been the province of the college and university. At any rate the professional teacher today still seems to be directed as much by the notion that he is there to transmit a knowledge and understanding of the monuments and themes of literature as by anything else. In a survey of American school programmes undertaken by the NCTE in 1963–6,[4] James Squire and I found teachers giving over half of their time to the study of literature; in comparison, our study in the United Kingdom (1967)[5] revealed that English teachers on the east side of the Atlantic spent only about one-third of their classroom time on literary study. In spite of what may seem an insignificant fractional time difference, we noticed that there were essential differences in the approaches to the study of literature. American insistence on analysis, the study of literary components and concepts and preoccupation with literary history were all quite foreign to the teachers of English in British schools. (An exception must be noted of course in the upper levels, particularly sixth-form work, in the English schools.) It is my impression, based on a more recent visit (1972), that these differences remain.

From the time of the Basic Issues Conference (1958) it became fashionable to think about English in America as if it were a stable compound made up of the elements of language, literature and composition; the next ten years were to reveal little professional consensus, however, and there was occasional antagonism to such a view, even though it was given some support by the NCTE, the Commission on English, and the U.S. Office of Education. Internally, the opposition developed on such issues as 'Which grammar?' or 'Which literature?' Externally, the popular view was still that English was an accumulation of skills, reflecting the language arts bias of the elementary schools and the accrediting agencies.

Along with every other aspect of education American English has undergone a kind of revolution, but it has not found any new role to its liking. Five years ago, in the heyday of federal grants for curricular development and teachers' institutes, the rage was for programming, planning, and sequential activities. A number of universities were singled out by the Office of Education in the mid-sixties to develop new and distinctive English programmes which would revolutionise the subject much as had been done in mathematics and science. The revolution was too late! Attempting to emulate the sister disciplines, English specialists set about working for more useful and varied 'structures' that could be identified as the quintessential English and, with some modification, be appropriate to the study of English from the elementary school through the far reaches of the university. For a time teachers worked closely with specialists in the universities to develop programmes which were then attempted as experimental or pilot projects in this innovative school or that enterprising system. Some of the ideas incubated in the project were in fact incorporated into school curricula.

This was also the time of the flowering of modern linguistics departments in the universities, and a number of the Project English centres gave over much of their effort to incorporating the findings of this nouveau riche discipline into high school English programmes. Unfortunately the promise was seldom kept. Although a number of textbooks now used in high schools and elementary schools reflect newer theories and insights into the workings of language than did their predecessors, the study of language and the understanding of the role of language in the schools is probably no more a living thing today than a generation ago.

Another major international difference to be found in the schemata of English is in talking, where we even seem to have a different lexicon. Americans don't talk of *talk*, they give classes in speech! Universities have departments of speech; when one says *speech*, one usually refers to someone addressing a group in a more or less formal way. The notion of talking as discussed by James Britton or as accepted by most British English teachers is not a concept that is understood in the same way. If we are not emphasising talk, we do make a great point of discussion, which tends to carry overtones of classroom relationships, democratic organisation, and of course classroom methodology – i.e. how skilfully one can organise 'discussion' to accomplish a particular pedagogical purpose. Once again, the important difference is one of attitude and purpose: between the spontaneity of *talk* in the British classroom, and the goal-minded purpose of *speech* in the American sense.

Virtually the same distinctions can be made with respect to student writing; and although our vocabulary tends to be much the same, we tend to teach writing differently because we have made different assumptions about it. As in talking, the ideal British teacher of English is inclined to think of writing as a natural if not an instinctive activity for a young person. Writing becomes a part of him, and there is generally much more emphasis on the act itself than on the end product. We have tended to teach writing as though it were an extrinsic skill which has become an artificial necessity of living. Yet we have assumed that it is mastered only with the kind of diligence and effort required of an airline pilot or a trapeze artist.

The expository mode, rather than the personal writing mode, has been supreme in American secondary education for many years precisely because it has been thought to be a better teaching vehicle – more susceptible to generalisation, and more compatible to patterns, analysis, and replication. Ironically, a student can learn a great deal about such writing and even learn to practise its virtues without becoming an insightful writer or a creative person. Personal writing (poems, stories, fragments, reveries, diaries) has been dominated by the no-nonsense term paper or by other manifestations of academic discourse because schools have been thought to be training grounds for universities, and it was assumed that universities were interested only in such discourse.

Creative writing has for years had a negative connotation among most practising English teachers, who either see no need to offer their pupils opportunities for such writing or else consider this work so non-literary, jejune, or capricious that it is not worthy of their reading. There is some reason to believe that the strongly didactic bias is shifting, but, as with so many educational reforms, a counterforce can be as grotesque as the malady.

During the fifties and sixties the profession turned inward in an attempt to define the discipline, to integrate its parts and to find controlling principles. If a present trend can be found it is in the opposite direction. Reformers seem to be outdoing each other in their attempts to enlarge the circle of English to include hitherto alien territory, and the results suggests that the subject is in a fragmented state with little consensus regarding ends or means.

One measure of fragmentation in the last few seasons has been the mushroom-like appearance of elective courses in English programmes throughout the country. Although the notion of English electives is not novel in the United States, the rate at which these special courses have grown and the strange variety now available is an index to a change in professional outlook from the lang-lit-comp view of a decade ago. A review of several articles in the April 1972 issue of the *English Journal*[6] reveals the following examples of elective or 'mini courses' as they were described by one teacher: Romanticism I, The History of the American Novel, The Expanding Universe of James Joyce, Legal First Aid, Black Dialog, Yoga I, II, and III, Student Rights and Civil Liberties, Wit and Humor in Literature, Trends in Contemporary Rock Music, Still Photography, Topics in Psychology, and English for the Garrulous. While one of the authors takes issue with this 'psychedelic supermarket' approach to English, pointing out the absurdity and the irony of such calculated fragmentation, its accommodation to faddish interests and its reduction of values to an unknown common denominator, the majority opinion represented in the issue seemed to applaud such efforts as giant steps away from what is apparently regarded as a too-confining English classroom. Another irony concerning the move to multi-elective programmes is that these courses often become content-oriented altogether, at times positively arcane, and thus work against the principle of spontaneity and participatory learning that launched them in the first place. In some schools certain of these courses are placed out of bounds to many students; in others, specific 'electives' are required of those intending to go to college or university.

It is difficult to discern a single voice among all the political overtones, the radical manifestoes, and the populist tendencies that one finds in the literature directed toward educational change; but much responsible criticism of public education has been timely and effective. From within the profession this criticism aims to broaden, enrich and enliven the whole educational process. One thinks inevitably of Charles Silberman, James Moffett, and James Miller – and of course all of those who were touched in some way by the experience of Dartmouth. Sparked by the insights of another English, they seem to guide us ever closer to the British view. Yet some of our reformers seem confused and contradictory. In what may only be a case of overstatement, two writers have described the role and attitude of the creative teacher as follows:

It [a creative curriculum] demands a teacher who has no firm and fixed answers and who thus expects none from the students, who lacks the courage of his convictions because he has few convictions and has learned instead to rely on the courage of his confusion, who is willing, indeed eager, to learn with and from the young people with whom he shares a classroom.[7]

Such a view of the English teacher may be understandable to those in the profession who have felt the constraints of the skill-centred curriculum and who know the values and pleasures of teaching for personal growth; but the prevailing orthodoxy (both in and out of the schools), conditioned as it is by behaviourist views and melting-pot attitudes, will find such rhetoric an easy target and one consequence could be retrenchment rather than reform.

At the other pole from such thinking is another attempt at 'reform'. Stimulated from outside the profession largely by ideas and methods borrowed from the competitive world of commerce, this movement attempts to specify aims and to rigidify methods by imposing new measures and controls on education generally. The touchstones of this enterprise are 'performance contracting', 'behavioural objectives', and 'accountability', and these expressions evoke distrust and outright hostility among most English teachers in the United States. In effect, the 'system' that encompasses the terms derives from the same philosophy that underlies diagnostic tests and standardised examinations, and teachers are no more sanguine about having such arbitrary measures applied to their teaching than they are towards using the time-established tests on their students. However, state legislators and local school boards are now adopting such strategies from industry and commerce to force education into a more productive and responsible mould. At the 1971 annual meeting of the NCTE a resolution was adopted by the profession which probably will not rebuff the quantifiers and simplifiers, but which represents the baleful view of American English teachers toward this trend.

English teachers recognize their accountability to various groups – to students, to colleagues both within and without the discipline of English, to parents, to the local community which supports the schools, and to the wider communities beyond it. However, they reject the view that their goals and objectives can be stated only in quantifiably measurable terms describing the behaviour their students will display at the completion of instruction.

Debates continue in America between the radical reformers and teachers who represent a more traditional view, and also between both these groups and those external forces that would superimpose criteria of teaching and learning alien to the humanistic elements that have always been thought to be vital to English study. In my view, it is likely that this new challenge from without – these new demands of the Philistines – will bring about a long-needed consensus in the profession on the proper role of English in the last quarter of the century. We are finally going to agree, I think, that our subject is not a composite of 'old iron, old bones and old rags', and that it cannot be circumscribed by writing, reading, speaking and listening nor anatomised in language, literature and composition.

After the quarrels and the conflict, I believe that the essence of English in America will be much closer to that English described by our British colleagues at Boston and at Dartmouth half a decade ago than to our own statements of that time. We will have come to learn that English is not the stable compound we assumed and that John Dixon's description, 'quicksilver among metals – mobile, living, and elusive', is much nearer the mark. Our predilection for analysis, form and sequence has in the past caused us to forget the dancer in our preoccupation with the dance. As stated in his presidential address (NCTE) in 1970 James E. Miller, Jr, noted that we will come to believe that we can 'turn from the text to the student and . . . consider our primary task the education of his imagination. We will be able to let the tradition fend for itself – as we have more important things to do.' In 1966 such a statement might have come from an English delegate at Dartmouth, but scarcely from an American representative. It is clear now, however, that a sea change has occurred and it is beginning to transform the teaching of English in our schools.

Even as this transformation occurs – and it is a change characterised more by ripples than flood tides – it seems to us that structural and philosophical shifts are occurring on the eastern side of the Atlantic. We are told that secondary schools are becoming more comprehensive, more democratic, and more 'American'. As the school-leaving age is raised to sixteen in the United Kingdom, and the expectation for some form of higher education grows, the role and function of the secondary school is modified. And although such change is bound to have its anomalies and oddities it is strange indeed that so many new (or apparently new) structures as the Open University, and the open classroom, as well as the new attitudes towards the teaching of English suggested in Boston and Dartmouth, should have come from an educational system that was thought to be narrow and elitist. Most American observers still find it strange, moreover, that even in the least conservative schools in Britain boys and girls usually wear uniforms and have been heard to 'sir' their masters.

Educational leaders of both countries must be wary of making easy parallels and of adopting programmes and attitudes that appear to flourish in their native soil. There are quite genuine cultural differences that often make us operate in rather different ways. What is palpably clear (or ought to be) is that transplants must be especially hardy varieties and that what often results after the first generation in foreign soil is a hybrid of no special character or value. But it is also true that certain happy accidents of time and circumstance help to create a hybrid that is unusually rare or useful, and we are inclined to think that our cousins' views and insights on teaching English in 1966 are beginning to find a comfortable soil and climate in the new world.

References

1. J. R. Squire, (ed.), *A Common Purpose, The Teaching of English in Great Britain, Canada, and the United States*, NCTE and NATE, Champaign, Illinois, 1966.
2. J. Dixon, *Growth through English: A Report Based on the Dartmouth Seminar, 1966*, OUP 1967.
3. H. J. Muller, *The Uses of English: Guidelines for the Teaching of English from the Anglo-American Conference at Dartmouth College*, NATE, NCTE, Holt, Rinehart and Winston, 1967.
4. J. R. Squire and R. K. Applebee, *High School Instruction Today*, Appleton, Century & Crofts, 1968.
5. — *Teaching English in the United Kingdom*, NCTE, Champaign, Illinois, 1969.
6. The *English Journal* is the official journal of the Secondary Section of NCTE.

4   Coming of age in Australia

GARTH BOOMER

> The world is yours, and you must take
> Your making, breathing, shaping way:
> That instant when the cord was cut
> Ended my brief imperial sway.[1]

Australia is about to enter a pre-figurative stage in the development of curriculum and in the teaching of English. Another dose of immaterial dialectic about the Lucky Country, you say? Just another Alice seeing Wonderland in a nutshell? Bear with me. Perhaps my generalisation is as good as the next man's and at least I begin with a learned anthropological allusion.

You may find the key to my text in a brief study of the evolution of cultures by Margaret Mead in a book called *Culture and Commitment*.[2] Once upon a time there was a post-figurative culture in which, since society was about as tranquil as the Sargasso Sea, stored wisdom could be transmitted to the young by respected elders. Then there came the co-figurative era of pioneering, where among other things the frontiers of science, agriculture and technology were extended, and in which the young and the old together had to make sense of a changing world by reference to the old. But, eventually, change began to happen so fast that the young said to the elders: 'I can no longer take your advice for you have never lived in my world. I must make my own meanings and then try to teach you.'

Now the elders in this Aquarian age can either resist such rebellion by tightening the economic and political controls which are still theirs to manipulate, or they can with dignity signify their willingness to listen by setting up a system in which dialogue between young and old can proceed with neither fear nor threat.

Emergence of this latest stage of pre-figurative culture is now, says Mead, a world-wide phenomenon but its dynamic or *modus operandi* can be most dramatically seen in Papua where transistorised youths are returning to the tribal village to help initiate their bewildered parents into a new age. Such a notion chimes nicely with my idea of what is happening in the field of education in Australia, and more specifically in the realm of English teaching in our secondary schools.

At present nothing is certain except that the major answers to the major questions will be determined not by theorists or university seers or teacher educators like myself (forlorn commentators from no-man's-land), but by the teachers of this and the next generation.

If I am to make some sense, it is necessary to provide a context for readers outside Australia. Each of the six states has a centralised system established along bureaucratic lines. At the apex of the triangle is the director-general and fanning out below are the various directors, superintendents, assistant superintendents, education officers and inspectors. In the last decade regional departments have been formed in an effort to localise administration but the essentially military structure still prevails.

Apart from one state[3] the major part of the curriculum in the final years of secondary schooling is directed towards external public examinations which aim to place candidates in some order of performance so that employers and universities may discriminate among those who seek entry. Scholarships to the university are usually awarded on the basis of performance in these examinations. In all but one state[4] English is a compulsory subject for those seeking to matriculate for university studies.

The syllabus for English courses leading to public examination is set by curriculum committees comprising university personnel, administrators and teachers, while syllabuses for all other courses in English are outlined with varying specificity by departmental committees of teachers, lecturers from colleges of education and inspectors usually supported by a more or less permanent curriculum research and development team. In the schools themselves there is also a hierarchy.

Now this sketch must look alarmingly post-figuratively inclined to our colleagues in the United States and the United Kingdom where, at least superficially, there is an official recognition of the value of free enterprise in education. Certainly it would seem to the casual observer that our whole country is equipped for control in education, and dedicated to a process of handing down by chain of command. But such a conclusion in 1973 would be premature. It would be to assume that bureaucracy necessarily implies imperialism.

While there is no doubt that historically education in Australia is permeated with imperialism and that vestiges of paternalism and arro-

gance still adhere in certain quarters, it can now be said that the last
ten years or so have seen radical changes in education as, paradoxically,
both administrators and teachers have found ways of using the system
to beat the system. In fact, I will suggest that what has been in the past
a largely restraining and restricting influence, 'the system', is now
becoming a powerful agent in the service of growth, change and variety
in education. Whether or not such growth will ultimately end in chaos
and despair depends to a large extent on the system's protection and
support of vulnerable teachers as they 'go it alone'. (Of course, we
can always rely on political intervention if innovation becomes
'unsafe'.)

Like most countries we have been pioneering in education in the
last decade. Wider changes in society, in technology, educational
theory and politics have forced administrators to innovate in various
ways – to devise alternative courses for the 'less able', to provide
audio-visual equipment, to introduce new subjects (road safety;
Malay) and, in line with our western allies, to build 'open plan' schools
and to set up a nation-wide spring cleaning to make way for New
Maths, New Science and New Social Studies. (Cynics might think
that there is something rather Pavlovian about our responsiveness to
overseas stimuli; but we are gradually growing out of our psychological and genetic tendency for the 'educational cringe'.)

Now the speed with which these changes have been imposed on
schools has meant that administrators have had neither time nor
sufficient understanding to issue clear instructions on how they should
be implemented. And so, because the administrators had to rely so
heavily on the teachers to make things work, a new spirit of partner-
ship in exploring new frontiers has developed (where teachers have
overcome initial resentment to impositions). For the teachers it has
meant a growth in self-respect and self-reliance; for the administrators
the adoption of a supportive and exhortatory role accompanied by
a curtailment of customary injunctions. We have seen a gradual process
of strategic administrative withdrawal from specific intrusions into
the content and processes of the educational programme.

At the same time, slowly but irrevocably, the external examinations
are being abolished, so that by the end of the decade it is likely that the
great Australian Inquisition will be no more. In general, administrators
in education are actively campaigning against the external examinations while, ironically, I believe that the majority of teachers would
still vote in favour of their retention.[5] Such has been the narcotic

C

effect of mass examinations and of reliance on sibylline administrators in times of indecision that many of our teachers are understandably reluctant to accept the unstructured loneliness of pre-figurative existence. And so our administrators are compelled to take a courageous and possibly brutal stand; they are not merely giving the teachers freedom but thrusting freedom upon them, knowing that if we are to survive the critical era of change, we need teachers with qualities of independence, resilience and creative energy; not good and faithful servants.

In South Australia in 1970 the director-general of education set an historic precedent by announcing that heads of all schools had freedom and authority to make their own decisions after consultation with parents, children and teachers.

It has, I think, been necessary to give this wider context before looking at English teaching in Australian secondary schools if only as a foil to some of the rather poetic flights of Holbrook[6] on educational administration in this country. What one tends to extract from Holbrook's account is a romantic image of a few dedicated teachers promoting 'love' (and creativity), often in the face of appallingly barbarous physical and cultural conditions and despite the obtuse indifference of administrators and politicians. This is patently naïve although it suits his wider theme of 'homunculism' in the antipodes. (Alas, the voyeurs who peek at Australia seem to leave either singing a fastidious refrain of distaste or loudly intoning *Waltzing Matilda* and swinging a boomerang.)

Like Holbrook, I am tempted to romanticise the Australian English teacher, not as a lonely idealist, but as the active campaigner. I am convinced that he has led the way in developing non-prescriptive syllabuses, new assessment procedures and child-centred approaches. Through his efforts, English is permeating other subject cells, drawing attention to language across the curriculum; questioning the habits and rituals of an outmoded pedagogy. But then it must be remembered that it is probably easier for teachers of English to be rebels. They are less constrained than others in the first place. English is not a 'content' subject; it is both an area of study and the medium through which and with which children learn; there is no consensus on its scope; objective evaluation of a child's writing is impossible; idiosyncratic style and charisma seem to be part of the English teacher's heritage; where English has been taught well in the past the emphasis has always been more on sharing (or at least drawing out) than on telling.

Despite my admiration for the English teacher, I shall try in this necessarily selective and therefore distorted commentary to avoid leaving the reader with a convenient stereotype, a mistake I believe Ian Hansen made in 1970 when he wrote:

Your classroom approaches [in England] are often extreme, the ultra-formal in one school ('Now write in your books a close paraphrase of the poem's last five lines') to the utterly permissive in another ('What shall we do this morning? Write something about something or have some expressive drama?') Australian teachers, true to their national conformist character, stand (in their defence it must be said 'stand uneasily') between formalists and permissivists, between USA and England. . . . Where extremists are to be found they are rarely noisy: the vocal ones are moderates urging the best of both worlds.[7]

I suggest that Dr Hansen, himself a confessed moderate, besides insulting the United Kingdom and the United States with clichés, has underestimated what I should call the militant voices of English teaching in Australia, the people who, with ever-increasing teacher support, have led the 'revolution'. It has been an almost disappointingly tame and bloodless coup, but quite clearly progressivism, if not radicalism, now dominates the national consciousness of English teachers. In 1973 Australia is not 'making the best of both worlds'; it is a bona fide partner in a world-wide movement, a burgeoning of life in the teaching of English. And it has its own distinctive personalities at the cutting edge of the advance. Significantly, most of them are teachers or at least closely involved in the practicalities of teaching, liberal educationists who have shown that 'the best practice is usually ahead of the best fashioned theory'.[8] They have influenced Australian teachers profoundly because they have talked frankly about strategies for the front line; they offer some ways that have worked for them and an approach that liberates the teacher from formerly unquestioned classroom ceremonies. At the same time they have read widely and thought incisively about the needs of children and the nature of their subject.

The campaign may be seen in better perspective after a brief survey of the last ten years of English teaching in Australia. In the early sixties official courses in English were still fairly rigid, setting down texts to be studied in the fields of poetry, novels and drama and suggesting final examinations of specified time and desirable content (e.g. two examinations of one and a half hours each: a 'free' essay, language exercises and a piece of comprehension in one; essays on poetry, play and novel in the other.)

Teachers and children suffered under the autocracy of prescribed books in a system where each child owned his own texts. Thus, even if the teacher disapproved of certain course books, he usually felt obliged to use them since the school would be faced with embarrassing questions from parents if, at the end of the year, a book still gleamed virginal and intact. The year's work at the lower end of the secondary school rehearsed the exits and entrances and the declamatory lines of senior school courses leading to public examinations.

Then, in the mid-sixties, things began to move. As more children stayed longer at secondary school, as some of the external examinations were abolished and existing external syllabuses became more relaxed, and as the writings from the 'creative' school began to have an impact on both administrators and teachers, alternative courses for the 'less able' were developed.

In retrospect it is more than a little ironical to observe that many of the 'new' approaches now accepted at all 'levels' had their origins in experimental work with the 'disadvantaged'. For such children, it was conceded, far more emphasis should be put on talking, on creative drama and project work. Perhaps some film and television study would be relevant; and, of course, Holbrook had already suggested that creative approaches might work with the 'rejected'.

It was as if teachers on the curriculum committees, writing out of years of frustration in preparing children for some distant examination course, poured into these new alternative courses all their hopes and suppressed beliefs about what English could or should be. Admittedly there was not even an incoherent philosophy, but these writings did represent a minor revolution in that they began to push out the 'content' frontiers of English.

From such beginnings change came quickly, not just at the junior secondary level but also in the content (and examination) at the upper end of the secondary school. In a brief space, I can only summarise a few significant developments.

1   Official courses became general syllabuses with advisory notes or handbooks containing suggestions. Basic ideas in alternative courses were incorporated at all levels.
2   As the wider scope of English (to include wide reading; creative drama; mass media studies; creative writing) was recognised,

the notion of an experience-based syllabus gained currency and work with themes and topics began to flourish. Some schools also began to establish a general studies programme.

3 By means of a levy system in which children contributed to a school book fund, sets of resource books of all kinds were established in English centres, and, by a gradual process of weaning, children came to 'own' fewer and fewer texts while gaining access to a growing array of materials. For instance, a school with five first-year forms might provide fifteen sets of novels where previously all had studied the same three novels. Thus the pre-ordained 'package deal' was replaced by a relatively free-choice curriculum.

4 Teacher programming became less visionary. In an experience-based course, one cannot predict in detail a whole term's work. Diary-form programmes in conjunction with projected outlines of small units of work began to replace the largely hypocritical long-range forecast.

Working as a consultant in the late sixties I was able to observe some of the effects of these changes on teachers. It seems to me that, when change is occurring as quickly as this, fads and extremes are inevitable, even necessary. Yes, we had our creative writing binge, to such an extent that, in South Australia, working papers and advisory notes now prefer to talk about writing in its various forms, since the term 'creative', has become a word for all seasons. Happily, it now seems that the 'creative writing lesson', that rather ludicrous paradox, is giving way to the comparatively leisurely and individualised writing that arises more naturally out of thematic studies or personal experience.

We also had the predictable instances of thematic ingenuity such as *The Old Man and the Sea* being used as an illustration of 'men at work'. (I am pleased to report that I have yet to see *King Lear* appear in 'the family'.)

Then there were those who persisted in teaching in strips, clinging to a belief in content and 'the course' to be completed. Where before there had been, say, six recognisable elements in English, now with the broader horizons there were perhaps ten or eleven. An already fragmented English was even more drastically anatomised. Result: confusion.

At this vital point in the evolutionary process teachers needed to find their bearings and they found some refuge and support in the theory that English is a unity; that reading, writing, speaking and listening should be seen as continuing and integrated activities in communication. They welcomed the thought that their job was not to teach poetry or novels or grammar but to help children to learn through using language in the context of interesting situations. But while this clarified their task, the challenge had not diminished. Teachers trained to teach Shakespeare and T. S. Eliot will not change overnight.[9]

This, broadly speaking, is 'where we're at'. As a brief index of the kind of guidance, 'inspiration' or support our teachers currently receive from official writings, I have selected the following general statements which seem to reflect the 'climate':

(1) (After many years of writing aims in English from the teacher's viewpoint, the 1971 Junior Syllabus in South Australia[10] is wholly oriented to the needs of children and *their* aims.)

'The curriculum in English should pay special attention to the following needs of the student if he is to grow and mature.

1 His need to feel accepted as an individual
2 His need for effective communication with other people
3 His need to be concerned for and involved in his social environment
4 His need to express himself freely, confidently and frankly
5 His need to make evaluations and responsible decisions in areas of concern to him
6 His need to recognize and appreciate emotional responses
7 His need to play
8 His need to be left alone.'

(2) (The same syllabus, representative of similar writing in other states, introduces its advisory notes as follows):

'The following notes are advisory only: in no sense do they set out to be prescriptive. They suggest some ways in which the intentions of the syllabus may be put into effect in student-centred learning situations. It is emphasized that they constitute a pool of ideas from which the individual teachers may make selections.'[11]

(3) (On the one aspect of texts in English it is uncharacteristically dogmatic:)

'It is clear that the student at this level should not be systematically taught formal English grammar. . . . It follows that course books based on an outmoded and discredited view of language and language learning are foreign to the aims and spirit of this syllabus.

Course books containing comprehension passages, sentences to be corrected and exercises on usage are not recommended . . .'[12]

(4) (In Victoria, home of the most radical thinkers, it is argued that English cannot be considered in isolation from the wider context of the school):

'Many of the assertions made about the teaching of English affect the organization of the school as a whole:

1 The school needs to draw up its own courses.
2 The school should provide for creative writing, wide reading, study of literature, experiences of drama, theatre, television and film.
3 The school cannot rely only on the English teacher to encourage mastery of language in its students, but needs a policy which all teachers recognize and which includes where necessary:

   (a) re-writing academic texts in language which students can understand;
   (b) having students use active discussion as a basis for understanding and using the ideas they are studying;
   (c) supervising re-writing of accounts which do not put ideas clearly.
4 Teachers who are to work together need time-tabled opportunities to consult each other about their work.
5 The time-table of the school should be flexible enough to accommodate a wide range of experiences and allow for some uninterrupted work on projects which require it.
6 Literature should be neither examined nor assessed.
7 Student writing should not be subjected to pass/fail marking or any other practice that suggests that writing is an activity intended only for the gifted.
8 School libraries must make books accessible to students by being well stocked, open for students to use, and not forbidding in their rules and atmosphere.'[13]

(5) (A paper on curriculum development presented to a recent UNESCO seminar made these assertions):

'We now accept as almost axiomatic:

that the spoken language is primary
that there is a close relationship between language and thought; language is the mediator of thought
that what and how we teach should be related to the stages of the child's mental and imaginative and emotional development

that language changes so that there is no fixed arbitrary standard of correctness

that traditional grammar is an inadequate description of the English language, and in any case should not be taught before the age of fifteen or sixteen to those who are interested in classifying and categorizing

that children learn language by using it in various modes in a wide variety of situations

that children need to use language for personal growth and development because it is through language that they learn to understand themselves and their world

that children need to use language for self-expression and for communication.'[14]

You may well ask: 'So what?'

Having admitted some amazement and pleasure that out of bureaucracies can come such vigour, it is necessary to see the effect of the challenge on individual teachers in the schools; for where there is ideology, there will always be those who seek shelter from thought under the doctrinal umbrella (which in this case is very broad).

I have already hinted at some of the idiosyncasies of the recently enfranchised English teachers. One of the corollaries of a non-prescriptive syllabus is the licence given to the teacher to indulge his natural (or unnatural) propensities. In this new climate the various styles are highlighted so that we can now discern, in relief from the more balanced practitioners, the frantic sufferer from galloping hysteria (trying in vain to keep poetry, novel, play, creative writing, oral skills, comprehension, composition, mass media, etc., simmering in five lessons a week); the *avant-garde* rider of hobby horses on the educational merry-go-round (e.g. creative writing; psycho drama; individual progression); the exponent of pedagogical input (a swinging metronome); the free-thinking muddler; the reluctant novice with a propensity to nihilism (allied to a fear of children); the distorted devotee (to film study, or to the lesser poems of J. P. Donleavy); the mindless marker; the press-ganged grumbler; the teacher of the theme, the whole theme and nothing but the theme; the exclusive Leavisite; the disappointed academic; and the rat psychologist ('hit 'em with the stimulus and watch 'em respond').[15]

These are, of course, caricatures indicating tendencies. Teachers will always be heirs to such infirmities and I am certain that Australia has no exclusive patent on the models.

The point is that teachers can no longer disown their methods by using 'the system' as a scapegoat; the responsibility is theirs. The new syllabus allows for pluralism; the wide range of resources imposes no content; a philosophy is offered but means and methods are optional.

While some teachers may be beyond redemption, at least there is now room for growth and my facetious survey of extremists needs to be weighed against a more optimistic account, such as Henry Schoenheimer's:

Teachers have stopped 'giving lessons', have, in effect, stopped 'teaching', or have ceased to regard this as their main function . . . only quite secondarily as the need arises are they in authority. And this is true . . . whether they stand by a fairly familiar literature and language programme, or whether they see English as merely one focal point round which the whole study of the human situation from the philosophy of Charlie Brown to the sociology and anthropology of the Arapesh may be legitimately organized. Subject title and material content may appear to remain the same; but the educative experience is altered drastically, is transformed.[16]

Such a happy situation implies teamwork. Which leads me to a crucial issue. Given a copious reservoir of resource materials, non-prescriptive syllabuses, external examinations independent of texts studied,[17] an established programme of in-service conferences and a central administration sympathetic to experimentation, the future of English teaching in Australia will, even so, be blighted unless everyone recognises that the *school* should be a learning centre for teachers as well as for children.

Accumulated wisdom and 'the tricks of the trade' can no longer be handed down. The old models don't fit the new scene. The puppeteer leader is an anachronism. And so headmasters are of crucial importance. If they continue to run schools in which teachers are streamed, constantly assessed, subjected to arbitrary routines and denied the opportunity to talk and plan together, great numbers of English teachers, like so many of our children, isolated and uncertain, will stop learning and play the withdrawal game.

We are now beginning to realise that, at great cost, we have almost completely ignored the headmaster in our plans for the 'new' English. And yet, it is quite obvious that if each school is to plan its own curriculum, organisation to allow for teacher co-operation is essential. If no *time* is given for faculty discussion it is likely that in the end, as a matter of survival, the faculty head will decree common programmes and the whole movement will be back to square one.

There is another problem. Despite the quite radical tone of current working papers and articles throughout Australia, there have been relatively few dissentient voices. One wonders, to use the distinction of Camus, whether there are too many revolutionaries and not enough rebels. Perhaps this acceptance can be attributed to the evolutionary progress of the changes; perhaps it is just that the ideas are eminently sensible and appropriate; it may even be attributable to the fact that never before have teachers been so closely involved in curriculum planning. But more fundamentally disturbing is the thought that the present agreement is one last salute to the royal curriculum writer. Even though he has abdicated perhaps he still commands a lingering deference.

Whatever the reasons there is the disconcerting feeling that we have come too quickly and quiescently to the new orthodoxy. The danger is that too many teachers may be happily going through the motions with little understanding and less direction. Are we akin to adolescents, who in revolting against the establishment, simply conform in another way?

Considering such reservations it was most fortunate that, at a time when we needed new questions and a clearer focus, UNESCO with the support of the Australian Association for the Teaching of English organised a national seminar on the teaching of English in Sydney in June 1972. James Britton and Roger Shuy[18] were key speakers and consultants.

One outcome of this most significant seminar was a resolution that we must examine the subtleties of language in education with more rigour. Teachers should be brought into closer contact with current knowledge about language, and research must be generated in such a way that practising teachers are involved in all stages of its operation.

For pre-service education of teachers the implications were clear. We need urgent action in the form of language-centred courses for all intending teachers, the greatest obstacle to this being the almost complete dearth of people considered 'qualified' to conduct courses in the role of language in education. In this respect, it seems that matters are little better in the United Kingdom and the United States. Once again, our immediate hopes rest on the ability of the teacher to find his own way, in co-operation with his brethren overseas.

While I have expressed some dissatisfaction with Ian Hansen's estimation of the Australian English teachers, I cannot deny that the present ideologies had their beginnings in the United Kingdom and that some would attribute this to congenital passivity. Our capitulation, first to Marjorie Hourd and David Holbrook and then to A. B. Clegg and F. D. Flower and later still to Frank Whitehead and John Dixon, was completed following the adoption of texts belonging to the *Reflections* family tree. (Texts by Geoffrey Summerfield, Michael Marland, Peter Abbs and Nancy Martin are highly regarded.)

But this phenomenon is not merely, I think, the customary genuflection of colonials to the motherland. If in Australia there had not been already a profound discontent with current practices, the new writings, like so many high-level tracts before them, would scarcely have rippled the surface of day-to-day English in the classroom. It was a classic case of 'what oft was thought but ne'er so well expressed' finding a response in the intuitions of our teachers, whose somewhat guilty, tentative and surreptitious experiments could at last be acknowledged.

Significantly, the Australian English teacher, as if instinctively, has remained suspicious of the taxonomies and specific behavioural objectives which have dominated curriculum planning in the sciences and in social studies.

Thus our stance after Dartmouth was at first unequivocally British. One looked in vain for major North American influences until recently when we discovered James Moffett, Neil Postman and the urgent voices of the de-schoolers and the socio-linguists such as William Labov and Roger Shuy.

The seventies are gathering momentum for international co-operation to find a sound structure for English based on a growing understanding of the place of language in education. If the catch-cries of the sixties were 'creativity', 'experience', 'themes' and 'child-centred', the seventies already promise to be the era of 'language'. If the old controversies were predicated on 'content' versus 'experience' and 'grammar' versus 'growth', there are now indications that the seventies will generate polemics on the place and value of literature and, on a wider scale, the position of English itself as a separate subject in the curriculum.

It will be a pity if, as a backlash at the sixties, the old dichotomy between language and literature is re-established. What seems to be required is a revaluation of the relationship between language and literature and society, along with a thorough analysis of our teaching of English literature in the universities.

Perhaps when the academics have subjected some of their long-standing myths to scrutiny, literature will be taught, and justified, with more conviction as a dynamic and formative influence in society. The linguists have rescued language from the frozen chambers of post-mortem study. Meanwhile, at least in Australia, we wait for the gurus of literature to show the way to life. We wait for some new questions and, unless they come, whole legions of English teachers will continue to treat literature either with a kind of disengaged, ceremonial respect or else as documentary evidence to support their own social theories. Eventually, failing these questions, our teachers may find answers to other questions from other directions and university literature studies may be pre-figured out of existence.

References

1 Rosemary Dobson, 'Child of Our Time', *Cock Crow*, Angus & Robertson, 1966.
2 Margaret Mead, *Culture and Commitment*, Bodley Head, 1970.
3 Queensland has abolished all external examinations.
4 It is not compulsory in South Australia.
5 Results of a recent questionnaire in South Australia indicated teacher support for public examinations in conjunction with some form of school assessment.
6 David Holbrook, *English in Australia Now*, CUP, 1973.
7 Ian Hansen, 'An Australian View', *The Use of English*, Autumn 1970, p. 32.
8 H. P. Schoenheimer, *English in Australian Secondary Schools*, Cheshire, Melbourne, 1972, p. xv.
9 At this point 'the system' can apply pressures with new forms of external examination. A cynical colleague of mine once said that the best way to change teachers is to change the examination requirements. In Australia, the nation-wide Commonwealth Scholarship papers in England have played a significant role in educating teachers. The papers, devised by the Australian Council for Educational Research, are independent of any specific courses or texts studied. They assess the candidate's ability to read and write in a variety of situations, using multiple marking techniques.
10 Education Department of South Australia, *English*, Junior Secondary Curriculum, January 1971, p. 1.
11 Ibid., p. 6.
12 Ibid., p. 43.

13 From a discussion paper prepared by the Victorian Secondary English Committee, 1970.
14 M. A. O'Brien, 'Teaching Methods and Curriculum Approaches Developing in English Teaching in South Australian Schools', unpublished MS.
15 Adapted from remarks I made in a paper to the annual conference of the Australian Association for the Teaching of English, April 1972.
16 H. P. Schoetnheimer, op. cit., p. xi.
17 The presen leaving examination in South Australia prescribes no specific texts for study.
18 Professor of Socio-linguistics, University of Georgetown, Washington.

Further Reading

B. H. Bennett and J. A. Hay (eds.), *Directions in Australian Secondary School English*, Longman, Melbourne, 1971.
David Holbrook, *English in Australia Now*, CUP, 1973.
H. P. Schoenheimer, (ed.), *English in Australian Secondary Schools*, Cheshire, Melbourne, 1972.
R. D. Walshe, (ed.), *My Machine Makes Rainbows*, Reed, Sydney, 1972.

Social Contexts

5   Whose language?

MYRA BARRS

A horror story first. A primary school child was dictating to his teacher a caption for the picture he had just painted. 'This is me mum', it went. Under the picture the teacher printed neatly 'This is my mother'.

Over the past few years the characteristic of books and conversations about English teaching has been the recurrent question, 'What are we supposed to be doing? What is "English"?' Many school subjects have undergone some degree of self-questioning and re-definition during the same period, but they have tended to emerge from the struggle with a new formula, in the shape of books, packs, hardware and software of all sorts; a package deal presented with the help of trendy graphics. Sometimes the thinking behind the facelift has been serious, sometimes it has just been a question of revamping the old syllabus. Very few subjects seem to have experienced the self-doubts, the uncertainty about whether they should continue to exist at all, that have marked the discussions about English teaching.

In the course of these discussions it has become clear that English has abandoned most of what could formerly have been called its content, the obvious stock-in-trade that serves as the justification for many other subjects. There are perhaps still teachers who see it as their main duty to prepare their classes for the study of great literature, and others who consider that ensuring linguistic competence is the first priority; but the majority of books and public conversations in the last ten years have been concerned with a vaguer and more mystical vision of the subject which has occasionally made it sound like a spiritual chest-developer – 'English for maturity' in fact or 'growth through English'.

From initiating children systematically into the difficulties of a public, adult language the emphasis has shifted on to the child's own language and its role in the development of each individual. Language has been seen to be a major means by which people express, explain and come to control their experience of the world. The role of the

English teacher has undergone a corresponding change. Rather than encouraging an approximation to certain approved models he has become increasingly concerned with individual language development, and with ways of providing a range of experiences and suggestions which may serve as a stimulus for different kinds of talk and writing. Recent research has offered objective support for the larger and larger place being given to personal writing in the English class, seeing this 'expressive' mode as a necessary preparation for later kinds of writing, more differentiated in their style and function. Moreover, the English teacher, because of the confessional nature of much personal writing, has sometimes developed into a sort of lay analyst, and progress in English has appeared to be linked to the healthy development of the personality.

Despite the note of irony that has crept into this summary it is clear that these developments and theories are of great importance and have been the impetus behind much of the most interesting current classroom practice. But considering their preoccupation with language they have been, until lately, strangely quiet on one important subject – they have not placed much emphasis on the extent to which a child's language is as much a social as an individual possession.

Let's go back to the anecdote I began with. It would be interesting to know what kind of reaction one would have had in reading it, say, twenty years ago. In a sense the teacher who corrects the child's caption is obviously doing what she sees as her job, though it might be generally agreed that she is going about it in rather a crude way. But in another sense the meaning of her action is perfectly clear. She is substituting school language for home language, or, more plainly, middle-class language for working-class language.

This is where the dilemma begins. For the language of school has always been the language of the middle class, of the dominant culture, the book culture. Yet when English teachers encourage personal, expressive writing, they are encouraging a child to bring his own language, the language of his home and street, into school. At some stage in the school there will inevitably develop a conflict between the traditional book culture and the largely oral working-class culture of the majority of children.

The exams that are often the goal of school, slow to change and needing to preserve some standard from which deviation can be measured may be the point of conflict (their influence often spreading much further down the school). So may the assumptions about what is correct language held by colleagues. And so, of course, may the teacher's own language habits, which will themselves, by definition, be middle-class habits. We must acknowledge that this conflict exists in schools and not simply hope that it will go away, which is the reaction of a good number of teachers. On the whole, more 'progressive' teachers would be unwilling to tell a child that his own language is 'wrong' and the school's is 'right'. But they probably nevertheless rely on the child's adaptability and powers of assimilation to ensure that his language will change and develop in imitation of the models they provide for him. The process at its smoothest is described in the following quotation:

Neither special practice nor examinations in 'oracy' are likely to become necessary, provided that the tactful correction of slovenly speech, the insistence that reticent boys should not be swamped by the garrulous, and plentiful opportunities for both formal and informal talk, in such contexts as discussion, debate and drama, continue to figure as they do. Regional eccentricities of dialect, incidentally, normally disappear of their own accord before boys leave school, and no teacher would attempt to superimpose 'standard English'.[1]

Any working-class boy who gained entry to that school had probably got rid of most of his 'slovenly speech' already. But a large number of children will be less quick to adapt their language. What about them? As the exams approach it may become necessary to explain to them how much of their language is 'wrong'. Or they may be abandoned by the school, academically speaking (and perhaps therefore abandoned completely).

To some people the dilemma I have been outlining may seem absurd. The advantages of middle-class language (more 'complex', more 'coherent') may seem too obvious to need justification. In this case the brisk and sensible way in which the problem is disposed of in the following passage will be very attractive:

It is very important that a sentimental attitude towards working-class language be avoided. Undoubtedly it possesses a certain dramatic vigour and colour which should be preserved. But it should also be recognized that such language forms are in some important respects limited in range and control . . . . in all cases the important factor should be that teachers should never give the impression to a working-class child that his culture in general or his form of speech in particular is in any way inferior to the culture of the school. The concept of appropriateness rather than right or wrong speech and behaviour should become the desired end.[2]

Yet this summary, though it appears to take a balanced view, is not altogether satisfactory. For a start, little enough work has been done as yet to show where the particular strengths of working-class language lie, or to prove conclusively that it is incapable of handling abstractions and complex ideas (rather than of taking certain syntactical forms). And secondly, though Lawton's emphasis is on extending language rather than changing it, on the whole the situation this passage leaves us in is awfully like the one where we started – children's language is to be valued, but they are to be persuaded that it is inappropriate (not 'wrong'). It doesn't seem that, even with this shift of attitude, the teacher is likely to meet with much more success in the classroom in changing the language habits of children. Probably as many or as few will prove amenable to persuasion, and those will also be the examination successes. But at least the teacher will feel newly justified in his unsentimental attitude.

It seems clear that school has always had a lot to do with social selection and with the perpetuation of an elite. Its main benefits have always been reserved for the upper and middle classes, or increasingly for those who were most able to adapt to its standards and values (the 'upwardly socially mobile'). Exams, the end and thus the meaning of school are primarily selective processes. All these are by now familiar statements. Yet, if one rejects the conclusion that hence school should be abolished, one is left with the question of what it should be doing. If it is not to exist to benefit only the middle class and the most adaptable of the working class, what ought it to be like? Might there be an education primarily designed to benefit the majority of children – and in whose language would it be carried on?

It is possible to divide theories of curriculum, crudely, into two kinds – those which take as their starting-point the individual child, and those which try to define (very variously) what children need to know about the world they are growing into.

Education which is 'child-centred' aims at giving free play to the natural interests and abilities of the child. His individual development, his moments of understanding and impulse to creativity become the central point of education. Yet although this philosophy has the great merit of putting the client, the child, first, and although it lies behind some of the most heartening movements in primary schools, its organic vocabulary is not entirely appropriate to the growth of children who are inevitably limited in their freedom to develop by the social conditions that surround them, and shaped by social forces. Obviously 'child-centredness' has been responsible for many of the developments in English teaching that were briefly described earlier (perhaps because of upward influences from the primary school) but obviously too it is not a sufficient formula for education.

Curriculum theories which concentrate on what children need to know about the world take countless different forms, from traditional academic ones which concentrate on passing on the accumulation of past cultures to modern 'integrated' ones based on the children's own environment. The thinking behind the latter kind of curriculum is obviously that the child is a social being and should be prepared for this role. Yet such preparation, even when it takes the most modern and attractive of forms, can easily degenerate into a form of training for society as it is, into an acceptance of your role – as in a girls' comprehensive where the integrated syllabus for the four years from the ages of twelve to fifteen was based on the family, marriage, child care and various aspects of housewifery.

There is a need to decide in schools what children need to know, and never was there a more difficult question. But another question, seldom asked, is whether, in an unequal society, all children need to know the same things.

It has seemed for so long that the most desirable possible educational situation would be a comprehensive school which could achieve a successful mixture of ability and class that now it may seem perverse to question this aim. Yet the mixed-ability, multi-racial class in which all social groups are represented may be a false ideal. It looks very like a concrete version of the famous phrase 'equality of opportunity' which even the Labour Party now finds hollow. And to pursue it may be to limit what can be done. It does appear, for instance, that the most interesting experiments in working-class education have taken place in situations where the school did not have to pretend to a position of social neutrality, where the children were a homogeneous group, and where the success of the experience largely depended on the students' growing awareness of their own position in relation to their society, which they expressed in their own language. I am thinking in particular of the situations that underlie the writing of such books as *Letter to a Teacher*, written by Italian school students from the school of Barbiana;[3] *Thirty-six Children* by Herbert Kohl, about a class of

Harlem school children;[4] and, more generally, *Paint House*, a book by, and about, an East End skinhead gang.[5] The writing of Paulo Freire about his work with adult illiterates in Latin America is also of great importance.[6]

These situations represent one way of responding to the fact of social inequality in terms of education. The other way, which is to look to education to redress the social balance, is the more familiar course, and cannot be said to have met with any marked success. Over the years a succession of educational changes have been presented as roads to equality: they have included secondary education for all, comprehensive schools, the raising of the school-leaving age and, now, nursery education. One can recognize these measures as necessary, desirable, and important objects of campaign, while at the same time finding the presentation of them as social cure-alls highly misleading. Even while we work with them, it is important to recognise their limitations, for to expect too much of them is to put an intolerable strain on schools and on teachers. Education cannot compensate for society. Comprehensive schools which attempt to propagate an ethic of social equality, while they continue to perform the usual function of sorting out children, are well on the way to being schizophrenic institutions.

There are a number of reasons why English teachers today, in thinking about their subject, should have gone on, as many have, to discuss the politics of education. Questioning the content of one's own subject leads naturally to an interest in the curriculum as a whole, and in the whole process of education rather than one specialist sector. There has been discussion of the kinds of knowledge that are permitted or excluded by school. (Area studies, for example, may be acceptable if they are exercises in local history, but unacceptable if they take in contemporary local politics.) English Departments in several schools have increasingly found themselves in conflict with the institution as a whole over what can best be described as the *style* of their teaching; and in the course of this conflict have been made aware both of the anti-democratic nature of the structure of the school, and of the 'hidden curriculum', which stresses the importance of obedience and conformity even in institutions which overtly favour creativity and individual choice.

Finally, the question of attitudes to language and educational methods has proved to be one that cannot be confined to a school context. The values reflected in these attitudes are intimately related to the values of the society that the schools serve. English teachers have necessarily become concerned with this relationship.

References

1 B. Phythian, 'English at Manchester Grammar School' in G. Summerfield and S. Tunnicliffe, *English in Practice*, CUP, 1971.
2 D. Lawton, *Social Class, Language and Education*, Routledge, 1968.
3 The School of Barbiana, *Letter to a Teacher*, Penguin, 1970.
4 H. S. Kohl, *Thirty-six Children*, Gollancz, 1968, Penguin, 1970.
5 *Paint House: Words from an East End Gang*, Penguin, 1972.
6 P. Freire, *Cultural Action for Freedom*, Penguin, 1972.

6 Do we expect too much
– or too little?

EDWARD BLISHEN

I think that if a prize had to be given for a fairly meaningless activity, widely undertaken in the best of faith, it might be conferred on the teaching of English as it is carried on in a great many of our schools. If the prize were to be awarded to a single practitioner, I myself, round about the year 1951, would have been a strong contender. There I was, in a London secondary modern, face to face with boys who might well have quarrelled with my very use of the word 'English' – 'What kind of English er yer talkin' abaht then, matey?' – yet proceeding along the conventional course. We were talking (I was talking) about nouns, and verbs, and adjectives – oh, very warily, in a gingerly fashion, but still I *was* talking about them, and about sentences, and phrases, and we (and I mean *they*) were writing stories, and short statements of opinion, and I was correcting their work as if I'd been a proofreader, and as if they were a proofreader's proofreaders. We were crawling about, very nervously and reluctantly, in the scaffolding of language. This was what English teaching was, and had to be; the syllabus, if you could hunt down a copy, required it. (This syllabus, into the gloomy bargain, prescribed the use of sets of *Threadbare English*, Books I to IV.) There were nervous modifications and hesitancies, in my case, because I'd been recently trained and had come under the influence of an unusual tutor, George Sampson-inspired, so that I had a blurred awareness of other possibilities; but this added only a sneaky quality to the solid, conscientious meaninglessness of the activity.

It's true that there are forms of this activity far superior to the shape it took in my hands, twenty years ago. Some spring from the existence, side by side with *Threadbare English* (which only the old lags, or of course the young ones, use nowadays), of *English Bubbling Over*, and similar course books much livelier than their predecessors. Yet my bothered conviction is that in rather few places does even this greater liveliness really make English meaningful to an immense number of children. The activity remains, with them, most enormously out of favour. I think of a boy I taught in London in those early days of mine whose potential capacity for language was large enough: I mean, he was reasonably articulate, skilful: but he was a spokesman for so many when he expressed his boredom with English. The roots of that boredom were clearly far back in his experience of school. 'Let me go to the woodwork centre', he'd beg at the start of every lesson – as if with just a little more pressure he could bring about the collapse of my pretence that English was a reasonable subject for a near-man of fourteen.

It seems to me that one of the first tasks of a teacher finding himself face to face with such attitudes is to ask why any human being is ever persuaded that it's a good thing to improve his command of language. Clearly, many small children have a natural persuasion that this is so. Reading, writing, amassing words and turns of phrase and so forth, are self-justifying achievements. It may well be marvellous, at first, in the primary school – gaining power over language. You're enlarging your world, increasing your grasp of it: cutting a dash, too, and proving your ability. Many children even from environments where ambition is low and experience thin in respect of language may feel the glow and flush and natural pleasure of speaking, reading and writing with growing resource. Some will need (many never receive) special aid if they're to feel this, of course – because they've always been verbally ill-fed, or because they have social or psychological or physiological reasons, or mixtures of these, for being particularly uneasy about language. But the simple fact that, for all of us, ability with words is an essential feature of our development, and one whose desirability goes, at this early stage, without saying – this simple fact will carry many along, for a while. A minority will continue to feel the force of it, because they live among adults who make something of words, or gain various advantages, evident ones, from an advanced or fairly advanced capacity to use words. But for very many indeed, and rather early on in their schooling, the fuss the school makes about English easily becomes a puzzle, a perplexity or a sort of blankness. What's it all about? Why this to-do about approved forms of speech, when the powers a child already has seem perfectly adequate for him, and for the world he moves in and expects to continue to move in? Why, similarly, the fuss about reading? And especially, why the fuss about writing? Who, if he can write a simple note and fill in a form, wants to go on increasing his power to write?

It needs more than pure liveliness to make headway against such feelings. It needs also, I believe, a deeper analysis of what's wrong. One has to ask oneself, for example, what harm is done by the fact that English is one of the two major elements in schooling that, from early on, can be seen as areas in which your quality and your deserts are decisively judged. You are good at numbers, or fair, or not much good at all. You are good at English, or fair, or really pretty bad and unhopeful. For an enormous number of children, English soon becomes associated with a sense of poor, and fairly unimproveable, performance. Some children are winged with excellence at arithmetic and English, and they are clearly going to fly upwards, out of sight. The rest are wingless, or can boast a few rudimentary feathers.

The number of children I taught in Islington who'd been made to feel they were simply inept with their mother tongue! The sense of ineptitude had become the very core of their attitude to English. Why persist with one's mediocrity? I remember, again as an archetype, the boy who came up from the primary school with a shattering jumpiness in the matter of apostrophes. It would be a small exaggeration to say that he'd been led to feel that between him and any success whatever in writing stood the apostrophe, a dragon hired to keep the unworthy at bay. Little Bolton had discovered a connection between this device and the letter 's'. So he surrounded the letter 's' with apostrophes, wherever it appeared: even in the middle of a word. Bolton, nervously attempting to propitiate the apostrophe, stood for so many others, aware of their mother tongue (in so far as it was something to work on, in school) only as an area of ineptitude.

So, whatever the teacher does where this has happened, he most certainly must find ways of re-defining English for his pupils. It must become something other than what they're not good at. The question of being good at it must be replaced by another feeling altogether. And then (another result of that deep analysis of what is wrong) he may have to rescue it from seeming to be merely a feature of social class. When I taught in my London secondary modern, it took me rather too long to conclude that one of the reasons for the resistance to English, as a school subject, was that most of my pupils were quite desperately afraid of coming to resemble teachers. They saw themselves as being taught, not a mother tongue, but the tongue of the middle class. A stepmother tongue, indeed! This is one of the problems of English teaching that, I believe, we widely fail to focus: that we have to persuade a great many children that we have a language in common.

And we may – teachers may – have to begin by persuading ourselves of this. In Devon once at a meeting of teachers I was asked what could be done about the local accent and idiom. I thought the questioner was concerned with preserving west country forms of English: but it turned out that, clearly no lonely eccentric, she was of the opinion that they ought to be destroyed. All over the place, it's my impression, we fail to prevent the children from suspecting that our teaching is a kind of subversion directed against them, in the matter of their being comfortable with a language – with the language, that is, in which they talk among themselves, and at home. Sir Bernard Miles, whose own two main voices were acquired in a Berkshire village and in Oxford University, has said:

You have a heart language, that's the language where your feet are planted, the basic soil of your being. And then you have a head language, that you use for wider communication – and for purposes of convenience, that perhaps has to be received, standard English. . . . But the heart speech is where you belong. You should never let go. That gives you terrific sustenance.

How much respect for the heart languages is there in our schools, in our English classrooms? One of the brightest boys I taught in my own early years in London was self-demoted from a grammar school: he hadn't been able to endure the constant war levelled there against his local tongue. It wasn't, when it came to the point, that he was against the acquisition of a language of the head. He was fully capable of providing himself with a received and standard tongue, spoken and written. But the assumption that he could be considered to have got anywhere in English only by forswearing all the turns and tones of his native Cockney – *that* he couldn't swallow. He put up against it, being the person he was, an articulate and resolute struggle. It is my experience that a very great many children put up that struggle silently, negatively, and that the measure of it is their lack of interest in the English lesson. They don't hit out; they stonewall.

If all this is so, what do we do in order to turn English teaching in such settings into an effective and positive activity, and stop it from being a dead and useless one?

What follows is based on my own attempt at an answer, in the course of ten years teaching in a secondary modern in an educationally dejected area of North London. I make this point because I believe very strongly that every teacher must look in himself for his own natural strategy, in this situation: he may pick up ideas from others, but in essence he has to work out his own answers. Right at the heart of it all, as I see it, must be a lively teacher being himself: trying to remove from English teaching the generalised, stereotyped, impersonal qualities that everywhere remain characteristic of it, and make so much more difficult the struggle to hearten and convince these children. I think we need a teacher who thinks of his classroom as a studio, or workshop. And never mind that workshop is a fashionable word in educational discussion! When Tolstoy taught Russian to the children of Yasnaya Poliana, the room was much more of a workshop than a classroom – with Tolstoy at times, it will be remembered, sitting at a desk, writing, while the boys crowded around and discussed how the writing should go, what turns of phrase might be considered. If wood and paint and clay are the materials that make it easy to apply the word workshop to the woodwork centre or the art room, then words, paper, books are the no less real and manipulable material of the English classroom.

I remember, indeed, an occasion when my own classroom, and our woodwork centre, became related – as follows. I'd found myself wondering what it was that constituted the thick and complex and therapeutic odour of the woodwork room, to which I confess I would retreat when my side of things became intolerable. Off to that island in the centre of our maze of playgrounds and lavatories: and past the fences shouting, in chalk, that half my colleagues were mad – off to the woodwork centre, where my eccentric colleague would cry: 'Down! Down on your faces! Here's the master in charge of English!' And the class would fall flat in postures which, fortunately for them, they'd studied in films about the Foreign Legion. And I'd stand and take in that life-restoring smell of resins and varnishes and wood-dust. . . . So, anyway, I got a class on to that: to trying to get their tongues, as it were, round that smell. And when we had a few satisfactory sentences and even a complete passage or two on the smells in the woodwork centre, we found it irresistible to attempt to account for smells elsewhere in the school, far less satisfactory most of them: some left from a fairly remote date, we guessed roughly 1878. A deep deposit of most despondent odours! . . .

The point is that, all over the place, woodwork centre and art room are popular places (while the English classroom is not), primarily because there's a sense of real work being done, with real materials, that as I shall hope to suggest in a moment, the English classroom can also provide. But first there has to be this determinedly lively teacher, who among other things will borrow an extra cause of popularity from the example set by the woodwork master and art master: the fact that both of these are participating teachers – playing captains! Sir paints in the art room, Sir is usually known as someone who also paints at home, away from school: and Sir saws and hammers and measures (and curses when he hits his thumb) in the woodwork centre, and is known to do these things when he's away from it. But think how few Sirs, or Misses, are securely known to practise English, in the classroom or out of it: in matters of speech, beyond the oral element in teaching itself ('Turn to page 27'), in matters of writing or reading! Especially the two last! Do we convince our children that we do much writing ourselves, outside the most stringent line of duty? Is it possible for them to feel that we are urging upon them an activity for which we have personally no great enthusiasm? Do we write when they write? Where is Sir's story, or Miss's poem? When did we last see Sir carrying a book, his own book? When did Miss last tell us about a book she was reading – or say to us something like: 'I was reading a story last night that made my hair stand on end, and if only we had five minutes to spare –' 'Oh go on Miss – we'll give you five minutes!'? When was there last such an exchange in the classroom? Are we able to feel that Sir or Miss not only urge the importance of reading upon us, but feel it themselves so obviously that we're totally convinced of the reality of it – oh, because you always see them with books, and a score of times a day a turn of talk in the classroom reminds them of a book – and because they read bits of books to us: bits that cause them delight, or puzzlement, or surprise, or scorn. . . .

One thing I'm absolutely certain about in this matter of attempting to make English real for those who have every reason for being indifferent to it: at the centre of the effort must be a teacher who, like the good art or handicraft master, uses himself, his own way with the materials of his subject – in this case, his own writing and reading and his general traffic with language – as a constant demonstration of the pure interest and value of increasing one's hold over the mother tongue. It's an honest demonstration that's needed, if the suspicion's to be thrust aside. Among the achievements that may begin to grow out of that demonstration may be the disarming of the children's fear of the social overtones of English teaching. Because the real answer to that fear lies in the truth that language, in some of its aspects profoundly affected by class, is in the end above class. Listening to, say, one of Conan Doyle's Sherlock Holmes stories, a child doesn't think of the language of the story as the product of a class – though it certainly is, speaking as it does with a late Victorian English middle-class voice – but as a classless language of satisfactory narrative. I believe there are two ways in which we can hope to overcome that resistance to English teaching which in so many of our children arises from their suspicion of the teacher's intentions, in social terms. The first is to busy ourselves so variously, so informally, so unsolemnly in language, in the classroom, that by sheer activity the suspicion is bypassed. The second is to put to employment the gift for language that is natural in most children.

That last sentence will seem a paradox. And in terms of what we actually do and expect in much of our English teaching, it *is* a paradox. I remember, in my early days in London, when I had duly concluded that I was working among children who in respect of language were sensationally handicapped – by experience, certainly, and perhaps by nature – I remember the shock of suddenly understanding that this conclusion was incompatible with a certain observation I'd made, during those first months, again and again. This observation, which I'd been too distracted to generalise, was that my boys were in fact extraordinarily able imitators and parodists. In classrooms and in the playground I'd heard my own accent, my own turns of phrase, closely copied, for purposes of anonymous derision. I'd noticed that boys could imitate a BBC announcer – and not the voice alone, but the phrasing. There was, in fact, a great interest, largely impish, in language, and real gifts of parody and satire. This discovery was the starting-point of a slow conversion on my part. I came to see, bit by bit, that I must make use of the boys' unconventional, informal interest in language – in the tones of language, especially. And this work, too, I believe, helped to take English out of the reach of social suspicion. We weren't any longer starting from the premise that there was a single acceptable form of English, of which the teacher was the (alas, so often dull) custodian, and which could prosper only if it drove out all other forms. Instead, we were interested in many different forms, and usages. I must say that, in my case, the conviction that this was one way of going ahead was reinforced by my experience as a writer – that is, as someone who had never in his life wished to be anything else, and who, as long as he could remember, had scribbled, scribbled, scribbled. Those driven by this strange necessity always, instinctively, experiment in tones of voice: they always, instinctively, listen for the ways in which things are said, for individualities of language. With several of my classes I set out on the making of a local dictionary and phrasebook. We made ourselves aware of peculiarly local phrasing, and would look for equivalents drawn from other settings, other atmospheres. So up the hill from Islington, up in Highgate village, they'd talk about someone being 'well-to-do', when down the hill, where we were, there'd be talk of his having 'lots of lolly' or being 'quids in'. Conceited in Highgate, a man would come down to Upper Holloway and find that we thought him one who 'reckoned himself'. Each of these languages, we observed, had its perfectly serious place, as a language of the heart – or the hearth. Each language, of course, was also amusing, or immensely interesting, for what it told us about its users. And each was very properly a source of full comedy, because each in extreme forms was capable of being entirely ridiculous. We listened, on holidays and other sorts of travel, to turns of phrase from elsewhere. My aim, slowly declaring itself to me out of the fogs of my actual practice, was to disarm the boys' suspicions by bringing about, as far as I could do so, a good-natured and interested feeling for the great variety of human usage, and the manner in which habits of language were related to personalities, ways of life, accidents of geography, and so on.

Much of the work I found myself doing from then on was of this sort – I mean, not taken from course books, but based on local listening, local observation and on exercises (mostly of a game-like sort) in tones of language. Behind all my other reasons for working in this way lay the fact that I found I could, by such methods, cause some excitement and curiosity among my boys left cold (as, I confess, I was myself) by conventional methods of working. But it meant we were getting away from that generalised, official, approved language that children are able to feel is being imposed upon them. There was all the material I wanted on which to base my work in the world of language in which we, particular groups of schoolchildren and their teacher, moved. So we were interested in the speech we overheard, in the streets, on buses, everywhere. We listened for the phrases and turns and patterns of speech through which people betray (so we may conclude) their natures. We tried to discover those habits of language that marked the bore, or the man or woman – or boy or girl – who is in the grip of anger, or of tenderness, or of greed. How did a vain man speak? Carefully, good-naturedly – what about our own habits, tics, oddities of usage? (Sir's included.) We listened, much of the time, simply for words. It was, again, woefully late in my teaching that I understood what a passion most children have for words, purely and simply. We bury that passion, pretty effectively, under much of our formal classroom work in English, or in work in words that may seem to be a reproach levelled at the children's own comfortable idioms and usages. But here we were, listening for words and hunting them down, and vying with one another in pursuit of them, comparing and matching them and trying to fit them into the dictionaries or amused or amazed to observe that they wouldn't quite match their official meanings. . . . The important thing, in my experience, was to keep at the core of it this interest in the language with which we were ourselves surrounded, this or that particular group. Not, of course, merely the language of speech overheard, or language that was locally ours: but also the language of radio and television, of newspaper and comic, and the language of books.

But at the heart of it was *our* detective work, *our* local observation, *our* discovery of the connection between a man or woman, boy or girl, and the way he or she used language. And so on.

Teachers say sometimes: but we can't work like this. We must rest much of what we do on the generalised material of the course books, of exercises found in such books, and on similar material. The other method is too exhausting! My reply to this is not an abstract one, but is based on my own experience. I think teachers shrink often from this exploratory and improvisatory work because they believe the bulk of it, including the decisions as to how to proceed, must be carried by them. The truth is that, once the spirit of such work is established, much will be done by the children themselves. They become, very simply, more involved and far more interested. And when one begins to think in terms of what is offered by occasions, by opportunities arising, then ideas begin to flood in. There are so many kinds of work that spring naturally and copiously from attempts to examine such a question as: how can a thing be said? In how many different ways can a thing be said? How do changes of word alter what is said? Or perhaps we shall decide to concentrate, this week, on language so used that we are made to feel sad. Who can find a passage, anywhere, in a book or in any printed thing, that will bring tears to our eyes? Can any of us write such a piece? Next week, or the week after, we shall be trying to make each other's hair stand on end. We'll have long-range tasks of this sort, requiring thought and vision and revision, and we'll have sudden sharp tasks, to be done within the next ten minutes. Write down, quickly, what happened just before you came into the room, at the beginning of this lesson. Nothing happened? Then give an account of that nothing (I remember some surprising accounts of nothings). A passage from a guide book to our town – but we want people to come, so dull conventional guidebookese won't do. But now we want a passage from that guidebook designed to keep the tourist, however eager, at bay. One sentence only, as interesting as you can make it, about something you saw on the telly last night. One *word* only on the same subject. Has someone got something to read to us this morning? . . .

And in the middle of it, the teacher, sharing things: being in the middle, in this busy and informal way, partly because his concern is that his charges should work better and better, more and more efficiently. In simply and naturally displaying the workings of his own self-critical processes, he can, I believe, do more than by any other single step to show his children how to work on a piece of English until it's tolerable. And this he needs to do because he must give his pupils an attitude to correction, to the whole process of working over a piece of writing or a spoken statement, that won't be like the monstrous, utterly unserviceable approach that is the mark of most conventional classroom correction. There is a calculation that is never likely to be made, but that would, I suspect, produce the most depressing results: it would weigh the time spent all over the country by English teachers in the meticulous and incessant correcting of children's work, against the real effect of those corrections in terms of the children's understanding of them and of improvement flowing from them. It's a disease, this habit – even a beloved disease. It rests on a tradition that the English teacher is a species of conscientious mechanic. Each piece of work done by a child is like a car driven in for service. The teacher dons his overalls and drops into the inspection pit. Every fault must be set right. To do nothing about, say, a misspelled word or a misplaced or missing comma would be like ignoring a loose nut on the wheel of a car, or a faulty clutch. And this vast and useless operation adds to children's sense that writing is that which one does in order to create the need for correction.

Many teachers become so nervous when there's any suggestion of economy of correction. They see standards slumping – they see it all ending in that wilderness of blots to which, the Black Paper people declare, new forms of English teaching are leading. I have to be personal about this. I have the writer's usual stern obsession with the

D

machinery of language. As a teacher, I wanted my children to become more and more efficient, contantly to increase their command of the machinery. The proof is everywhere that old mechanical forms of correction, old mechanical methods of all kinds, produce no true increase of efficiency. This is partly because we are most likely to master the mechanics by having our attention on the substance of what we are doing, not on the mechanics themselves. In addition, we must have a reason for caring about mechanics. With all that, it's much the same as with morality. It's in actually doing that we learn the techniques of doing: not through sermons, homilies, exhortations. So we need the English workshop, with much going on, and the teacher working alongside his pupils – we need that, if we're to create a true and effective appetite for some command over the machinery of language. Little Bolton's progress was barred by that damned apostrophe because the apostrophe had been dealt with in the abstract. He got over the barrier once he was busy with writing; so preoccupied with that, and with his desire that it should be readable by others, that the not terribly difficult secrets of the apostrophe were suddenly laid open for him.

I have to be cryptic about another aspect of this work that, to me, is of the greatest importance. I believe it is essential to attempt to revive the association between the spoken and the written. One of the dreadful general blights on English teaching, I believe, is that so soon in a child's schooling the connection between what's said and what's set down, between the voice and the written word, is shattered. In a good infants' school, the children are perfectly aware that in writing they are employing a splendid extension of the power of speech. An extension, of course, with its own qualities, its own advantages. You can shape and consider and reconsider what you write. But still the basis of it is the voice, the tongue. Too soon we're taught to write for the eye, unhearingly. It's another reason, I believe, why work in English may seem so awfully unreal – this separation of what one would say, with one's tongue, from what one's led to say, with one's pen. Again, to try to retrace one's steps is actually to make things more interesting. There are hundreds of pleasant ways in which writings can lead, in the classrooms, to readings and speakings. . . .

And there's another association that I believe to be important – between writing and reading. How often, how easily, the two activities are kept apart in the classroom! Or the reading leads only to hopelessly foolish kinds of writing – analytical dullnesses! There's an essay of Proust's in which he speaks of reading as being, very often, a spur to writing. You want to go and do the same! Children feel this desire, too, but it's so often balked: so that books, instead of seeming what they in fact are, especially resourceful examples of work we all attempt to do, come to have no connection with us at all. . . .

I return to a statement I made near the beginning: that the question of being good at English, or no good, must be replaced by another feeling altogether. My experience is that, even with children who've become pretty dispirited or demoralised, this can be done; but it needs a teacher who believes himself that the question of a child's flair for his own language, and achievement with it, is only one matter among a complex of matters. The important question is whether one can help any child to be as resourceful and happy with his own tongue as he's able to be. I believe that if we think in such terms, then much of the conventional matter and manner of English teaching becomes point-less, because it really arises out of English as a medium for testing and assessing – aided and abetted by elderly and not deeply considered ideas as to means of imparting skills in language. What we're left with then are our children, their need to enjoy and develop their power over their own language; and ourselves, with our need to enjoy teach-ing. Ten years of work with children many of whom were deeply discouraged has convinced me that what arises out of *that* situation – whatever methods come naturally to any particular teacher – is work-shop English: improvisatory, opportunistic, much of it very local in inspiration and quality.

7   Beyond self-expression: English and the community

KEN WORPOLE

He [the writer] should never say to himself, 'Bah! I'll be lucky if I have three thousand readers', but rather, 'What would happen if everybody read what I wrote?' He remembers what Mesca said beside the coach which carried Fabrizie and Sanseverina away, 'If the word love comes up between them, I'm lost'. He knows that he is the man who names what has not yet been named or what dares not tell its name. He knows that he makes the word 'love' and the word 'hate' surge up and with them love and hate between men who had not yet decided on their feelings. He knows that words, as Brice-Parrain says, are 'loaded pistols'. If he speaks, he fires. He may be silent, but since he has chosen to fire, he must do it like a man, by aiming at targets, and not like a child, at random, by shutting his eyes and firing merely for the pleasure of hearing the shot go off.[1]

For many children, writing in school, or as Sartre puts it, 'firing merely for the pleasure of hearing the shot go off', at the secondary stage becomes a rather pointless activity, and one can understand their attitude. As far as they are concerned, most of them feel that they know how to write, and question the object of regularly producing work which is perhaps more frequently criticised than praised. Fortunately, most children are generous enough to assume that even if they don't know the reasons for their endless activity, the teacher is fully aware of its purpose. Their trust is very touching although I wonder if English teachers really deserve their confidence. Of course, it is not too difficult, given a few minutes of thought, to produce what seem to be convincing explanations for demanding that children write, such as 'It enables them to sort out their ideas and present them in the coherent and structured style which writing demands', or, as followers of David Holbrook might put it, 'In their creative writing they can externalise their own interior conflicts and by means of dramatisation and projection come to some kind of resolution . . .' Incidentally, the problem with the second kind of rationale is that any piece of writing contains not one but two psychological contents: that of the child who writes and that of the teacher who reads what has been written. There are also the more explicitly 'functional' explanations which ultimately legitimise the work of the school: that so many pieces of written work are required for the course work component of an external examination, or that lack of literary skills will handicap the child in the employment market.

I personally don't find any of the above arguments totally convincing and I am sure that were we to confide in the children we teach that these were some of the reasons for their activity, they could, without too much difficulty, find fault with all of them. They could argue, for example, that they are quite capable of discussing ideas without needing to write about them; that the teacher has no right, and is most probably not qualified, to 'psychologise' about the stories and poems that they write; that the Certificate of Secondary Education examination is irrelevant to many of them and is a very arbitrary reason for writing, and that the job they are intended for does not even demand that they think, let alone write.

I think that much of our uncertainty about this issue arises very clearly from the areas of discrepancy between the study and the teaching of English. Teachers study English either at a college of education or at a university; in both cases, although perhaps slightly less so at the former, the content of the course is almost entirely devoted to literary appreciation: the study of, by definition, published works of creative writing in a number of different literary forms. There is little or no expectation that the students themselves will write and very little questioning of the whole idea of the distinction between writers and readers (which, since the roles imposed within the cultural industry are simply mirror-images of those imposed by the economic system, we might equally well call producers and consumers). Similarly, the study of non-literary forms of writing, other uses of literacy, the sociology and history of communications, are all either marginal to or absent from higher education English courses. Have we yet worked out whether there is, in fact, any theoretical difference at all between the kinds of questions and judgements we take to a 'classic' literary text and those we take to a piece of writing produced in an English lesson?

(A brief autobiographical note: during my five years as a grammar school pupil, from which I escaped twelve years ago, it was never once suggested that the boys in our class could write poems. We naturally assumed that poetry was written by rather effete, and certainly eccentric people with names like Tennyson, Browning and Rupert Brooke. We have come some way since then, but for many of us it is still difficult to break away from our traditional ideas about literary production, so that we can begin to think of the children we teach not only as writers, but as authors.)

Now obviously, the deep study of literature is highly relevant to much of our motivation and sympathy for writing when we are in the classroom. And while we are on teaching practice, using the ideas about how to stimulate the children to write which are generated in the 'professional courses' we undertake, we find that the children are very responsive to our efforts. Unfortunately, the 'stimulus-response' model of English teaching, while sustaining us during a short period of teaching practice, seems unacceptable when we are faced with the prospect of five years' work in English in the secondary school. One begins to realise this when one overhears a boy, walking across the playground as the snow begins to fall, turn to his friends, due to be taught English next lesson, and say, in a deliberately loud whisper, 'Oh, I suppose we'll have to write a poem about being out in the snow!' The model is, in the end, unacceptable because it is a tautology; it is self-rationalising and ignores the question we started with: why should children write?

I think that we can answer that question with regard to younger children by saying that they write because they enjoy it as an end in itself: 'Firing merely for the pleasure of hearing the shot go off.' Very young children are fascinated with words and enjoy making (and illustrating) stories of fantasy and adventure. There is also the important source of motivation with primary school children that arises from the relatively high 'significance' of the class teacher for whom the work is written. This factor is considerably weakened in the secondary school where the pupil only sees the teacher for perhaps two to three hours a week and often for only one year, when he or she is replaced by another English teacher.

In the secondary school, particularly from the third form upwards, there is a much more frequent resistance to writing, and often the students' arguments, if we acknowledge them, are not without foundation. They realise that their writing situation is a very artificial one, and even if they are only writing for the teacher they often realise that their story or poem will not get the sympathetic attention it deserves because a teacher teaching six classes a week will, theoretically, be reading and marking at least one hundred and eighty other stories, essays and poems as well. Faced with this situation I think we must completely open up the discussion and take a new look at hitherto accepted views of motivation, reasons for writing, class-cultural attitudes towards knowledge and the sociology of literary and cultural production.

The dominant debate in education today centres on the question: why do so many working-class children fail in school? Much of the debate focuses on issues which are of particular importance to English teachers: language and culture. The argument about language now almost exclusively takes its bearings from the theoretical models offered by Bernstein. However, quite different perspectives are now being proposed by, for instance, Harold Rosen in this country, who asks for a more thorough understanding of the historical dimension to the variety of working-class cultures that still to some extent shape and consolidate structures of attitudes and feelings.[2]

Two misconceptions about 'the working class' continue to obscure and divert the debate on 'educability': the first is that the working class is an undifferentiated mass with a mechanically controlled set of cultural responses, and the second is that working-class cultures have always been almost exclusively oral. With regard to the first point there are the depressing findings of Goodacre[3] concerning the inability of many teachers to make any valid inferences about children based on parental occupation, and the general ignorance of teachers about degrees of skill and responsibility within working-class occupations. Secondly, we probably need to remind ourselves that during certain periods of our history working-class people were quite capable of producing highly literate responses in political affairs, and of reading and understanding works of theory that would tax many of us teachers today. It is appropriate to note that most social historians date the beginnings of the radical working-class movement from the formation of the London Corresponding Society, a group of mostly skilled artisans concerned with the propagation of radical ideals by means of debate, correspondence and pamphleteering. In 1817 Cobbett's *2d Register* was selling between 40,000 and 60,000 a week, whereas the circulation of the leading daily, *The Times*, during the same period was between 5,000 and 6,000. Between 1791 and 1793 Thomas Paine's *Rights of Man* had sold 200,000 copies in a population of ten million. It would be more true to say that there was a conscious move by the ruling class to divert the working class away from serious reading and written propaganda, towards the passive consumption of diversionary reading.

Radical writers continued to expand the public, John Wade's *Black Book* selling 10,000 an issue, and Cobbett's *Address to the Journeymen and Labourers* selling 200,000 in two months. But it was here, precisely, that active measures were taken against the expansion on the grounds of *the political dangers of too widespread reading.* The heavy taxation of newspapers was supplemented by a series of prosecutions aimed at killing the whole radical press. A different response to the same danger was the development of cheap tracts, of an 'improving kind', designed to counter the success of Cobbett and others, and these were heavily subsidised in this first stage.[4]

What I think one can generalise from history, because there have been many other periods of intense working-class organisation and self-education, is that within working-class cultures, reading and writing have been foremost social activities, shared activities that have not been seen as ends in themselves but as genuine means of communication between men towards an understanding of common problems and mutual enlightenment. And again I think one can generalise also by saying that within certain kinds of middle-class cultural settings, particularly literary and educational ones, reading and writing have been regarded as being ends in themselves, without necessarily any 'functional' overtones. The extreme example of this latter kind of attitude is the allegedly true story of an Oxford college reunion at which the toast was, 'To pure mathematics: may it never be of any use to anyone!' The culture behind such an attitude would, of course, be incomprehensible within any kind of working-class framework. Yet I think that in much of our English teaching we, with some uncertainty perhaps, find the 'non-functional' approach to reading and writing closer to our own intellectual position than what we assume to be its opposite: presumably lots of spelling, letter-writing practice and comprehension exercises on newspaper articles. In actual practice many of us pretend to solve the situation by doing both. I believe, though, that there is an alternative to the highly individualistic 'self-expression' approach, advocated by probably the majority of English teachers at present, which is not at all functional to the employment market but is potentially far more liberating and creative than much of our work at present.

I suggested at the beginning that for many of our students writing for its own sake seemed irrelevant. And I think that that kind of attitude is closely connected with class in that what essentially defines class is the relationship with the means of production. In economic theory, and in fact, the working class are the producers and this is very much a determinant of cultural attitudes as well as occupational ones. In our education system, almost right up to post-graduate level, education is essentially non-productive, and it might be that this feature rather than any other is the source of the 'clash of cultures/values' that most of our sociologists talk about. I think that what we now have to consider, as a matter of real urgency, is how English teaching transforms itself from essentially individualistic and reflective activity into a form of cultural production for others. That is, that we begin to think in terms of the work we do having some social and cultural purpose that goes beyond the confines of the classroom walls.

What makes this situation now possible, to an extent that has not previously been envisaged, is the accessibility of schools to the new reprographic technology. This is not the place to raise the question of the relationship between technology and the new kinds of cultural forms that it makes possible, except to say that in this country we have never really taken the theories and practical possibilities seriously. Again I think teachers in general, and perhaps English teachers in particular, have fought shy of contact with technology, which they often regard with suspicion, or have simply seen it as a helpful aid which enables them to do the old things more easily. The case is, though, and this may seem paradoxical, that the new media technology is potentially much more democratic and amenable to local and individual control than older methods of communication. The move from letterpress printing to photo-lithography provides an appropriate example. With letterpress printing one had to have, to start with, a very expensive composing machine as well as a highly skilled compositor. Each letter of print was cast in an expensive and very heavy metal alloy. Consequently, book production overheads were high, and the addition of illustrations in the form of block engravings made the production of printed material expensive except for books with potentially high sales. Also, once a book had been printed one was faced with the problem of storing all the printing blocks at great expense, or melting them down again in which case reprinting became impossible. With photo-lithography, the image can be produced on a typewriter and then photographed. The photographic negatives can be stored very easily and used again as desired. Illustrations present no separate problem except that they may have to be converted into 'half-tones', which is a simple process. Photo-lithography also means that the author is in control of layout and design since the original art work becomes the photographic plate, whereas with letterpress there was no such flexibility. Today, there are schools which possess their own offset duplicator which can print on hard glossy paper copies of a child's original writing and illustrations.

We have, then, the technological potential now to abolish completely the traditional distinction between writers and readers (producers and consumers), providing we ourselves are prepared to re-think our notions of literary production. It is not simply that one wants to make such changes on wholly theoretical grounds; we have to realise that it is the present system of, in this case, children's book production that is based on an outdated and elitist conception of literary production. A modern trend in children's readers provides an exemplary case. We are now finding, in the commercial publishers' lists, reading schemes which 'are directly relevant to the modern urban working-class child', with breathless titles such as (I characterise) *The Jesmond Alley Crew Go Mugging*. In many cases the contents of such readers are very crude and false projections of working-class life, written without empathy or imagination. One wants to ask, surely, 'If you want a direct and true account of everyday life in a city-centre tower block, why not ask a child who lives in one to write it?' At this point we in fact confront that peculiar ideological and mental block which cannot possibly conceive of democratising the process of literary production. I believe that we teachers have to begin to start this process ourselves. It might now be relevant to discuss some of the projects that different children, parents and teachers have been working on in Hackney which provide an idea of how this theory can work very well in practice.

Our first production was a children's reading book, illustrated by photographs, which used a story-line set very specifically in Hackney. This was done with the help of a friend who lived in the area, a very good amateur photographer with a professional understanding of printing processes. The four main characters in the book were played by four first-form boys from the school where I teach. To start with, we outlined a story, which was endorsed by the boys taking part, and then during the days of a half-term holiday took a series of photographs on location which matched the sequence of the story. Once we had developed and printed the photographs, we wrote out the narrative in full and again had this ratified by the boys as to its imaginative authenticity. The story was then sent to be typeset and when we received that back we were able to lay out the book exactly as we wanted. The cost of producing *Hackney Half-Term Adventure* – the title was a compromise of sorts – was £300 for 3,000 copies, which retail at 20p each, of which 1,200 copies have been sold so far in the ten months since it was published. Distribution for the book has been almost completely handled by a local bookshop/community centre, although several local newsagents were persuaded to sell it.

In retrospect, I think that the book would have had more vitality had it been written by the children. However, as it is, it has been enthusiastically read by local children who quickly recognise the location of the photographs as being ones that are familiar to them.

During a discussion with a fourth-form English class about children's reading books they made very much the same kinds of criticisms that many teachers would make: that the settings are remote, mainly rural; that the characters are even more remote, the ubiquitous genteel middle-class, pre-war family of boy, girl, mother, father and faithful dog, Rover, and the language within the books inert and inconsequential. It then seemed obvious to ask them to produce books themselves which could be used by younger boys within the school. Since we have a number of cheap cameras in the English department, they were also able to illustrate their stories. Two groups of boys chose to make books as single assignments for their CSE course work folder. Knowing that the book was intended for younger boys, each group 'borrowed' two boys who then became the central characters in the stories. Both groups planned their books in terms of the camera shots that they wanted to take and once this was settled they went out for the morning, under supervision, with the younger boys and took their photographs. The settings they chose were mainly the favourite play sites used by the boys themselves: by the canal and on the marshes. After the photographs had been printed they worked in their groups, and after a few lessons each group produced a collectively written text to accompany the photographs. The books were then duplicated with stencils cut on an electronic stencil cutter which permits the reproduction of photographs. The end products, although perhaps rather crude by commercial standards, were very well received by the younger children.

One of the most important features of this idea is that the language and syntax used in the books are precisely those used by the children themselves: their key words rather than ours. There is also the fact that because the younger, less enthusiastic readers themselves become the characters in the stories, there is the maximum possible identification, and this is obviously very closely linked with motivation. Another crucial difference between this kind of local, democratic process of book production and that of the commercial publishers is that this kind of reading book not only benefits the readers but there is also the very important educational and social experience involved in the production. New ways of working together and planning are involved and an interest is developed in picture composition, layout and writing within a new kind of context. The concept of authorship begins to lose its traditional aura and the activity of writing acquires a genuine social purpose; the pupils are genuinely helping each other.

Obviously this process is apposite to 'the great reading problem'. Although we now seem to be preoccupied with scientific models for the teaching of reading skills, it is very probable that the important questions of motivation and cultural relevance required in wanting to learn to read have been relegated to a rather insignificant position.

In the past year a number of new titles have been added to the English department stocklist: *The Soldier's Story*, written by a fourth-form boy and illustrated by one of his classmates; *The Red Bus and Other Stories* by six boys from one first-year class; *My Best Friend*, two longer stories by two other first-form boys: *Vivian Usherwood: Poems*, now also available in a glossy printed public version, and others are in the process of production. It is not too difficult to imagine the situation, a highly desirable one, I believe, in which most of the reading material available within a school would in fact be produced by the children themselves and other members of the community. This is not to propose that the very good, commercially published books by many of the better children's writers should not be used, but the community-produced books could well replace much of the 'hack' material that schools at present are forced to use because of the lack of an alternative. In many cases, though, we are filling gaps which the commercial publishers have never tried to tackle, particularly with very short stories for the slow readers who are nowhere near Alan Garner, John Rowe Townsend, Philippa Pearce and others. One is also breaking down the mysterious aura that books have for many children by presenting them with material that has been written by their own friends, and not by some faraway author whose books can seem a form of mental intimidation.

In our own case a school publishing programme would certainly be assisted by better reprographic material – we need now, I believe, an offset duplicator and a plate-maker – but most schools should be able to get access to better equipment through a resources centre or a teachers' centre.

Outside our particular school similar projects are now happening. We have recently produced a collection of social and historical documents about Hackney called *If it wasn't for the houses in between . . .* which has been designed like a 'Jackdaw' and contains a selection of historical maps, photographs, extracts from locally based novels, copies of local General Strike newspapers, a selected glossary of cockney slang and transcripts of tapes made with older members of the community. Perhaps some extracts from the local autobiographies provide some indication of the quality of experience which has been made available by means of the pack:

When I was fourteen in 1904 and left school my headmaster gave me a letter to a couple of firms who had apprenticeship schemes. And of course in those days there were no labour exchanges; decent employers always used to ask the headmasters to send along their brighter boys for apprenticeships. One I remember was a Mr Sparrow who turned out to be a sculptor who wanted a boy who was clever at drawing and of course I took along some examples of my work and he was quite satisfied with me. He said to me, 'You're a very small boy, aren't you? I shall have to give you some boxes to stand on, won't I!' I said 'Yes, Sir, does it make any difference?' He said, 'Oh no.' 'Because after all,' I said, 'Nelson was a small man and look where they put him in Trafalgar Square.'

'If you were ill you were expected to go to school and if a boy was away, the teacher, or the headmaster, would send another boy round to his house to see why the boy didn't come, and if he was ill to try to persuade the parents to let the boy come. He needn't do any lessons, he'd just sit in front of the class, but it was imperative that he came. In winter months, practically every day there would be five, six, seven or eight children all sitting round the fire, their heads resting on their arms and their arms resting on the fireguards. The children should either have been in bed, or, possibly, in hospital. But the thing was that they were present! And that was all important. . . .

I often would argue with the teachers over politics. Even at that age I had a fair knowledge about politics – I was about nine I suppose at the time. I used to go to Victoria Park every Sunday on the huge piece of ground allocated for the purpose of people holding public meetings and I used to listen to the various speakers there. There were all brands of religious thought, and politically, they were mainly left-wing . . . and for my age I learned quite a lot from attending those meetings.

I still remember my father's friend telling him how his little son died. It could only have been a few weeks old. His eyes were red with crying. The remaining children were sitting around a wooden table with newspaper for a table cloth. After my father gave him the few shillings he had collected, he was asked if he would like to see the baby before the undertaker arrived to screw down the coffin. I believe it was the thing everyone did in those days. My father said he would and told me to stay put. This I would not do. I held on to his hand and insisted on going with him. After giving me a scolding, he told me I could come with him. On an old chest of drawers in a room with three beds in was a little white coffin. My father's friend slid back the lid and amid tears said to my father, 'What about him, Bill?' meaning me. My father replied, 'He's all right,' and beckoning to me, said, 'Come and have a look, boy.' He lifted me up to see the dead baby. I have never forgotten that face. In my tiny childish mind, I got my first glimpse of peace.

As an entry into the study of history, by looking at the historical process in terms of the locality, the pack has been very successful and in fact sold out of the initial print order of 750 within two months. Again, this pack was distributed by just one local bookshop – the only local bookshop – and has so far been bought mainly by parents for their children and for themselves. We have used it in school and found the children very interested because so much of the geography of the items is recognisable to them and they can begin to make connections with the past. The pack was produced quite quickly, with the design and layout being done by a local sixth former, and cost £300 for the 750 copies which sold at 60p each. It was initially subsidised by the Hackney Teachers' Association and Centreprise Bookshop, although now that we are reprinting another 1,500 copies, it is likely that the project will make quite a substantial profit which will be used for further community-produced books and collections of materials.

Another very successful local publishing venture was the production of a very attractively designed collection of poems by a local thirteen-year-old Jamaican-born boy who was for the first two years of his secondary school spending part of his time in a remedial education department. This thirty-two page volume, printed photo-litho, recently went out of print after selling 500 copies within two months at a cover price of 5p each. This kind of sales figure compares very favourably with what a nationally known poet might accomplish with national distribution. I believe that the literary quality compares equally favourably:

The Sun Glitters As You Look Up

The sun is shining bright!
The sky is blue!
The clouds are no longer there.
It glitters as I look up!
Bright it is, bright as my sister's face!
The sun looks like a face without a body.
Just round. With a nose and two eyes.
If only that beautiful face could come down.
It will be mine.
And I shall shine with it.
As dim as I am now I will be brighter.
Even brighter than the sun itself.
So it shall be.
And I shall be as dim as ever.
For it shall stay there for many years to come.

Blob Blob

Have you seen a blob?
The man that runs out of your fountain pen?
They wipe their feet on my paper;
I hate those men.
If I had a gun
I would shoot the men
Before I use the ink.

Snow

Snow is cold
Snow is good
Snow has no taste
Tom is bad
Dick is crying
The tramps are home
My mummy is gone
Rain won't come

My sister is crying
Tea has no taste
Tea has no sugar
And I am upset

                                    Vivian Usherwood

Within the next two months there should be four new printed
volumes of stories and poems, each written by a local schoolchild,
available within the community and for use in schools. As well as
that, two other larger projects are planned for production by the
middle of the year. The first is to be a sequel to the history pack
which will look at Hackney from the beginning of the Second World
War up until the end of the century. It will include transcripts of
interviews made by schoolchildren with local people, including their
parents, about what it was like to live in Hackney during the war:
effects on family relationships, work done, questions of community
feeling, and so on. It will also use interviews made with local people
living in high-rise flats, as well as other kinds of housing situations,
with comments by the children themselves. Also, local interest groups,
such as tenants' associations, playgroup organisations, trade unions,
residents' associations, local authority sub-committees, amenity
groups, etc., will be asked to write about and be interviewed about
their own recommendations, hopes and fears for the quality of life
in the future Hackney. As much as possible of this recording work,
as well as layout and design, will be done by schoolchildren.

The second major project involves the production of a paperback
book containing four local autobiographies. This has arisen out of a
Hackney WEA class which has been working on a course entitled
'A People's Autobiography of Hackney'. So far about twelve lengthy
tape-recordings have been made with local people, asking them to
talk about their lives. At least two of the tapes, one made with a clerk
who left school in 1912 at the age of fourteen, and who for frequent
periods of his life was unemployed, the other made with a seventy-
two-year-old ex-shoemaker who talks about learning the trade from
his grandfather, are more than three hours long and immensely vivid
and fascinating accounts of life in the past. Such transcripts will form
the published autobiographies which, again, will probably be of
considerable use in schools. But, also one is enabling the community to
become conscious of itself by the flexibility of the means of communication now available. There is so much knowledge, so much creative

ability, that has so long been ignored, within any community, that can now become public as part of a completely new kind of educational process of people talking and writing and illustrating for each other, quite independent of the legitimised forms of public communication.

Which is why we must become aware of the opportunities made available to us by the new technology, and acquaint ourselves with its workings and educational possibilities. There is not time here to mention other kinds of possibilities of communication on a local basis which cassette tape-recorders, video-tape cameras and play-back machines, as well as other technological developments, offer us. They exist and demand to be utilised.

These ideas are not original; the possibilities that the new media technology makes available in terms of democratising the cultural process have frequently been considered in other countries – certainly more so than in Britain.[5] Our efforts to work along these lines in English teaching will be complemented by similar developments elsewhere in the curriculum: I am thinking of the move towards community service in the upper school, of the idea of utilising elementary scientific knowledge in the interests of the community by making ecological studies of the local environment (testing different kinds of local pollution) that now take place in a number of schools. English teachers can make themselves central to this process by the ways in which their work becomes available to the wider audience. This could start, and the English departments in a number of Hackney schools have worked together on this, by persuading the local newspaper to regularly feature children's work. It could then go beyond that point by the production within and between schools of books of stories, poems and discursive essays in which children begin to write for others. Eventually there is the wider readership of the whole community, who themselves can produce for the children.

At present our system of education is based on the idea of the children as passive consumers of knowledge which perhaps prepares them too neatly for their adult functions as consumers of material and cultural production. We perform a disservice to the children we teach if we confirm them in their roles as consumers only, or, by practice, never suggest that their writing is anything more than 'self-expression'. In short, they must become authors, and we have to locate their audience, and to make available to them the means of production.

References

1 Jean-Paul Sartre, *What is Literature*, Methuen, 1950.
2 H. Rosen, *Language and Class*, Falling Wall Press, 1972.
3 E. J. Goodacre, *Teachers and their Pupils' Home Background*, NFER, 1968.
4 Raymond Williams, *The Long Revolution*, Chatto & Windus, 1961; Penguin, 1965, p. 186. My italics.
5 The ideas in this essay have been strongly influenced by the writings of Walter Benjamin. Two of his essays in particular are appropriate to the argument: 'The work of art in an age of mechanical reproduction', in *Illuminations*, Cape, 1970; and 'The author as producer', *New Left Review*, no. 62, 1970. A writer who devoted a great deal to the potentialities of the book was El Lissitzky, whose essay 'The book' is available in *El Lissitzky: Life – Letters – Texts*, Thames & Hudson, 1968. For the debate on the relationships between the media and technology and the democratisation of culture, one recent essay seems to me to be outstanding: Hans Magnus Enzensberger, 'Constituents of a theory of the media', *New Left Review*, no. 64, 1970.

Further Reading

The following suggestions for further reading are all books that seem to me, in different ways, to tackle the main issues that I have tried to outline in my essay. Central to these issues is the problem of cultural democracy.

W. Benjamin, *Illuminations: Essays and Reflections*, Cape, 1970.
J. Berger, *A Fortunate Man*, Allen Lane, 1967.
William Morris, *News from Nowhere*, 1891 (Routledge, 1970).
R. Williams, *Culture and Society*, Chatto & Windus, 1958; Penguin, 1961.
— *The Long Revolution*, Chatto & Windus, 1961; Penguin, 1965.
E. P. Thompson, *The Making of the English Working Class*, Gollancz, 1963; Penguin, 1968.
School of Barbiana, *Letter to a Teacher*, Penguin, 1970.

8   The case for diversity

ANTHONY BURGESS

The job may get no easier, but the means for the job get better. Schools are less barren than they used to be. We are growing used to the Schools Council and the projects. In their wake (not to mention the publishers') have floated cargoes of courses and kits, sheets and booklets and books. They expand the resources at the teachers' disposal and we are learning how to use them. Indeed with the notion of 'resources' has developed a new way of looking at the basis from which a department operates.

Reprographically (if the equipment is there) it is not that much more difficult to reproduce fifty copies of a child's story now than to correct it. Tape-recorded discussion, making a tape with a group, film-making, tape–slide programmes, photo-plays, class magazines, newspapers, 'collections' of a class's work or an individual's, photographs, montages – all these options are much more open than they used to be. With better staffing they could be more open still. But given a department working together, common planning of some areas, double time-tabling where possible, team-teaching (Tony Adams[1] and Michael Marland[2] have contributed as much as anybody to this way of working), quite new possibilities can be envisaged. Not all schools are working in this way of course – it may not seem right for all – but the channels are opening. None of this is specifically restricted to English teaching.

It is help when it is needed. Diving a bit below the surface, one can point to two broad themes (I think) at work beneath the changes. The first is a very general matter. It has been the search to give a real meaning to the goal of educational equality. Quite simply the new comprehensives and secondary moderns presented us (increasingly perhaps) with challenges which simply could not be met within the terms of the old pedagogy. We have had to make our way along that direction. Teaching being what it is, too, a goal of that level of generality is not one that we make constantly explicit. Nevertheless, I believe it is one goal which has given impetus to the desire to make pedagogy as good as it can be (and indeed that it should be). The point about the theme though is its breath. To master that dimension takes us beyond specific matters of teaching into organisation and finally of course into debates about the sort of society we want to make. One of the things which has been happening to our conception of English teaching recently has been that it has been encountering the impact of a new sort of debate about equality.

Secondly, though, behind the new developments, lies the impact of what L. E. W. Smith[3] has called the New English. Putting it negatively, the 'growth' model (as John Dixon[4] called it) destroyed our faith in two things. It questioned the adequacy of explicit instruction in skills either to provide a rationale for what we should be doing, or even to be effective in terms of its own objectives. As the research evidence indicated, the road to effective use of language lay precisely through active use, not through exercises, practice paragraphs, dummy-runs, drills, prescriptive grammar teaching and the like. Secondly, it laid other questions at the door of literature. Particularly it questioned a view of literature which located its importance in a past cultural heritage to be imparted. This was not merely to say that the literature of the past should be taught for its relevance now, but to locate the reasons for teaching it in a different sort of rationale – within the individual's private and personal reflection on experience and articulation of his own view of the world.

I should add – to be quite clear – that none of this in any way questioned either the concern for children to develop an effective use of the language or the fact of literature's importance. Rather it subsumed these concerns within a new kind of vision, which gave central place to the active participation of the child in constructing his own picture of experience and to the role of language (including literature) in this. As Nancy Martin puts it in two separate epigrams, in the new vision the concern with the mechanics 'should have its place, but be in its place';[5] while the veritable 'white whale' before us became 'not learning to talk and write, but writing and talking to learn'.[6]

Not surprisingly then, the opening of the English classroom to the individual interests and experiences of the children who comprise it, the attempt to develop a pedagogy which not only recognised these but saw them as the essential material of an English course – this has entailed the development of a much more flexible organisation. It becomes necessary to accommodate divergence – more than that, to develop an environment which is as rich as one would like it to be.

No doubt one could point to the impact of mixed ability teaching too. But then isn't the real point about that that English teachers were readier for it than most?

Nevertheless, despite developments, the fact of educational inequality remains. I think it is worthwhile to pause on this point. Not that the English teacher can resolve this alone, of course, nor that it is alone his responsibility. But then it is difficult to foresee a goal for English teaching which remains neutral towards general difficulties in the educational system. Would we either want it or in practice be able to have it? For given that the teacher of English is concerned broadly with the development of the pupils' language, he is concerned (clearly enough) with one of the most general dimensions of educational achievement. There are many people interested in that. As one looks to the future, isn't it the impact on the teaching of English at other levels of educational debate (and the contribution in turn which English can make to them) which seems most significant? Teachers of English have to meet – and to make – challenges with regard to the ways in which effective use of language is acquired and what kinds of use are worth aiming at anyway. The necessity is not likely to diminish.

Equally, whatever the understandings *we* draw as teachers from the study of language, these have to be projected into the situation of the classroom; and hence, necessarily, into the interaction of classroom with school, school with community and so on. There are issues at that level of thinking about the job which need to be made more explicit.

Initially the questions are very general: they revolve around the *definition* of the equality at which we aim; also around how we represent the polarities of the debate. In many respects the *interpretation* of inequality of achievement turns on the way such questions are settled. There are delicate decisions involved. How in fact *do* we settle them, either in theory or in practice? As the Coleman Report[7] proposes in the American context – and from an administrative point of view – our definition has shifted in recent history from a concern with providing equality of access to a concern with guaranteeing equality of outcome. The point of view underlies the research in this country into the correlation of achievement with social class. If there is anyone who still thinks that equality of access will of itself guarantee equality of outcome, then the research, among others, of Douglas *et al.*[8] should disabuse him.

This much perhaps is fairly familiar. On the other hand, have we not been facing recently a conflict in our versions of equality which extends beyond that contrast? There is a story, for example, invented by Bernard Williams[9] of a race for which some are trained and specially prepared by virtue of their monopoly of the facilities and some are not. That is one way of looking at the issues. But the two points which are increasingly pressed concern whether, for the large majority, the race is worth running at all, and whether the fact of the race serves the interest of the participants or the interest of the convenors. Just to tie that down, let me extend the analogy in a slightly different way. The central question concerns not so much whether our educational system is fair – in the sense that the prizes are proportionally distributed among different social groups – but whose interests are served by the kinds of prizes being offered. It is the point of view which underlies much of the literature of the de-schooling movement. It has also been developed in a powerful way by a recent set of essays edited by Michael Young.[10] The opening of Professor Bernstein's[11] essay puts the point rather formidably as follows:

How a society selects, classifies, distributes, transmits and evaluates the educational knowledge it considers to be public, reflects both the distribution of power and the principles of social control.

Now there is no pretending this is an easy point to focus within the traditional terms of the debate. One has heard a lot recently about working within the system and working outside it, which is a useful version of the argument in so far as it does not divert us from thinking about what sort of system we want. It directs us also to the way in which the definition of equality as an aim and the interpretation of inequality of achievement are linked; and provides a perspective on the interpretations suggested by Professor Halsey[12] in his recent report on the Educational Priority Area experiments. Inequality of educational achievement, he suggests, can be explained in three ways: those which locate the failure in ' "cultural deprivation" in the sense of inadequate social parenthood', those which locate the failure in the working of the school, and those which 'put the emphasis on the opportunity structure of society'. Now in terms of his classification this point in fact links the second and third sorts of interpretation. The explanation (potentially) which is given of the failure of the school is one which relates its curriculum and pedagogy to the same distribution of power which determines 'the opportunity structure of society'.

We may add the recommendation that work in EPAs should be marked by diversity of provision and diversity of curriculum, recognising that diversity of provision implies at the conceptual level that equality may consist in the recognition of a diversity of interests in forming the way the education system is predicated.

We can then define the equality debate in terms of two alternative positions. On the one hand is the position which seeks equality of outcome, presupposing a *uniformity* of educational content and a uniformity of interests that the education system should serve. The other position presupposes a *diversity* of content and a diversity of interests to be served, seeing equality as a discriminatory recognition of the need for this diversity. The critical question, perhaps, for those seeking equality of outcome is whether a fairly proportional achievement (supposing we could get it) would in fact serve the interests of all social groups equally.

The importance of this choice is shown at the point where the concerns developed from within the framework of (say) English teaching collide with broader concerns about the future structure of society. Matters of this kind are difficult to resolve. But we can avoid vagueness about them. So often, for example, this sort of debate is joined at a level which envisages as the only relevant polarity a conflict of aims between the individual as servant to the technological needs of the future (whose needs?) and the individual as independent master of permanent educational values (whose values?). Common to both points of view is the assumption that the structure of power and rewards in a society will remain essentially static. What we rarely do is to focus on other directions of social change in the community at large which might be sought by pedagogy defined in relation to them.

It does make some difference, I think, whether the context of English teaching is one which envisages an increase in upward (and downward) social mobility, but which leaves the basic flow of power and rewards unchanged; or whether it envisages some sort of basic re-distribution of that flow. From the point of view of equality as diversity, for example, we might want to give weight to the proposal of Coates and Silburn that '. . . schools, themselves could become, to a degree, centres of social regeneration: growth points of a new social consciousness among the poor, which might at last bring poverty under attack from its sufferers, no less than from the all-too-small battalions of liberal welfare workers and social administrators'.[13]

It is a long-term view of course, but so also is the view which rests on equality of outcome. And there has been too much failure and too little change associated with that view. I believe increasingly that it is with the recognition of diversity of interests that we shall have to settle. Perhaps, though, in the end, it will be political will and personal nerve which will settle the matter for most of us. At any rate let me try to focus a number of the issues as they impinge on the teaching of English. We shall have to decide, first, how positive we see the role of that pedagogy as being, how actively it should seek to press on social change, or whether it should merely be compatible with it. From either the stronger or the looser formulation, though, we should still need to attend, secondly, to the priorities of the English classroom in terms both of content and uses of language. While thirdly, we should need to recognise that the role of the school and its relation to the community can no longer be regarded as peripheral to the concerns of English teaching.

Chris Searle, the London teacher, for example, told a story at a conference recently, which has stayed in my mind. It illustrates the ways in which the issues interconnect. He had been teaching, over a year, one boy, among others, with whom he had a certain amount of success – success in fact where others had failed. In particular the boy had come to value writing about himself and his area. But the point of the story was simple: the boy had left. Before long he had been before the courts and was in a remand home, where (as the point was put) his writing was not much use to him. Nor had it in fact helped him to deal with the practical challenges of his situation and environment. The question which was posed to us then was what in real terms the use of the teaching had been.

No doubt we could restrict the application of the story (and in other ways modify its thrust). There will always be individual failures. But it is capable of more general application than that. The point really is that it directs us as much to the evaluation of our successes, as to our failures. There is no need to rehearse here the general criticisms of a response which latches on to innovation merely as a way of motivating the less able pupil! But once critical attention is directed at the level of 'success', choices between a merely compatible or a directly positive pedagogy, or between the various possible priorities of an English classroom become central. It is those sorts of quandary the story catches.

It is no criticism of the theory of the New English to say that the content – what counted, that is to say, as the experience of the pupils – has been left open to be articulated on the ground. Rightly that was construed as a matter to be resolved by the teacher, not by the theorist. Given then the teacher's concern with motivated and effective use of language, hasn't it sometimes been the case that what that language was used about, what it was used to explore, has been settled less decisively than it might be – on the principle often of what works? Fairies and fantasy in the first year (but not after), myths, some projects on this and that, periodic returns to topics like loneliness, a few social themes in the third and fourth years: it has all been a bit piecemeal.

This is old-fashioned caricature perhaps. But, in general, are there no priorities with regard to the issues which we want to make central – priorities, not merely in the sense that this will get them going, but that it is important that it should? And if so, what? And if so (too), how do we reconcile the implications of some decisions as to content with the possibility of individuals also working on their own and developing their own lines? It is a delicate matter. What is important emotionally may not be what is crudely 'relevant'. Where you start is not necessarily where you go. None the less, I believe that we may have accepted too readily the criticisms of *Reflections*[14] (for example) as too sociological: it was marked by a sense of priorities at least. Might not too Geoffrey Summerfield's[15] often quoted doubts about the 'ad hoc excitements' of the New English be best explored along the dimension of content? The other response – the search for a very finely articulated progression of linguistic skills – smacks too much of a psychologistic hangover.

There are still critical questions too to be answered at the level of which use of language is made central in the English classroom. Those questions are no easier. Given a model of equality of outcome we might sketch a rough consensus such as this. There are languages of prestige and power in our society – the accepted (some might say official) languages that we have developed to control our environment and (indeed) to control ourselves. Command of these languages would be the important matter to aim for and en route to such command would lie first literacy and second standard English – necessary stages towards some sort of selection among the ends. The point is, though, that while, on the other hand, there might be evidence to suggest that acquisition of these languages had to be seen as a developmental matter – further that it was best developed from an initial basis at any rate in the individual's own language – our pedagogy could be quite easily adapted to accommodate such findings without the need for any basic revision of ends. The goals could remain the same.

If there is truth in this, how happy are we with the consensus? For the principle of diversity suggests at any rate that we might probe it. There are issues both of (in the broadest sense) culture and of educability. About the first there is this at any rate to be said: that accepted use is no guarantee of intelligent or effective use. Acceptability too is a cultural and therefore an historical matter: criteria are defined by some groups and not by others and criteria change. The point, I suppose, to consider lies with the way our own role presses on the definition of cultural expectations. The matter of educability in relation to language has been taken up recently in a paper by Harold Rosen.[16] Citing the work of the American linguist Labov[17] he argues there that the evidence to date of any basic deficiency in working–class language (in particular as an explanation of low working–class achievement in school) needs to be closely examined. Weakness there may be as well as strengths, but that would be true of middle-class language as well. At any rate he suggests we are far from establishing any such case as would lead us to think that working–class language was inimical to reasoning or logic. Perhaps his main point though is with the need to address ourselves again towards the study of the issues. Any such study (one might suggest) will need to direct itself to the role of situations in affecting our language use and to the interaction of different 'language communities' (in Gumperz's phrase[18]) within the culture. Coates and Silburn make the point that 'Self-confidence, no less than material welfare, is a crucial lack of the poor'. [19] Most teachers of English will recognise the force of that in connection with the use of language made central in the English classroom. It would not be surprising, after all, if with a great number of the expectations of the culture defining one's language as at best 'ordinary', that turned out to be the case for many. Do we need to seek positively for ways of redressing the balance?

Much of this points of course to the sort of places schools are, or have been, and the sort of expectations which help to shape the interaction of the classroom. The central thrust of *Language, the learner, and the school*[20] was directed to that point. Since then we have had the extension of the concept of 'expressive language' – the language in which, as James Britton has put it, 'we are likely to rehearse the growing points of our formulation and analysis of experience . . . our principal means of exchanging opinions, attitudes, beliefs in face-to-face situations.'[21] Yet it is clear that to find ways of realising the possibilities of expressive language is a job we are only just beginning to tackle. It is not merely that the belief that the language of publication is necessarily the langage of thought dies hard: we need to look too at the way in which the institutional context affects the possibilities of language use. The point drives us outwards from the English classroom – to the context of the school and to the total context of a culture defined by the differing, possibly the conflicting, interests of different social groups. New possibilities are growing. The development of groups of community schools with a positively (not ascriptively) oriented community curriculum is an exciting prospect. So too is the formulation of the notion of action research (on Halsey/Midwinter lines) directed at tackling the problems of innovation. There is a sense in which that is no more than the basic job. One can see too the lines of a positively oriented working-class pedagogy forming: the predication of that will depend no doubt on the thrust towards change more generally within the community. But then our situation is now one of change rather than stability. In its context, choices about the future of society, about the role of the school and about priorities in English seem increasingly less easy to separate.

References

1 A. Adams, *English and Team Teaching*, Pergamon, 1970.
2 M. Marland, *Towards the New Fifth*, Longman, 1969.
3 L. Smith, *Towards a New English Curriculum*, Dent, 1972.
4 J. Dixon, *Growth through English*, OUP, 1967.
5 N. Martin and J. Mulford, 'Spelling, etc.', in A. Jones and J. Mulford (eds.), *Children Using Language*, OUP, 1971.
6 N. Martin, 'Stages of progress in language', in J. Britton (ed.), *Talking and Writing*, Methuen, 1967.
7 J. S. Coleman *et al.*, *Equality of Educational Opportunity*, US Government Printing Office, Washington DC, 1966.
8 J. W. B. Douglas, J. M. Ross and H. R. Simpson, *All Our Future*, Peter Davies, 1968; Panther, 1971.
9 B. Williams, 'The idea of equality', in P. Laslett and W. G. Runciman (eds.), *Philosophy, Politics and Society*, Blackwell, 1964.
10 M. F. D. Young (ed.), *Knowledge and Control*, Collier Macmillan, 1971.
11 B. Bernstein, 'Classification and framing', in *Knowledge and Control*, op. cit.
12 A. H. Halsey (ed.), *Educational Priority*, Vol. 1, *Problems and Policies*, HMSO, 1972.
13 K. Coates, and R. Silburn, 'Education in poverty', in D. Rubenstein and C. Stoneman (eds.), *Education for Democracy*, Penguin, 1970.

Middle Years

9   The sixteen-year-old leaver

ANDREW MACALPINE

Where to begin? That must be the first question that all but the most narrowly trained teachers of English confront themselves with on their first day at school. I find myself faced with the same problem. 'English' in the secondary school can mean anything from poetry writing with Creole-speaking West Indians to a study of Dostoyevsky with a grammar school sixth form. The teacher's question, 'Do you consider *Lear* the greatest of Shakespeare's tragedies'? might elicit anything from 'Eh?' to a ten-minute monologue, depending on where it is asked. Would you consider that making an 8-mm film on robbing parking meters should be classed with a lesson on the full stop under the same general heading of 'English'? My own particular starting-point is the fourth and fifth years of an urban secondary school and I shall attempt to show this as a separate area of concern. The following passage can be seen as part of an attempt to define this separateness. It is taken, very unfairly, from a companion to this book, *New Movements in the Study and Teaching of History*. An exercise is described where the children are told that a wallet has been found containing the following objects:

A recent photograph of a young lady
A recent newspaper cutting of a wedding
A membership card of an exclusive golf club
Two one-pound notes
A number of printed cards, with the same name and address on them
An Oxford class list (explain) of 1939
An airmail letter from Turkey
A DFC ribbon.

They are then asked to write 'as much as they can *reasonably conjecture* about the owner of the wallet'. Given this exercise, a child of fourteen wrote:

He is most probably of the upper class. These are the reasons pointing to this assessment: (a) He belongs to an exclusive golf club. (b) He carries printed cards. (c) He has been awarded the DFC. (d) He went to Oxford. He most probably has a cheque book, because a person in his position would be more wealthy than the amount in his wallet suggests. Perhaps he is careful with his money, and never carries more than he immediately needs.[1]

As an exercise forming part of a history syllabus this seems admirable to me although I am not competent to judge. What interest and concern me as a teacher of English are the implicit assumptions made about language. We are told that the writer is fourteen and later on in the piece it is implied that this kind of work is for children of 'average' ability. Looking at the passage quoted from the standpoint of a teacher in a creamed London secondary school one can only feel unease. The instructions themselves containing the words 'reasonably conjecture' suggest a high level of comprehension on the part of the pupil. The pupil's response shows that these expectations were realistic. His use of words like 'probably' and 'perhaps' clearly indicates that he understands what 'conjecture' means and his sophisticated deductions are clearly expressed. However, before the reader (making my sort of assumptions) has a chance to recover from a sense of surprise at the level of ability he is told that the boy's work 'can, of course, be criticized on the grounds of commission and omission'. The clear assumption here is that there is an even higher standard of literacy which we could expect fourteen-year-old boys to attain. I would like the reader to consider now some fourteen-year-olds that I know and through whom I am constantly making my own assumptions about language.

In a recent project on advertising fourth-year classes were given a copy of an advertisement for Kentucky fried chicken which appeared in a local newspaper. It announced a special offer from a branch in Trafalgar Road, Greenwich, and featured 'Colonel Sanders' as the originator of the recipe.

On the back of the advertisement were a number of questions which the pupils were required to answer. The first three questions were as follows:

1 What is the name of the man in the picture?
2 Write down everything in the advertisement which is printed in very large type.
3 What does KFC mean and what has recently happened at 186, Trafalgar Rd?

Before the reader dismisses these questions as absurdly simple, let us look at some examples of answers that 'average' pupils at my school gave.

In answer to 1: '1 The name of the man in the picture is? Colonel Sanders.' 'his name is Colonel Sander's.'

In answer to 2: '2 Everything in the advertisement that is printed in very large type are. KENTUCKY FRIED CHICKEN HAS ARRIVED!' 2 These are the words that are Printed in very large type are Kentucky Fried Chicken HAS ARRIVED + 7p OFF.'

In answer to 3: '3 KfC stans for kentucky fried chicken at 186 trafalgar Rd they are surving kentucky fried chicken.' '3 It means Kentucky Fried Chicken. The thing that has happened recently at 186, Trafalgar rd is that 7p off of chicken and chips with a certain voucher.'

So a typical fourteen-year-old as *I* see him will produce work similar to that quoted above. As the questions on the advertisement became more difficult so the level of response deteriorated until a situation was reached where questions like: 'Is it important to have Colonel Sanders' name on the advertisement? Why or why not?' elicited no response at all.

Let us turn from written work to oral. The level of *my* pupils' understanding of the spoken word is often more in line with the first of the two answers I suggested might be given to the question about *Lear*. On a more technical note Carol Chomsky has written a book entitled *The Acquisition of Syntax in children from 5 to 10*[2] and in her book uses tests such as the following:

1 A pupil is blindfolded and the other pupils are asked whether he is 'easy to see' or 'hard to see'. If the reply is 'hard to see' then the follow up is 'How do you make him easier to see?'
2 Children are asked to say what John said to Mary when he 'told her the time' and what he said when he 'asked her the time'.

I tried these two tests on two classes of fourteen-year olds and the results showed quite clearly that, according to Chomsky's criteria, many children at fourteen still hadn't acquired basic structures that middle-class children can be expected to acquire by the time they are eight or nine. More than half the children in one fourth-year class of (for the school) average ability thought that the blindfolded pupil was hard to see although they had an uninterrupted view of him. Many of these

E

children suggested that if we took off his blindfold it would make him easier to see.

On the second question – distinguishing between 'ask' and 'tell' – the failure rate was not quite so high but nevertheless the two were often confused. The ability of our pupils to listen effectively is probably one of the most neglected areas of education. When we look at the above examples or when we discover that a fairly intelligent twelve-year-old doesn't understand the word 'valley' then we should look closely at our assumptions.

Most writers trying to communicate theories about teaching and learning will back up their general points with specific examples of children's work. My point is that these specific examples either confuse or alienate the reader because they are not familiar to him. The examples I have quoted I hope indicate the kind of assumptions I am making. I propose now to describe in more detail part of the background to these assumptions – that is to say the type of school where one might expect to find the language features I have picked out. Let us then picture (or recognise) an urban secondary school (eleven to eighteen-year olds). The buildings are either old, or cramped, or both, and facilities for science, music, drama, games and technical studies are poor. The school competes for its intake against the ever-present grammar schools and even against one or two purpose-built comprehensives. Thus the number of children in the top ability band is very restricted. Coming into this poor educational environment, then, are many children who have already failed at school and are, even at eleven, actively hostile to the whole educational set-up. In many others this hostility shows itself later and increases with each succeeding year until they leave. How then do the difficulties inherent in this situation manifest themselves? Here are a few specific examples of the kinds of problem that teachers, particularly younger, less experienced ones, encounter.

1 A teacher will usually find that there is at least one (and often more) really difficult child in his class. The sort of pupil, for instance, who will walk in and out of the room when he feels like it, throw books, pick fights and generally make any attempt at formal teaching impossible. Obviously there are a number of ways in which a teacher might try to cope with this problem but one of the more obvious ones is to enlist the help of a senior colleague. Such a course of action, while in theory sensible, often produces no results or even negative results. The senior colleague will rarely have time to spend long with the

offender and frequently in the offender's eyes the teacher has been defeated by referring the child to someone else and exploits his victory as soon as he returns, unchastened, to the classroom.

2 Calling a register – an activity much satirised by writers (see B. S. Johnson, Edward Blishen *et al.*) – is all too real an experience for teachers. It involves either controlling a whole class or else abandoning control and noting down children as one sees them – a very lengthy process.

3 Children consistently forgetting, or not bothering, to bring something to school to write with thus involving the teacher in the time-consuming and, at the end of the lesson, frustrating task of giving pens out and taking them in.

4 Older children easily develop habits of lateness or simply fail to turn up for lessons. This will involve teachers in what a colleague has referred to as 'sheep dog trials' i.e. the rounding up of recalcitrant pupils. A member of a fourth-year class I had last term regularly used to turn up half an hour late for the afternoon session and decided after a week or two that 'You teachers are always one period ahead of us'! As an episode in a book amusing enough – as a factor to be reckoned with when teaching a particular course, another barely tolerable pressure.

5 What do you do with a fifteen-year old boy who just sits at the back of the class saying 'Bollocks' over and over again?

6 And when you enter the staff room to escape and enjoy the delicious relaxation of a non-teaching period the cruellest blow of all can fall in the form of a substitution. Even when you know your classes and are able to prepare material for them lessons can be dismal failures. Being asked to take a class you have never seen and for which you have had no time to prepare can be the last straw.

Some of the above situations are, to the practising teacher, so grotesque and absurd that they find their way, in literary form, into highly humorous accounts of life in a school. This may serve the needs of our more creative colleagues but it does little to alter what, is in fact, a most distressing situation for so many teachers – bad enough, all too often, to force them not only out of a particular school but out of teaching altogether.

I have tried to convey something of the situation that very large numbers of sixteen-year-old leavers find themselves in. If we are to assume for the moment that school is still an acceptable form of education then how can we organise our English teaching so that it appears to our pupils to be of some interest, relevance and validity? At Thomas Calton we have tried to devise a course which will appear in this light and which attempts to provide for the kind of variety that English means to us. The two passages that follow are both concerned with language but similarities end there. The first is a poem written by a fifteen-year-old girl in an English lesson; the second is an extract from a tape-recorded conversation between a young shop assistant and a customer. First the poem:

Violence

All day long they would argue
All night long they would fight.
The man caused the rows
The woman tried to defend them
Why was it they occurred?
Through silly little things
He would go on and on
Causing hurt and weariness.
This kind of thing lingered
He would rub it in
With a nauseating pain
Without a warning he would pounce
The children ran towards their mum
Protecting her from the heavy fists
Screams of fear would echo out
The man slowly backed away
Falling to a chair
To cry like a baby
Who had lost his mother
But still the following day
He would start again
Hammering out insults
To cause the violence
Used once before.

What the girl describes in the poem are the relationships in her own family. She was able to write this piece because she had developed two things: trust in her teacher and the ability to use written language to convey her meaning. It is common for English teachers to concentrate on developing this kind of writing by responding correctly to whatever their pupils write and thus building up their pupils' confidence. Compare then the skills necessary for that kind of work with the skills necessary for analysis and action on the second passage.

A customer approaches a young assistant behind the sports counter in a large store. The customer is anxious to buy some inexpensive tennis balls. All the tennis balls on display vary considerably in price, with one particular brand of ball being remarkably cheap. The customer asks the assistant why these balls are so much cheaper than the others. The following conversation ensues:

Assistant: Well like for practice – you know – championship and that – you can knock about a bit.

Customer: Are they made of some different material?

Assistant: Well like for practice – you know for a championship against a wall like – they're all right.

Customer: They would stand up to an ordinary game.

Assistant: Well they're practice ones like – championship – you can knock about a bit you know.[3]

This kind of oral stumbling is all too common among sixteen-year-olds and they progress naturally into low-paid, low-status jobs like the one being done so badly by the assistant above. What kind of course will help these children to express themselves, in speech, more confidently and effectively without sacrificing the traditional aspects of English teaching such as reading and personal writing? The Certificate of Secondary Education syllabus which we have been doing does not really seem to come to terms with the natural diversity that language demands of its courses. The only *prescribed* work is the study of four set books. Formal exams hold sway and course work still only represents fifteen per cent of the total marks in a course which should span two years. As to oral work it is all very well to state, as does our Board's syllabus: 'The purpose of the oral test is to give the candidate an opportunity to demonstrate his powers of personal communication and his command of spoken English, *the importance and usefulness of which is at least as great as that of written English*'[4] (the italics are mine) but the fact that this particular board only makes available fifteen per cent of the total marks for oral work suggests that the gap between the wish and the reality is very wide. And the wish is not only on the part of teachers. A Schools Council report on school leavers published in 1968 shows that a large numbers of children would appreciate more attention being given to spoken English.[5]

This then was one of our starting-points for a school-based syllabus – what the examination board refers to as Mode III – a syllabus devised by the subject department in the school, *for* that particular school, marked by the staff themselves and only moderated by the Board.

The second area where our views were different from the Board's was in the importance that should be attached to course work. The children we are dealing with do not, for the most part, work towards distant goals. They will not willingly sacrifice the present for a doubtful future and thus to start working at the beginning of the fourth year for an exam which will not be taken for two years makes unreasonable demands. The allocation of a much larger number of marks for course work is immediately seen by pupils to be both fair and logical and motivation quickly improves. In addition, formal exams with their intense pressures do not reflect the reality of the sixteen-year-old's outside world. The reading, writing and talking he will be doing after he leaves school will not be done under exam conditions.

The third aspect of our English teaching that particularly worried us was the reading. We may sometimes be successful in teaching pupils the important business of using books to find answers to specific questions. In spite of a concentration on 'literature' we rarely manage to teach children to turn to fiction for pleasure. The American situation does not, of course, exactly parallel our own but it often shows what lies in store for us. In America it has been reported that half of the college graduates never read another book after leaving college. The students 'live in a world hostile to school-taught literacy . . . a child who is not successful at obtaining right answers through reading, and who does not learn that reading can serve the purpose of pleasure, is likely to learn that reading is good for nothing except the pain of recurrent failure'.[6]

The problem for the English department, having analysed the situation, was to devise a course which incorporated solutions to the problems discussed above at the same time as taking account of other possible constituents of a CSE course and including them where possible. In fact one of these 'possible constituents', mass media work, has become a focal point for each term's work and each of the five projects – advertising, television, newspapers, film and magazines – form the basis for a term's work. The five projects illustrate vividly the problems that a teacher or a group of teachers has in selecting material. It would be quite rational to build an English course round the mass media. On the other hand many schools will have little to do with anything as contemporary and non-literary. Language is used in so many diverse ways that the choice of what to include in a two-year syllabus for fifteen- and sixteen-year-olds may eventually appear arbitrary. Nevertheless, the choices have to be made and justified. We have decided on the following programme of work to be done during the fourth and fifth years. (The proportion of the total marks is given in brackets.)

WRITTEN COURSE WORK

(a) *Personal writing* (fifteen per cent). Stories, poems, free verse, dialogues, etc. The poem 'Violence', reproduced above, would fit well into this category.

(b) *Book reviews* (ten per cent). In discussing the problems of learning to enjoy reading we were considerably influenced by Dr Daniel Fader, author of *Hooked on Books* and director of the University of Michigan's programme 'English in Every Classroom'. The Fader approach works on the assumption that the resistance is not so much to books but to irrelevant books. Various experiments in America inspired by Fader have suggested that even among poorly educated people with no background of learning the *right* books can be very successful. We accepted this principle and while not managing to wean ourselves from the in-depth, formally examined approach (see below under 'set books') we devised a system which seems to encourage reading whereby over the two years of the course pupils are expected to read twenty to twenty-five books selected from a list of a hundred. Nearly all these books can be obtained in paperback (a basic Fader point) and at least a quarter of them are in the Pan/Macmillan series 'Topliners' – a series specially designed for adolescents with all the attractive looks of a normal paperback and yet short enough and simple enough not to deter children with below-average reading ages.

(c) *Set books* (five per cent). Two novels and a play must be read in depth and are examined formally at the end of the course.

(d) *Mass media* (ten per cent). This section has already been referred to. One of its great advantages as a series of projects is that it enables the teachers to get close to the pupils' own interests – particularly through the work on advertising, film, television and magazines. It is commonly assumed that the popular press has an automatic appeal for teenagers. The *Daily Mirror* was once said to be written 'by office boys for office boys', but the reading age of twelve or thirteen is already too high for many of our fifteen- and sixteen-year-olds.

(e) *Poetry folder* (five per cent). Pupils are given a wide choice of theme and asked to select poems from available anthologies and write their own – all to be related to the chosen theme.

(f) *Functional English* (five per cent). This can be divided into active and passive. Under active can be included activities like letter writing (all types, i.e. for jobs, to the papers, personal, etc.), descriptions (e.g. eye-witness account of accident), instructions (e.g. a note to your brother telling him how to look after a rabbit while you are away on holiday). Under passive we can consider reading and following instructions and directions, filling in forms, etc.

I have shown how our particular English department chose to tackle two of the areas we considered most in need of reform, i.e. the amount of marks allocated to course work and the use of fiction for exam purposes. Perhaps more interesting to us than anything else was the challenge to our imagination and administrative ability that the greatly increased emphasis on oral work demanded. How could we justify to the Examining Board our desire to make thirty-five of the total marks available for oral work? On educational grounds there was no problem. Most Thomas Calton children will do very little writing after they leave school but they will almost all spend most of their working lives in situations requiring the ability to communicate orally. Our course is designed to develop and test this ability. In part this is being approached in a fairly traditional manner through group discussions, short talks, interviews and even the reading of short passages as is contained in most Mode I syllabuses. It is in what we have called 'role play' that we have tried to break away from traditional approaches to oral work and produce something as relevant to adult speech situations as filling in forms is relevant to adult writing situations. Under this heading of 'role play' we put our pupils in as large a variety of speech situations as possible – reflecting as closely as possible the oral encounters they already have and will continue to have after leaving school – for example, dealing with hostility, dealing with one's own anger, obtaining information, handling the totally unexpected, complaining effectively, using the telephone.

To simulate the above situations is not easy, but the method we are using appears quite effective. It involves using cards on each one of which a particular individual's situation is described. In each set there may be anything up to half-a-dozen cards. For example we may have a 'pawnbroker set' whereby card A describes the pawnbroker and how he tries to pay out as little as possible for pawned good. Card B in the same set describes a customer with a watch to pawn and some idea of its real value. There is no dialogue written on the cards and the pupils have to talk (rather than act) out the situations. Another set might be concerned with a theft in a local supermarket and there may be cards for a couple of customers, a shop assistant, the supermarket manager and a policeman. In each case the card tells them what sort of person they are and what they have, or have not, done. Each situation must be talked out. There are endless situations that can be prepared and simulated in this way.

All that I have written about CSE will probably have given the reader the impression that our scheme does not cater for brighter children. In fact it is only recently that we started the transition from high-flying fifth-year groups taking O level to unstreamed classes in both fourth and fifth years. The introduction of unstreamed groups demands a less formal approach – a 'homogeneous' group (can such a thing exist in a school?) can be talked to as a group. Mixed ability classes require the teacher to look on the class as a collection of individuals rather than as a group. This means constant teacher movement round the class with children working at different speeds and arriving at points at different times. Work set either has to be varied to suit the needs of children at different levels or else it should be sufficiently open-ended to enable brighter children to progress beyond a point that might be reached by the average child. It is the latter approach that we have had to adopt, as we now enter every pupil for CSE English. Accompanying the introduction of unstreaming in the fourth and fifth years is the phasing out of O level language and literature as a fifth-year exam. Bright pupils who want to do an A level course in the sixth form use a Grade I pass in their CSE rather than O level literature as their jumping-off point.

Although our Mode III's emphasis is on language and communication we still retain the in-depth study of set books and among the hundred books which can be selected for reviewing are many (*Great Expectations, Silas Marner, Jane Eyre, Pride and Prejudice,* etc.) which provide a natural link with A level. Naturally we would like to see A level moving in our direction away from its 'pure literature' approach. This feeling is increasingly widespread among teachers in schools such as the one I have described, where intelligent children are penalised by their lack of background. Middle-class children at grammar schools may be no more intelligent or hard working but will usually be far better read and thus at a considerable advantage doing A level literature as it is at present.

References

1 M. Ballard (ed,). *New Movements in the Study and Teaching of History*, *Maurice Temple Smith*, 1970.
2 Carol Chomsky, *The Acquisition of Syntax in Children from 5 to 10*, Research Monograph, MIT, 1970.
3 D. M. and G. A. Gahagan, *Talk Reform*, Routledge, 1970.
4 Metropolitan Regional Examinations Board, Regulations and Syllabuses, 1972.
5 *Enquiry into Attitudes of Pupils, Parents, and Teachers towards Schooling: Enquiry I: Young School Leavers*, HMSO, 1968.
6 D. N. Fader and E. B. McNeil, *Hooked on Books*, Pergamon, 1969.

Further Reading

E. M. Halliday, *Linguistic Sciences and Language Teaching*, Longman, 1964.
D. Barnes, J. Britton and H. Rosen, *Language, the learner and the school*, Penguin, revised ed., 1971.

10 Literature for fourteen- and fifteen-year-olds

MICHAEL MARLAND

One sometimes shudders at the sheer impossibility of it. One remembers what literature has meant and can mean to oneself – those moments when life coheres and flashes to extra intensity through the personal impact of a passage of writing. One remembers other people's cherishing of phrases, passages, or whole works for their importance as turning-points in their lives. Those moments are perhaps all summed up in the autobiography of the deprived Negro who was to become an international author, Richard Wright. In his book, *Black Boy*, he says of his discovery of reading: 'It would have been impossible for me to have told anyone what I derived from those novels, for it was nothing less than a sense of life itself.' Against this one remembers the inevitable limitations of school – the large numbers, pressed men, cut-up time, remote relationships, and the didactic tradition of analysis and a linear approach to learning. The gap between the potential of literature and the reality of school is difficult to close.

And yet one of the few certainties of secondary education is that a good story, vividly read aloud, will grip virtually any group of pupils on virtually any occasion. The sheer humanity of literature is its point of access – literature is 'a dialogue about life', 'a storehouse of recorded values' (to use two hackneyed but true definitions). Its raw material thus offers more points of connection than any other part of the traditional curriculum. Here lies the hope.

There is also a very close relationship with the whole of language teaching. We have come to see growth in language as central to personal growth, and the gradual mastery of more and more complex language as parallel with the mastery of experience. We thus encourage the pupil to create his or her own 'literature', growing out of each person's individual experience. Here is the point of contact with writing, for we shall relate each pupil's writing to suitable echoing and prompting pieces of literature.

There are three past traditions that have to be touched on before I come to the core of our work in 'the teaching' of literature. There was the 'exegesis' tradition, which put explanation of words as the key use of books. There was the 'heritage' tradition,[1] which saw the central aim as handing over a traditional regard for the accepted classics. Finally there was the potent force of the 'discrimination' tradition[2] which concentrated on helping pupils choose between the best and the less good, especially by carefully paired passages. Each of these traditions has a value to the classroom. At its worst the first meant Shakespeare reduced to word games, and novels stretching over months used as exercises in dictionary scanning. Its best legacy, though, has been its regard for detailed understanding. Some modern approaches use the text as a springboard for leaping off so rapidly that the pupil is never encouraged fully to push towards understanding difficult passages. The worst of the second tradition was its tendency to offer up texts for reverence rather than personal significance. Its best legacy, and one that needs re-discovery today, was its sense of tradition, and realisation that writers do have a relationship with the past – and the future. The third tradition also had its unfortunate extreme: at times teachers and pupils found more reason to demolish the supposed weak, and the continuous search for objective judgement (Eliot's definition of criticism as 'The common pursuit of true judgement') frequently pushed to one side the need for an emotional involvement with literature. Perhaps *its* best legacy has been the insistence on supportable reasons for preference – a discipline which even the weakest pupil can manage, and which is often lacked in some of the dismissive discussions of today.

In putting forward what I take to be the best of the current tradition, I am very well aware that it is not new – except in emphasis, and also that the best of those three past traditions needs weaving into the fabric of today's teaching also. However, today's emphasis is surely on the sharpening and extending of the range of response. The focus is on what an individual can make of the words on the page by relating them to his knowledge of language, his experience of life, and his grasp of literary methods. This differs from the third, or 'discrimination', tradition crucially in that it places its emphasis firmly on the positive response, hoping to aid discrimination by plentiful involvement with what is appreciated. Teachers today are also willing to realise that it is not only the first-rate which can have a value. Not every passage explored needs to have eternal value (here is one difference from the 'heritage' tradition), for the goal is the overall literary grasp, and a piece that proves in the long-run to be only second-rate may have first-rate value en route. The 'response' tradition, as I shall call the present focus, naturally looks to passages that involve pupils with themes and experiences that concerns them, and modes of expression that, while possibly stretching, are comprehensible. The aim is to help the pupil understand and enjoy the full range of adult literature by learning how to respond to what he can genuinely, personally, and fully take *now* – and to avoid those pieces that must wait for even greater maturity. The discipline lies in sifting the appropriateness of a reaction, and seeing behind the surface of a word its significance to the wider context. For all but the most verbally and historically sophisticated, these criteria normally lead to recent, or at least twentieth-century, writing. It is extremely difficult to develop a personal response if too many words have to be explained, if the general idiom is strange, and if the settings have few points of recognition.

The lines of choice are not, though, merely the negative ones of avoiding too dense a verbal battle and too remote a setting. Each teacher needs to be widely read in twentieth-century literature, although unfortunately not many training courses are at all thorough in this. The teacher will search for characters with which the pupil can identify (thus the popularity of Barry Hines's *Kes*, or Stan Barstow's Vince in *The Desperadoes*), or at least understand substantially. They will look for situations that strike the pupil as important, for problems that provoke, and for backgrounds that intrigue. The books that chance has been largely responsible for leaving in the school stocks of the past too rarely had these opportunities for impact. Now there is a wide range.[3]

The novel is still the dominant literary medium of the age, despite the fresh popular life of drama and verse. It is no wonder that schools have built so much of their work around the novel – 'the great book of life', as Lawrence called it. However, there are acute technical pedagogical problems of studying a novel as a class activity, and these have barely been explored. It would somehow seem too rigid, too mechanical, too boring – too American even! – for a college of education lecturer to give a course on ways of handling the novel. Yet I have come to feel that such a technical analysis is needed.[4] There has been a definite, and I think regrettable, decline in the class study of whole novels. This has come from admirable distaste for the routine 'reading round the class', from a greater stress on personal choice and individual response, and from the growth of thematic work. However, the decline has also come from our bafflement as teachers about how to 'do' a novel with a class. The novel is designed to be read by an individual, silently and virtually privately, at his own pace and in long stretches of time. This is about as far as you can get from the 'Thursday five we'll do the novel', which spreads chunks over the term. If most of us had to read like that we'd give up.

The problem revolves around the need, first, to blend the continuity of the novel with the need to dwell on significant passages, and, secondly, to blend the clarification of plot and sequence with individual response. These problems are considerably less difficult with the short story. It is lucky for schools that there is such a wealth of short stories from which to choose. Despite the supposed uncommerciality of short stories in general publishing, excellent collections continue to appear, and many skilful selections have been made from these for school use. The short story uses the same devices as the novel, but has to do so with a deft intensity that gets the reader into the story rapidly. Descriptions, feelings, and dialogue are threaded together so that the point is reached rapidly. Most pupils can hold the entire story in their mind while a snatch of dialogue or a particular incident is being discussed, and it is this technique of probing the significant moment and relating it to the general span of the story that is the main approach to such teaching. The ways of doing this are fairly varied. Specific oral or written 'comprehension' questions are an old but useful tool for helping pupils clarify important points in the story for themselves. Such questions should be used a *teaching* device rather than testing checks. It is important to explain difficult words or references to the pupils, and not pester them with attempts to force definitions or explanations out of them if they are not likely to be known. In the first sequence of *The Lord of the Flies*, for instance, I've seen teachers probe for geological or geographical answers, swooping with delight on the need to understand the word 'fulcrum' at one point: 'Ralph used one hand as a fulcrum and pressed down with the other till the shell rose, dripping.' The temptation is to insist here on definition by the pupils – which is both difficult and distractingly unnecessary. The need is for a gesture and phrase to make the sense rapidly clear.

Key passages can be selected by the teacher for a vivid reading himself or a *prepared* reading by pupils. At other times the pupils themselves should select these passages, and justify their choice. They may be asked to find a passage that shows Billy up in a good light in *Billy*

Liar, or select the passage when we first sense Rose's affection for Allnutt in *The African Queen.* Other devices for focussing are for the pupil to select passages that they think could be cut if cutting were needed, or to write in additional dialogue for certain characters.

Plays have many of the advantages of short stories – even a full-length play is in fact quite short. In addition the fact that they are written entirely in dialogue makes them more amenable to class reading. It is usually better to choose the cast in advance, and arrange for them to prepare their parts. In the classroom the readers can sometimes be grouped together. The reading should, in other words, have at least something of a presentation feel about it. Because of the relative shortness of a play even examination preparation is possible without distortion of the words. The notion of the producer is the key here, and the detailed exploration of the text can be via the need of a production analysis. Which sections should go fast? What kind of actor would be best for this part? How should the scenery be arranged in this act? And so on. Writing can be on such analytic questions, or, and this is especially successful, take the form of added dialogue.

The drama of the sixties was particularly suitable for school study. As drama has recently become less dependent on story-line and characterisation (in the theatre at least), and its qualities less attractive to pupils, poetry, curiously, has come nearer to their appreciation. Its vocabulary and syntax have simplified, and its themes have become more direct. The vogue for spoken poetry had made much of it more accessible. Most teachers slip poetry in alongside other forms where there are relevant connections, spending a little time in analysis, but relying on considerable and frequent exposure, rather than extended study of fewer pieces. Alternatively poetry is related closely to the pupils' own writing, and thus its form is appreciated from the point of view of a fellow craftsman. However, this does not mean that an occasional continuous 'burst' of poetry reading will not come off, especially if the choice is subtle and wide ranging. It is wise to choose poetry in which there is a clear and strong attitude, feeling or incident. Battling through a piece which needs so much explanation that its tender point is lost after the effort is pointless for all but the most able.

It is more than a mere sop to the age to insist that the literature of broadcasting should be included. Radio and television have stimulated a remarkable variety of very good drama. Surely any school work in literature is aimed beyond the moment of study towards helping the pupil's future grasp and enjoyment. We must, therefore, include television drama at least, because it is such a significant part of the adult's literary experience in the widest sense. Despite the fall in television viewing in the late adolescent years, television drama is still the most familiar medium for our pupils. That is a second reason for including it in our work, and the third is that the clear stories, definite characterisations, and comprehensible dialogue of many television plays make them especially accessible to pupils of a wide range of abilities. There is not a great number of such plays available for schools, but I have produced editions of *Z Cars*, *Scene Scripts* (the BBC schools series), and five plays on the theme of generation difficulties: *Conflicting Generations*; and David Grant has edited a collection of *Steptoe and Son*.[5] Each of these has themes which are likely to intrigue most of our pupils (the Steptoe scripts have considerable depth and sympathy); they demand close attention to the implications of remarks and the interaction of dialogue and character, and they encourage discussion of form (e.g. 'Why does the scene end at *this* particular point?'). Further, the scripts can be used for a wider exploration of television drama, its techniques and form. The script studied can be compared with current programme output which the class are asked to watch. Radio drama, it must be admitted, is a far less popular form. Yet it has made its mark on the age, and a number of important writers have started with radio plays and return to them. The emphasis on words is ideally suited for the purposes of education, and the rapid flow of the story assists. A number of radio plays have been published, but the best for schools is that produced by Alfred Bradley, head of BBC Drama North: *Worth a Hearing*.[6]

I have spoken of the forms of literature separately, and so they must sometimes remain. However, a time in the year should be put aside for a sequence planned around a theme, to show the inter-relatedness of writing and to simulate in the classroom the way in which the responsive mind makes connections. In such a run of work a few key texts are read by the class; groups study other books, and report back to the full class; and all the pupils read privately from a specially prepared reading list. Ideally films, records, music, press-cuttings files, research and interviews are combined – the fact supporting the fiction, and the literature enriching the fact. The dangers of such an approach are, first, that there could be too much concentration on snippets rather than complete works, and, secondly, that literature could be warped to fit 'the theme'. However, if these pitfalls are guarded against, a thematic unit of work, say, twice a year is valuable.

A further dimension that must be present is the pupil's privately chosen reading, which should for substantial sections of the year be encouraged by a regular private reading session if at all possible. Book lists can be issued as starters, and there will be close liaison with the library. 'Reading diaries' can be kept, and sometimes reports given to the others. The essence, though, is individual response and discussion.

A considerable part of the work of the school in this field must be to familiarise pupils with the range of literature. The school should 'speak' books. This can include such simple schemes as displaying new library books in cases around the school, having lists and posters in suitable places, and exhibitions from time to time. More elaborately it could include a permanent paperback bookshop. My experience of successful ones in two comprehensive schools and observation of others suggests that these contribute powerfully to the literary life of the school.[7]

Such a flexible use of books as I have briefly described has considerable organisational problems, and schools need to scrutinise their selection, stocking, and issuing procedures very carefully. Too often a teacher is lumbered with a set of books for which he has no enthusiasm, at a moment when he is not ready, and for a period of time which he feels is inappropriate. The principles are clear: selection should be shared so that ideas are pooled and there is a regular reviewing of the available literature. Meticulous cataloguing, numbering, and stocking methods must be devised. Sufficient spare stock must be held to allow for flexibility, and individual teachers must be able to reserve books ahead, according to the sequence of their work. In addition there must be stocks – especially of verse and prose extracts – available for immediate spur-of-the-moment access when a particular passage will just fit into a context. Many schools have carefully maintained home-duplicated stocks of sheets for this – with author, title, and theme cataloguing of specimen sheets. A vigorous literature programme is not possible for the individual teacher as a loner: it depends on departmental planning of resources, for, paradoxically, individual flexibility depends on tight departmental organisation.

The central conflict in the teaching of literature is the stress between group needs and the requirements of personal response. The central aim of the work is surely to assist the personal response. This includes the intangible task of trying to sensitise and heighten that response, but also it must include the intellectual task of helping pupils understand the workings of literature. There is a didactic task, which may not be the heart of the matter, but is essential to it. The temptation that faces the teacher today is to so over-react against the 'mechanical' teaching of, say, novel plots or play characterisation in the past, that the pupil is given insufficient technical help. The teacher must help clarify, and must always connect the technical preparation with the emotional content.

What can be achieved, though, is an enriching of the personal reading by the group sharing. This is partly a matter of tactful but precise technical explanation, as I have said. It is also a matter of creating shared experiences. A clue is given by Alan Sillitoe when he writes of his idea of the 'ideal story': 'a narrative spoken aloud by an illiterate man to a group surrounding a fire in the forest at night, or told by a man to his friend in a pub, or at the table during dinner-hour in a canteen.'[8] This group sharing is vital. It can come from teacher reading, audio reproduction, or pupil talk. The teacher is well advised to build up some such warm shared experiences from time to time. More subtle is the way in which individual responses can be pooled by careful and pointed questioning to enrich the group response. The private reader ideally likes a 'sounding board' companion on whom he can bounce his response, to test reaction. The teacher hopes to capture in the classroom the strength of such an interchange by the group reactions, constantly leading outwards to the pupils' experiences and observations of life, but always returning by quotation, direction, or questioning to the text. In these ways he hopes not only to heighten the present response, but also to educate for the future.

References

1 For an account see J. Dixon, *Growth through English*, OUP, 1967.
2 See especially F. R. Leavis and Denys Thompson, *Culture and Environment*, Chatto & Windus, 1935; and Denys Thompson, *Reading and Discrimination*, Chatto & Windus, 1949.
3 I have developed a list of recommendations in the Appendix to my *Towards the New Fifth*, Longman, 1969.
4 For a good start see Kenyon Calthrop, *Reading Together*, Heinemann Educational Books, 1971.
5 All published in Longman Imprint Books.

6 Blackie, 1967.
7 For a practical guide see Marilyn Davies 'Paperback bookstalls', in *The Practice of English Teaching*, Blackie, 1971.
8 See his own introduction to *A Sillitoe Selection*, Longman Imprint Books, 1968.

Further Reading

T. Blackburn (ed,). *Presenting Poetry*, Methuen, 1966.
S. Bolt, *The Right Response*, Hutchinson Educational, 1966.
K. Calthrop, *Reading Together*, Heinemann Educational Books, 1971.
M. Marland, *Towards the New Fifth*, Longman, 1969.
G. Owen, and M. Marland, (eds.), *The Practice of English Teaching*, Blackie, 1970.

Techniques

11   The study of language

FRANK WHITEHEAD

It is seldom that one's advice is acted upon, and when this does happen one may find oneself nervously contemplating the consequences. In my book *The Disappearing Dais*, published in 1966, I included a chapter of which the basic recommendation was that 'no attempt should be made to teach children knowledge about the grammar of their own language until they reach the age of at least 15, and preferably 16'. It would be unpardonably egocentric to suggest that my own voice has been the decisive influence which has in a brief period of years changed the practice of most English schools; but it does seem to be true that for one reason or another it would be difficult now in 1973 to find more than a handful of schools in England where any systematic attempt is made to teach pupils about the structure of their own language. One will, of course, find classrooms in which from time to time incidental reference is made to the main parts of speech, usually in the context of a discussion of the pupil's own writing, and one can sometimes hear of a lesson in which a teacher draws from recollections of his own grammar school tutelage some garbled definition (to the effect perhaps that 'an adverb is a word that describes a verb') which he dictates to his class as a nugget of wisdom they would do well to memorise; but anything more developed and systematised is certainly rare in the main body of the English secondary school.

The change seems to have been brought about by two main factors. In the first place the developing consensus about the central aims of English teaching has in certain respects spread so widely as to become almost universal. The inculcation of knowledge or information is no longer an important objective of English teaching. The vast majority of English teachers would now hold that their main aim is rather to develop the student's ability to use his mother tongue as sensitively, flexibly and effectively as possible, for a wide range of purposes and in all its modes. This recognition that English is for our pupils their mother tongue has inescapable consequences. We are bound to perceive that the mother tongue is learnt for the most part outside the classroom, and that even for that part of his life the child spends inside the classroom much of his language learning takes place within lessons in other subjects. Similarly, we cannot fail to realise that the mother tongue is learnt largely by massive practice, intuitively and incidentally, and that the conscious learning of rules and their subsequent application play a minimal part in contributing to the competence which all pupils achieve in some variety at least of their native language. Finally, it is becoming increasingly clear that the acquisition of one's mother tongue is intimately linked with the development of thought processes, feelings and values, so that we are all increasingly aware that 'practice' of language in school, if it is to accomplish anything, can never be a merely verbal procedure (of the kind once enshrined in exercises instructing the pupil to 'put this word into a sentence'), but must actively involve at all stages the pupil's own thoughts, feelings, experiences, and motivations towards communication. Given this experiential emphasis in English lessons, it is understandable that fewer English teachers than ever before should find a place in their crowded timetable for explicit study of linguistic structures and that such study should be seen as contributing little to the over-riding aim of developing effectiveness of language use. As a matter of fact, as Brian Hollingworth has recently shown, there has never been much unanimity about the utility of grammar teaching as an aid to productive writing and speaking, and the scepticism expressed by experienced practitioners even in Victorian times had sometimes a distinctly modern ring to it. Here for instance is a quotation unearthed by Hollingworth from an American book *Teaching the Language Arts* published in 1900:

It would be hard to say whether those who speak and write good English but who cannot parse, or those who parse well, but cannot speak and write good English, is the most numerous host. Men learn to use their vernacular by using it; the controlling factors are imitation and habit working through association and literature. Speech and writing are arts and must be learned by speaking and writing.[1]

More recently the findings of research have reinforced the intuitions which result from practical experience. Particularly influential has been the succinct summarising of the empirical evidence published by Andrew Wilkinson first in *NATE Bulletin*[2] and later in *The Foundations of Language*.[3] Wilkinson convincingly documented the essentially negative relationship between knowledge of formal grammar and proficiency in writing; and the message seems to have gone home.

Admittedly the researches summarised by Wilkinson were all carried out with traditional grammar 'sometimes referred to as 'tradgram'); and it is at least arguable that some of the inefficacy here revealed is a consequence of the failure of 'tradgram' to describe truthfully the patterns of the English language as we actually use it. Thus it might still be possible in theory to claim utility for the teaching of a 'modern' descriptive grammar based on recent advances in linguistic science – if an agreed pattern for such a new grammar were in existence. Here we come to the second main factor mentioned above. 'Tradgram' is by now thoroughly discredited; but such is the confusion of warring factions in modern linguistics that no alternative has yet presented itself in a form that could be commended for school use. During the 1960s there have in fact been four main schools of linguistic thought (two American and two British) contending with one another for pre-eminence; and while it would be an exaggeration to claim that their approaches have nothing in common, it is nevertheless true that their assumptions and procedures are so diverse as to make it improbable that their conflicting claims can be reconciled in the foreseeable future.

The two American schools may be mentioned fairly briefly since they had little direct impact on teachers in Great Britain. From 1933 to 1957 American linguistics was dominated by a version of structuralism which derived principally from the work of Leonard Bloomfield. American structural linguistics of this period set much store on the formal analysis of a language by objectively describable procedures which in theory exclude any need to rely upon meaning as traditionally understood. Thus in analysing the sound-system of a language evidence is drawn solely from the patterns of distribution of individual sounds, which are found to be grouped together in a small number of distinctive classes called phonemes each of which acts as a unit in the contrastive system. Once this phonemic system has been established the linguistic scientist can move on to apply a similar purely formal and distributional analysis first to the smallest units of meaning (morphemes), and subsequently to larger units of meaning (words and sentences), so that ultimately the language has been fully described in terms of an interlocking hierarchy of levels, building up logically from phonemics to morphemics to syntax. (Thus A. A. Hill's book *Introduction to Linguistic Structures* actually bears the ambitious sub-title *From Sound to Sentence*.[4]) In practice structural linguistics concentrated most fully on the phonemic and morphemic levels of analysis, while at the level of syntax it proved more difficult than had been anticipated to demonstrate Fries's claim that 'the signals of all structural meanings in English are formal matters that can be described in terms of forms, correlations of these forms, and arangements of order'.

In part at least it was the failure of post-Bloomfieldian linguistics to fulfil its proclaimed programme that left the way open for a radically different approach, which was signalled in 1957 by the publication of Noam Chomsky's *Syntactic Structures*.[5] It should be noted that the term 'grammar' as used by Chomsky expands its scope to include almost all that we normally mean by 'linguistics'. Thus 'transformational generative grammar' is a comprehensive linguistic theory whose aim is to present in a system of rules everything that is implied by the linguistic competence of a native speaker. As Chomsky himself puts it: 'A linguistic description of a language is an attempt to reveal the nature of a fluent speaker's mastery of that language.' The system of rules adumbrated in Chomsky's 1957 version of his grammar falls into three parts. First come the 'phrase structure rules' to generate the 'terminal strings' which embody the basic structure of all sentences. Second there are the 'transformational rules' which operate on the phrase structure terminal strings to generate the more complicated forms of structure which underlie any actual sentences in a language. These transformational rules are in some cases obligatory (e.g. those which specify the tense of the verb) and in other cases optional (as with those which transform an active form to a passive form, or those which link together two or more simple strings to generate a more complex structure). It should be noted that both these sets of rules work at a high level of abstraction. The semblance of real language only arises at the third stage, when the output of phrase structure rules and transformational rules are converted into utterance by the application of morphophonemic rules (leading to speech) or morphographemic rules (leading to writing). On the whole Chomsky displays rather little interest in the manifold variety and complexity of actual utterances; but in the later (1965) version of his theory (which incorporates certain revisions to the rule-system described above) he gets a good deal of mileage out of the contrast between the 'surface structure' to which post-Bloomfieldian linguistics confined itself and the 'deep structure' which only transformational grammar can reveal. It is true that analysis in transformational terms does make it possible to take into account the difference we intuitively feel to be present in certain pairs of sentences which would be treated as structurally identical by the 'immediate constituent analysis' of structural linguistics. Thus the surface similarity of the two (invented) sentences 'The war was started by 1939' and 'The war was started by Hitler' can be distinguished transformationally as arising from two fundamentally different deep structures. However, fresh insight into linguistic material is rather rare in the writings of transformational grammarians, and on the whole one gains rather the impression of an elaborately comprehensive re-arrangement of kinds of understanding which are already familiar from other linguistic approaches. For its own specific purpose a systemisation of this kind may have its value; and it is certainly the case that Chomsky's formulations have stimulated an impressive amount of experimentation by psychologists, particularly in the field of early language acquisition.

Whatever their merits in their own field and at their own level, do either of these theories have any potential as an approach to teaching secondary school pupils about their own native language? I should have thought myself that anyone who had studied in any depth at all either post-Bloomfieldian linguistics or transformational grammar would be bound to answer that question with a resounding 'no'. In each case the details of the theory are intellectually exacting to master, yet the whole point of the theory resides in the way in which these details are combined together to make a coherent interlocking system. To simplify the theory as a whole seems impossible without distortion, yet to extract from it a few of the more 'teachable' parts seems pointless. Surprisingly enough, nevertheless, attempts have been made in American high schools to teach both structural linguistics and transformational grammar; and success has even been claimed for these attempts. Thus from 1956 onwards a number of high schools used a textbook by Paul Roberts which offered a simplified version of Fries's structural syntax, while more recently one can read accounts of teaching to eighth graders or above topics taken from transformational grammar, such as tree diagrams, rewrite rules or transformation rules. It must be admitted that the rationale for such teaching seems to be one of those products of the American national consciousness which do not readily survive a transatlantic crossing.

There may be some relevance, however, in examining the status attributed to the elements of a linguistic theory by its adherents. Thus Robins has drawn attention to the fact that three viewpoints are possible in regard to 'the status of the abstractions employed in the description and analysis of linguistic form'. In the first place it can be maintained that 'the constants abstracted in an analysis, if the analysis is correct, are in some way inherent in the actual material of the language under analysis'; this is undoubtedly the viewpoint maintained by the American structuralists we have referred to. Alternatively it can be held that 'the linguist's abstractions are also abstracted, albeit unconsciously, by native speakers of the language as the result of their having learned the language in childhood, and are part of the content of the speakers' minds or brains'; this view, which attributes at any rate a psychological reality to the elements of a linguistic theory, seems very close to the view implied by Chomsky as manifested particularly in his constant appeals to the speaker's 'intuitive knowledge' of his own language. The point to be made here is that each of these two viewpoints, in its own rather different way, favours the idea that the concepts in question deserve in some sense to be known, and may consequently be thought to lend credence to the further idea that if they are not known they ought to be taught. By contrast we may turn to the third possible viewpoint, namely that 'the linguist's abstractions have no other status than as part of his scientific terminology' and are justified by their utility as tools to be used in the process of linguistic analysis. This viewpoint is the one particularly associated with the dominant British school of linguistics, and was indeed given explicit formulation by its leading figure J. R. Firth. ('Our schematic constructs must be judged with reference to their combined tool power in our dealings with linguistic events in the social process. Such constructs have no ontological status and we do not project them as having being or existence. They are neither immanent nor transcendent, but just language turned back on itself.') It may be suggested that there is a consonance not merely accidental between this standpoint and the relaxed and undogmatic attitude taken up by most British teachers towards the inculcation in their pupils of linguistic concepts.

Firth's highly original and influential linguistic theory can perhaps best be studied in the volume of *Selected Papers* edited by F. R. Palmer.[6] It is possible here to mention only a few of its most outstanding features. For Firth the raw material for linguistic study is language events, whether spoken or written, within 'the inter-related processes of personal and social life in the flux of events'. Within this matrix of experience linguistics focuses its attention particularly on the language features ('the text duly recorded'), but ultimately full understanding of an utterance demands that it be referred back to the 'context of situation' within which it occurred. More specifically and ambitiously 'the object of linguistic analysis is to make statements of meaning so that we may see how we use language to live'; but since language is a complex phenomenon it has been found impossible to describe any piece of it 'at one fell swoop by one analysis at one level'. Instead we must isolate features of the utterance on a number of different levels and study each level one at a time. Firth sets forth and explores brilliantly four 'intra-linguistic' levels – syntax, vocabulary, phonology and phonetics – and each level contributes its own component of meaning, meaning being treated in each case as 'function in context'. These dispersed elements of meaning only fuse together in a whole, however, when we move to the extra-linguistic level of 'context of situation' at which level it becomes appropriate to consider not only the internal relations of the text itself, but also the social and personal context, 'the human participant or participants, what they say and what is going on'. In general the central characteristic of the theory is the way it splits up 'meaning or function into a series of component functions. Each function will be defined as the use of some language form or element in relation to some context. Meaning, that is to say, is to be regarded as a complex of contextual relations, and phonetics, grammar, lexicography and semantics each handles its own components of the complex in its appropriate context.' Central to Firth's conception is the proposal that in our comments on an utterance we should move freely back and forth between levels, aware that each level has its own specialised techniques of analysis appropriate to it, but aware also that in the end the fragmented components of meaning must be referred back to the total situational context and to those 'living processes of persons maintaining themselves in society' within which any utterance is deeply embedded.

It will be clear that the 'tradgram' of the school textbook has always confined itself to topics drawn from one only of Firth's levels of linguistic analysis, and that historical accident apart there seems to be no compelling reason why this particular level should be singled out as the only one worthy of attention in school. Young people have, I believe, their own natural interest in language; but experience suggests they are most likely to find relevance in the less abstract and more directly human issues associated with Firth's 'context of situation' level. Indeed several years ago I made the suggestion that: 'In classifying a variety of different contexts of situation, in relating them to the different "registers" or social categories observable in language (such as colloquial, slang, technical, scientific, journalese, literary), and in considering the different functions which language may serve in such contexts (e.g. exposition, narrative, quarrelling, gossip, persuasion) the pupils would be working at the level which is nearest to their own interests and their own capacities.' The real difficulty about attempts to introduce their more vital kind of sociological linguistics into the classroom is that one cannot get very far at the 'context of situation' level without feeling the need to draw upon classifications and categories drawn from the more abstract levels of syntax, morphology or phonology. Even if these concepts are introduced only incidentally, they demand of the student an intellectual maturity which is rare below the age of fifteen or sixteen; and it seems therefore that under present conditions the obviously proper place for such work is the sixth form. (In those schools which enjoy the freedom to plan their own English syllabus which is conferred by an internally assessed examination there would perhaps be a good case for making a start with the fifth form, at any rate among the more able pupils.)

As it turned out, however, the main impetus in recent years towards a rethinking of the place of language study in the secondary school curriculum has come not directly from Firth, but from one of his associates, M. A. K. Halliday. Halliday has acknowledged explicitly his own indebtedness to Firth, and has sometimes been called a 'neo-Firthian'. In fact he represents, in his own person, the last of the four warring schools of linguistic thought mentioned in an earlier paragraph. It is doubtful, however, whether Halliday's elaborately schematised 'scale and category grammar' has much in common with Firth's theories beyond the use of a considerable amount of common terminology. Certainly 'scale and category grammar' is essentially monosystemic, in contrast with Firth's determinedly polysystemic approach; and Halliday, moreover, seems to attribute to his own categorisations a degree of 'reality' which is very much at variance with Firth's nominalist-inclined view of linguistic constructs as no more than 'tools of analysis'. It must be said indeed that if one were deliberately looking for a system of linguistic analysis that could not possibly be simplified for teaching at school level Halliday's comprehensive and intricately interlocking systematisation would be a natural choice.

However, Halliday took over from Firth a strong interest in the human and social purposes for which people use language, an interest which shows to advantage for instance in an article published in 1970 on the varied functions of language in the experience of pre-school children and the way in which these may be presumed to affect the models of language which they form intuitively in their own minds. It is this concern with the functional variety of a language that seems to have been most in evidence in Halliday's involvement, in the 1960s, with the process of curriculum development. This started in 1964 with the formation of the Nuffield Programme in Linguistics and English Teaching, a lavishly funded enterprise in which a number of teachers and linguists came together under Halliday's direction to examine in an open-ended way the relevance of modern linguistics to work in schools. In 1967 responsibility for the project was taken over by the Schools Council, and the outcome at the secondary school level was the publication in 1971 of a volume of practical suggestions for teachers, *Language in Use*,[7] followed in 1972 by *Exploring Language*,[8] a more theoretical exposition of the underlying ideas. *Language in Use* consists of 110 units arranged in three broad groupings, the first being concerned with the nature and function of language, the second with language in relation to the individual user, and the third with the relationship between language and society. Each unit provides an outline for a series of lessons but, with the exception of a few units which are based on an accompanying tape, the material for these lessons has to be either sought out and supplied by the teacher or devised collectively by the pupils, a procedure which has the merit (supposedly) of ensuring that any examples used are both current and appropriate to the level of maturity of the class but which may have the disadvantage of throwing rather too heavy a burden upon the ingenuity and resourcefulness of the average teacher. Here are a few representative unit topics: sports commentating, persuasion, intonation, regional speech, weather forecasting, operating instructions, how we use slang, being tactful, reticence, talking on the telephone, technical terms, applying for a job.

Its sponsorship ensures that *Language in Use* will be widely influential, and the only valid verdict on it ultimately will be that of the teachers who use it with their classes. A provisional impression is that it represents a step in the right direction in its emphasis on context of situation and on the social variety of language function, but that a mistake has been made in defining the target area too widely, in that adaptability to a wide age range of pupils has been purchased at the cost of a disconcerting loss of specificity and, at times, a vagueness of intention that may even border on the enigmatic. It would have been better, I believe, to concentrate on the needs of, say, fifth-formers and to insert a rather more explicit theoretical framework within which

6 J. R. Firth, *Selected Papers 1952–59*, (ed.) F. R. Palmer, Longman, 1968.
7 P. Doughty, J. Pearce and G. Thornton, *Language in Use*, Edward Arnold, 1971.
8 — *Exploring Language*, Edward Arnold, 1972.

Further Reading

N. Chomsky, *Syntactic Structures*, Mouton, The Hague, 1957.
P. Doughty, J. Pearce and G. Thornton, *Language in Use*, Edward Arnold, 1971.
— *Exploring Language*, Edward Arnold, 1972.
J. R. Firth, *Selected Papers 1952–59* (ed. F. R. Palmer), Longman, 1968.
M. A. K. Halliday, 'Relevant models of language', *Educational Review*, vol. XXII, no. 1, 1969.
B. Hollingworth, 'Traditional grammar and the use of English', *The Use of English*, vol. XXIII, no. 3, 1972.
R. H. Robins, *General Linguistics: an introductory survey*, Longman, 1964.
F. Whitehead, *The Disappearing Dais*, Chatto & Windus, 1966.
A. Wilkinson, 'Research on formal grammar', *NATE Bulletin*, vol. 1, no. 2, 1964.
— *The Foundations of Language*, OUP, 1971.

F

12 The uses of television

NOËL HARDY

The views expressed on this chapter are those of the author and not neces-sarily those of the Inner London Education Authority.

As a teacher producing television programmes I am troubled by the exclusive term 'educational television'. Justifiably or not, it sounds forbidding, calling to mind the conventional classroom or formal lecture hall. It conjures up in the mind the twentieth-century electronic equivalent of the magic lantern slide lecture, placing it solidly with stockroom shelves, stacked with visual aids and audio-visual books. It frightens away from educational channels many of those who might enjoy and value them most. That includes many students and teachers of English.

Yet the great power of television, commercial as well as non-com-merical, is that it continues to educate us long after we have left the confines of the classroom. Although to many it is seen merely as a frivolous fun medium, it can nevertheless replenish our store of in-formation, stimulate our imagination and perceptions, challenge our standards and affect our judgements. In the sum of what it offers it represents a profoundly liberal educative force.[1]

What passes for educational television, however, still so often seems to be little more than the provision of glorified audio-visual textbooks; life tidied up into a series of teaching points, sequential, incremental, developmental. However much these kinds of programmes may com-mend themselves to educational administrators with an eye to assess-ment and accountability, they are of no more relevance to the learn-ing of English than was the self-fulfilling prophecy of the eleven plus examination.

Such programmes contradict certain central beliefs of English teachers which may, at this point in time, be formulated thus: the crucial importance of individual development and the central role that lan-guage plays in it; the rejection of a content-centred curriculum in favour of a child-centred approach; an emphasis on autonomous, non-competitive learning situations as prerequisites for growth; non-authoritarianism.[2]

The kind of television material that is valuable in this context is that which makes good use of the medium regardless of whether it be produced by children themselves, by local closed-circuit networks or by the national networks. In this chapter I hope to be able to show some examples of how television can make its unique contribution as well as reinforce and enrich the teaching and learning of English.

It is interesting to observe that whereas we all accept film as an integral part of our English resources, relatively few call upon the facility of television. Because film is now universally recognised as an art form, it has gained a certain respectability which, as yet, television has not achieved. Who would deny, however, the depth of imaginative experience presented in such a television play as John Hopkins's *Talking to a Stranger*, and its value in the classroom?

For most people, and that includes our children, theatres unfortunately remain socially and geographically remote. For the older generation, cinema and radio helped democratise the experience of drama.[3] Today television has provided universal access to it.

A decade ago Newsom pointed out that television 'has the prestige of a medium that belongs to the outside world', that children, like their elders, spent on average rather more than two and a half hours a day watching it.[4] As Hilde Himmelweit states, this represents about a third of their available weekday leisure time. More time is spent on television viewing than on any other leisure activity.[5]

Clearly television is the major cultural experience for most of our students. If for no other reasons, these are sufficient for us to be more creatively concerned with television in its many aspects than most of us at the moment would appear to be.[6]

For some detailed consideration of broadcast television drama, its value in the classroom and some practical suggestions it is worth seeing the notes and the chapter entitled 'Thinking about television plays' in *Conflicting Generations*, edited by Michael Marland.[7] This includes scripts by, among others, John Hopkins and John Mortimer. A complementary volume entitled *Z Cars* contains a useful introduction by Ronald Eyre about the original conception of the series from a writer's viewpoint, and about how the series gradually changed its nature as it progressed through the years.

This chapter is not the place to enter into a wider discussion of the role of television in the school context. To what degree, for instance, should it merely reflect current approaches rather than lead? Schools television, however, both network and closed-circuit, has in the main been grafted on to the already existing rigidly subject-segregated structure of education. Thus this medium, unique in its potential for cross fertilisation of subject disciplines, for integrating the school and the real world, for providing a synthesis of imaginative and factual experience, verbal and visual imagery, has in the past been denied its proper exploitation. The development of television as a means of personal expression and communication, as a means of providing a creative synthesis of experience in the way that a poem does, is not encouraged by the administration which demands that certain programmes fill the history slot, others the art, science, social studies or English slot on the timetable.

To this must be added the surprising unwillingness of many teachers to share as equals with their children the experience of a television programme. There is a resistance to a television content and presentation with which they themselves may be somewhat unfamiliar.

Children are the most televisually sophisticated audiences we have. Without succumbing to the extremes of McLuhanesque enthusiasm, I would suggest that this first television generation, who are not exclusive products of the literary tradition as are teachers, are in many instances better able to 'read' television programmes than we are. They accept techniques of inverted exposition, the juxtaposition and superimposition of visual imagery, the condensed and visual shorthand now used to establish situations, to signify changes in time, mood and place that ten years ago would have seemed almost unthinkable. Compare the speed and pace of films made in the fifties with films made today and you will see how much more slowly they moved, how many details were included in the setting of scenes and in the establishment of relationships. Similarly with television commercials; when commercial television was first introduced into this country it was thought that the absolute minimum time required to get the simplest message across was at least one minute, more often than not two or even three. Compare this with what can be packed into a thirty-second commercial today!

No teacher of English expects every child in a group to grasp all the subtleties, ambiguities and layers of meaning in a poem, any more than he or she necessarily comprehends all. What is important is the individual's personal response to the poem. Yet when it comes to a piece of imaginative television this principle so often seems to vanish. There seems to be an automatic assumption on the part of the teacher that each child must understand every single frame, must distil every ounce of symbolic meaning from the visual imagery for the programme to be effective. What so often follows the transmission of a more experimental kind of programme, such as an audio-visual collage on the theme of loneliness, is a straightforward, teacher-directed exercise in comprehension, rather than a mutual exploration of the nature of the individual response evoked.

A documentary programme may quite appropriately be followed by some comprehension activities. An impressionistic programme, however, blending film montage and stills, evocative sounds, music and drama, juxtaposing words and images so as to extend meaning rather than dictate a single restrictive response, invites a different kind of follow-up.

The analogy between treatment in the classroom of a poem and of this kind of programme, is, I think, apposite. No matter how much individual or group analysis there is of the various components of a poem and the way in which these contrast, complement and fuse, we may at some stage encourage a synthesis. Having discovered perhaps something of the way in which the poem works, we are concerned to encourage the individual to articulate his or her personal response to the stimulus. The exact nature of this response will, of course, depend upon many variables but it may take the form of further discussion, or personal writing, the preparation of an atmospheric script for tape recording or improvisation. The poem may on the other hand simply be encountered and left as an enjoyable experience.

It does not seem to have occurred to many teachers that exactly the same sort of approach can be brought to viewing the kind of montage programme described earlier. Instead of regarding it as providing any kind of aesthetic experience to be mutually explored with the children, they persist in using it merely as more material for comprehension.

Television is still too frequently regarded as a visual aid.[8] It is sometimes seen as being opposed to literature. Rarely is it viewed for its own sake. A large proportion of the output of schools television for English and the humanities consists of direct teaching programmes, however much they may be disguised. At best the television presentation can only be regarded as sugar on the pill. An enlightened illustration of this is the series *Middle School English* made and transmitted by the ILEA ETV service. It aims to 'teach' the different registers of language, the difference between oral and written language, as well as a graded sequence of language structures (for example, instructional or explanatory). Each programme has a central teaching point which is set out and explored in a variety of short sequences using a humorous or visual method of presentation. Each programme point is encapsulated in a twenty-second sequence which draws on techniques usually associated with advertising and is repeated at intervals throughout the programme to restate the theme (e.g. 'and remember with every sentence there's a free full stop').[9]

These programmes achieve what they set out to do with imagination and efficiency. Being fast moving and entertaining, an element often lacking in education and in schools television generally, they certainly do not bore. To mix metaphors, however, our televisually sophisticated children can smell a teaching point a mile away. What they see during school hours, they rightly expect to be of at least the same standard as on the screen after school. Anything that falls short of this invites frustration and criticism.

A recent meeting of LATE[10] welcomed the increasingly imaginative presentation of programmes but confirmed that creative teachers of English do not feel such a need for this kind of television. What they do expect television to provide is material that they cannot possibly assemble or bring into the classroom themselves. As wide and rich a variety of source material is required as can, in its own right, complement the already existing resources of the teacher – stimulus material which can be developed in any way according to the individual initiatives and enthusiasms of those viewing.[11]

There is no doubt that where such programmes exist the response from those viewing is positive and fresh. While I was visiting a school to watch the transmission and subsequent follow-up to such a programme, one girl volunteered: 'You can't watch a television programme in school as escapism or entertainment. You always have to learn something but last week's programme was somehow different.' On my questioning her further, and the rest of her group seemed to agree, she explained that most television viewed in school tended to bore because 'it taught one thing only'. Others commented thus:

'We enjoyed this programme';
'It made you use your brain more';

'It makes you think about it more because it was unusual';

'It wasn't pumping it into you but left you to make up your own mind';

'It left you to make your own decisions.'

These comments were occasioned after the viewing stimulus programme from the humanities series, *You in the Seventies*. If I illustrate my argument by referring to this one series only it is not because it stands alone (cf. *Scene* BBC Schools; *You and the World* IBA Schools) but simply because it is the one most familiar to me. The aim of this series is to provide stimuli and materials that will serve as a starting-point for discussion and other activities in which language, spoken and written, has a central role, e.g. individual and group work, research and reporting back, outside enquiry, creative writing, drama and role play, preparation of scripts for tape recording, photo plays and film making. These programmes, originally conceived for fourth- and fifth-year pupils as well as liberal studies students in the sixth form, aim to appeal across the ability range and to cut across the curriculum. Dealing with controversial, human issues, they do not preach nor moralise. Each programme is open ended.

Topics are grouped around themes which include the family, society, the environment, the individual in a technological society, groups and community identification, personal relationships.

The issues about which the programmes are concerned are some of those on which people hold strongly conflicting opinions. These opinions or points of view are portrayed, sometimes in extreme forms, in the hope that they will prompt individuals to formulate their own ideas and feelings in the light of their own and others' experience. By testing their views in discussions with others, it is hoped that they will be helped towards more mature and considered judgements.[12]

The television programmes are accompanied by teachers' handbooks and pupil packs. Care has been taken in the compilation of the handbooks in an attempt not to sabotage the open-ended nature of the programmes, nor to narrow the range of individual responses.[13] For ease of reference and for descriptive convenience various activities are separately treated although English is now seen as a unity.

In designing this project the production team recognised the importance of allowing teachers as much information as possible in advance of the programme. Thus the first section of the notes includes not only a synopsis of each programme but wherever possible relevant

script extracts, texts and character profiles. Section two offers suggestions for discussion arising directly from the programme. For those
wishing to make a greater use of the series a third section contains
further evidence and factual information together with suggested
project topics. Material is provided which can be duplicated, trans-
ferred to work cards or put on to tape. The fourth and fifth sections
offer suggestions for creative writing and ideas for improvised drama
and role play. The last sections offer select bibliographies (poems,
plays, fiction and non-fiction) and also include non-print media,
i.e. films, records and tapes. An important final section provides lists
of organisations able to supply further information and prepared to
talk with our pupils.

In order to facilitate purposeful talk in the classroom, whether between individuals or in small groups, a number of pupil packs have
also been devised which run parallel to the themes of the programmes.
These consist of original resource materials, press cuttings, cartoons,
statistics, questionnaires, photographs, which, it is hoped, may further
help discussion. The packs are by no means comprehensive.[14] They
are conceived merely as starters which may serve to encourage students
and teachers to discover and supplement the material for themselves.

All this may sound suspiciously like a mammoth glorified textbook
of the kind that I was earlier attacking, but here there is an essential
difference. Unlike the textbook, which is didactic, nothing that is
presented in the notes, the packs or the programmes is intended to be
prescriptive. Although we may sometimes fall short of our aims, the
programmes themselves are not visual aids but by implication make
statements or raise questions in their own right.

The response to these programmes and the way in which they are
followed up is as diverse as are the interests of the individuals watching. To generalise, therefore, would serve little purpose. Very often,
however, where schools are streamed it is the bottom streams or non-
examination groups that are viewing. Feedback[15] from viewing a
programme which presents a series of images of old age serves to demonstrate how television can successfully stimulate perceptive discussion. Comments one teacher: 'The overwhelming feeling was that
this programme had gradually planted in the conscious and subcon-
scious mind a strong impression of the burden of time and its slow
passage; it had stimulated compassionate and copious discussion.'
Another teacher reports that 'the lower streams apparently had most
to say. They retained a strong visual memory' which no doubt moti-

vates their expression in a way that print media would not. At another school two girls in a small, mixed-ability, early leavers group were stimulated to write about their own views of old age. One girl who intended to leave and be a telephonist remained studiously silent throughout discussion, but had taken a passionate interest in following up this programme. As a result she not only began to write once more but also discovered for herself the poem 'Beautiful Old Age' by D. H. Lawrence published in the pupil pack. Considerable inter-generational communication was established as a result of the pro-gramme: visits to workshops for the elderly and to old peoples' homes as well as subsequent social work. Space prevents me from further practical documentation.

So far in this chapter we have been concerned with the professional provision of television programmes for classroom consumption. It is worthwhile considering two entirely different examples of the possi-bilities that open up for English teaching when the students themselves have access to television studios. One is an account of the creative use of television at Millfield School, Somerset, where the school itself possesses its own mini-television studio. The other is where a compre-hensive school links with a local technical college which has television facilities in order to create its own CSE Mode III syllabus in TV and Communication.

For the following account of work at Millfield I am most indebted to Peter Turner, head of the educational resources faculty, under whose direction the work took place. At this school they have been quick to appreciate that television can be used as a means of personal expression.

English teaching, in recent years, has placed great emphasis upon the individual creative work of the pupil and a television studio lends itself to this. Television can be used as a medium of expression like speech and the written word. It can be used as a new challenge that can be issued to pupils of all ages. Once they have learned the principles of the medium, the teacher can say to those in his charge:

'Here is a television programme. What do you want it to say?'

An individual child can be given the opportunity of producing a programme of his own choice (one might almost say 'in his own image'). The remaining members of the group can be required to take that part chosen for them by the pupil preparing the programme. Thus one child is the master of the medium and has the freedom to create the programme while the others co-operate to bring his ideas to the screen. Once the programme has been recorded, and replayed, then and only then may the producer's ideas be questioned and analysed.

Each week the teacher selects a new programme producer who is given several days to prepare his programme.

Creative work in English can be extended to the preparation and production by pupils themselves of material which by its nature builds up their critical faculties. Television productions involving pupils can explore dramatic and visual effects, and combine poetry, drama, areas of light and shadow as well as sounds from the electronic effects generator.

Over a period of several weeks, using the videotape recorder in the assemble edit mode, programmes can be created from selected contributions.

The resulting montage often has an exciting visual impact which exceeds the sum of the individual contribution.

For anyone unfamiliar with the making of a television programme, I must point out that even the simplest programme represents a pooling of effort and is the culmination of a complex, co-operative venture. The actual process of creating with television provides the children with numerous and real opportunities for rehearsing many different kinds of language.[16] At the same time they are learning for themselves some of the unexplored potential of the medium which culturally dominates our lives.

The value of television as a force for integrating subjects and cutting across the curriculum is also recognised at Millfield:

There can be great value to the English specialist in combining with other subject specialists to prepare an integrated studies project for television presentation to junior pupils. Role playing by the pupils may be used to write a number of subjects. Thus television is used to add flesh to the bare bones of a factual subject. English, History and perhaps Geography can be linked together as well as Art and Music. Research for a programme on Nelson could be done in History, maps prepared in Geography and the script composed in English!

This is a simple illustration of the way in which television can aid subject integration and enable children to experience as a unified body of knowledge the usually fragmented content of separate disciplines.

It is not difficult to see how this could be applied on a much more imaginative and ambitious scale. This kind of venture might also spark off discussions between different departments within the school which might, in turn, lead to the consideration, if not adoption, of a language policy across the curriculum.[17] It is common today for children in remedial groups to enjoy and be greatly encouraged through drama. Peter Turner finds that children derive much benefit from extensive work in the television studios.

Many of the pupils in remedial groups will be disorganised. They seem incapable of assembling themselves, their books, let alone their ideas. They appear slow to start any project and once under way they may still lose all the materials in their safe keeping. These are the children who are constantly in trouble with authority. In the television studio, these children are asked to complete a television programme within forty-five minutes and for once they cannot avoid being organised. As there is nothing for them to bring with them to the studio, they have nothing to forget and the session is able to get under way without the usual feelings of frustration and guilt. The method is time-conscious and the children have deadlines to meet. Their desire to perform on television and to see themselves overcomes any desires to opt out. A few of these children are likely to be hyperactive and are usually the most disruptive elements in the class. They have a great deal of energy, much enthusiasm but are unable to channel either into their work. They speak without thought and constantly seek to be the centre of attention. Any attempt to impose discipline usually results in anger and resentment. This kind of child, however, finds that he cannot dominate the three areas of activity within the television studio. He cannot present, create artistic effects with cameras, and produce all at the same time. Co-operation, he finds, is necessary. Because the hyperactive child finds that he cannot control the medium on his own, he is often willing to become a member of a team to make his contribution more effective.

The instant replay facility of the videotape recorder can play a unique part in boosting a child's confidence as well as encouraging a critical faculty. The programme is replayed at the end of a lesson so that pupils can see the results of their work immediately. This kind of work holds their attention for longer periods and heightens their concentration. Whatever they have undertaken, they can view their contribution in relation to the whole. This not only gives them a sense of achievement, it gives them an opportunity to evaluate for themselves.

My own experience while teaching certainly confirms this. After the mobile television unit from Goldsmith's College had recorded some drama periods, the pupils were able to watch this continuous video-taped observation. I am convinced that they learnt more from seeing themselves in action as others see them than from any amount of talk with me.

This was a rough and exuberant group of third-year boys from severely impoverished social and cultural backgrounds. As soon as the playback started their absorption was total. The amount of inter-personal talk and perceptive observation was remarkable. Rarely did the discussion become superficial. They were seriously concerned with details of characterisation and motivation. Unwittingly they were discovering language in action for themselves. With no prompting from me they were involved, sometimes quite vehemently, in dis-cussing the appropriateness of certain speech, gesture and action in relation to the emotional context of the scenes they had earlier been improvising.

Whether or not I am correct in believing that those children learnt a lot on their own about language and communication, their teacher certainly did. He also learnt some horrible home truths about his teaching: how easy it is to dominate, to intrude at the wrong moment, to prejudice response by the framing of assertions.[18]

It may be asked how pupils in the majority of schools who do not have their own television studio facilities can actively participate in any form of television. At the time of writing at least one English de-partment known to the author has formed links with a local technical college that possesses its own closed-circuit television studio. Together they have devised their own Mode III CSE syllabus in communication and television. This course, which is the first of its kind in London, is designed to achieve the following aims: to develop verbal, graphic and dramatic communication skills through the medium of television; to develop the ability to make judgements on the quality of television programmes: to design and produce television presentations that re-quire both individual and group contributions.

There is unfortunately not the space to consider this venture more fully. I mention it, however, to show that it is perfectly possible for schools to make proper links with other branches of education, to pool ideas, share expertise, and co-operate in forging a common sylla-bus. It represents one attempt at least within the traditional subject-bound curriculum to come to terms with the medium of television.

The area of education which concerns teacher training deserves a whole chapter all on its own. That I mention it last bears no relation to its overwhelming importance. It is, in fact, in this area that I think tele-vision can make one of its greatest contributions to education generally and especially in the teaching of English.

Although the networks have produced some excellent programmes which may be useful in teacher and in-service training they have neither the resources nor the time to cater adequately for minority needs and specialist interests. A local closed-circuit network such as the ILEA TV service is able to devote a large proportion of its output to the screening of specially commissioned programmes for teachers.

Those of us who have at some stage spent hours discussing the aims and new approaches to English teaching with sceptical colleagues or parents will know how frustrating an experience this can be. Experience shows that there is no substitute for actual observation of these approaches in action. To give a demonstration lesson in front of an audience of other teachers or parents is an exercise in artificiality. In any case it is often impossible for an audience to hear or see what is actually going on because of the nature of the activities.

A mobile videotape-recording unit allows us to share in the work of colleagues. Raw videotape of continuous classroom observation can be edited and with the addition of still photographs, film and commentary provide powerful material for discussion and appraisal.

I am not suggesting that television be used to inculcate a new orthodoxy. When videotaped classroom observation is shown to a group in the company of a sympathetic teacher, however, it tends to produce a greater understanding on the part of the viewers than any amount of abstract discussion.

Television, by looking at specific classroom situations, can help us towards a deeper understanding of such particular concerns as the nature of language, modern linguistics teaching and discussion. On the whole it is assumed that any[19] teacher knows how to handle discussion. With few exceptions, not enough seems to be done in this area at teacher training colleges, and yet this is one of the most subtle and difficult of activities. Through discussion and talk, children find out about themselves and explore the work, but classroom discussion is rarely a spontaneous exchange of opinion between pupil and pupil. It is all too easy for the teacher to dominate. On the other hand, if pupils are left entirely on their own, the result can be aimless bathing in predictable prejudice.[20] What methods are there of ensuring that the discussion develops constructively from the pupils' interest? What is the teacher's role? How large or small is the group? How are the groups organised? What factors affect the success of the discussion? These kinds of question are of vital importance to all of us. The series in particular that has stimulated much discussion in schools, local English centres, colleges and institutes of education is *New Approaches to English Teaching*[21] and some of the teachers' programmes in *You in the Seventies*. Some of these programmes are being used in other colleges outside London and reports suggest that they are proving of immense value.

Nowhere have I mentioned television as a means of distributing all that is best. Nor have I considered in sufficient detail television in the training colleges. This latter, especially, needs urgent consideration, for it is here that much requires to be done.

Television in education is still regarded primarily as a medium of instruction. Until this attitude changes there can be little hope of exploiting the full potential of television. What I hope I have managed to convey, however briefly, are some of the ways in which television can make its contribution to all that is best in the field of English and the humanities.

References

1 For evidence and detailed analysis of this see the section 'Television the liberal educator', in B. Groombridge, *Television and the People*, Penguin, 1972.
2 Cf. M. Barrs, B. Bryan and P. Griffiths, *Commission 7 Newsletter* at NATE International Conference of Teaching and Learning of English, 1971. See also F. Whitehead, *The Disappearing Dais*, Chatto & Windus, 1966.
3 See *Television and the People*, op. cit.
4 Cf. Newsom Report *Half our Future*, HMSO, 1963, para. 214.
5 See H. T. Himmelweit, A. N. Oppenheim and P. Vince, *Television and the Child*, OUP, 1958, p. 111.
6 See M. Marland, *Towards the New Fifth*, Longman, 1969,
7 *Conflicting Generations: Five Television Plays*, Longman Imprint Books. The introduction originally appeared in *The Use of English*, Spring 1967.
8 G. H. Bantock, 'The implications of literacy' in *Education, Culture and Emotions*, Faber, 1967: 'A school should use it [television] not as an aid but as a disseminator of experience.'
9 *Middle School English*, Series for third-year remedials of secondary school, produced by Glyn Edwards and Jan Martin, ILEA TV Series.
10 Meeting held by LATE at the ILEA TV Centre on 11 March 1972.

11 Teachers may like to view some of the programmes from the following series: *Vision On*, BBC TV; *Scene*, BBC Schools TV, produced by Ron Smedley; *Images*, produced by Charles Warren, ITA Schools TV; *Music Alive*, directed by Brian Kenny and Glyn Edwards, ILEA TV; *You in the Seventies*, directed by Noël Hardy, ILEA TV.

12 Guy Rogers, Staff Inspector Secondary Education, quoted in the introduction to *You in the Seventies, Teachers' Handbook*, ILEA TV Services.

13 See *Teachers' Handbook* published for the Schools Council Humanities Curriculum Project by Heinemann.

14 Thirty or forty items as compared with two hundred or so items in the Humanities Curriculum Projects packs.

15 Information compiled from reports gathered by David Dyke, Liaison Unit, ILEA TV.

16 Cf. 'Language is learned in operation, not by dummy runs.'

17 D. Barnes, J. Brotton, H. Rosen, *Language, the learner and the school*, Penguin revised edition 1971; and *English in Education*, vol. 5, no. 2, Spring 1971, NATE with OUP.

18 See note 13.

19 Cf. *Language in Primary Education*, directed by Barbara Wethey, ILEA TV.

20 Alasdair Aston, Inspector for English, ILEA, *Teachers' Handbook* for *You in the Seventies*.

21 *New Approaches to English Teaching* (ILEA TV), series devised by Michael Simons with extensive handbook by Alasdair Aston, aims to 'show teachers at work and pupils learning. It covers such areas as talk and the role of the teacher, including theme work and the Humanities Curriculum Project, talk in small groups and group work, outside enquiry, writing, film making, tape-recording and resources as well as remedial English. The handbook, which is full of useful information, contains sections of classroom transcripts.

Further Reading

Carnegie Commission on Educational Television Report, *Public Television: A Programme for Action*, Bertram Books, 1967.

J. P. Gay, 'What do all the people who exist in the world do? They die', *Sight and Sound*, Winter 1972–3.

B. Groombridge, *Television and the People: a Programme for Democratic Participation*, Penguin, 1972.

Stuart Hall, *The Popular Arts*, Hutchinson Educational, 1964.

A. P. Higgins, *Talking about Television*, Educational Department, BFI, 1966.

Marshall McLuhan, *Understanding Media*, Routledge, 1964.

Denis McQuail, 'Television and education', in James Halloran (ed.), *The Effects of Television*, Panther, 1970.

Guthrie Moir (ed.), *Television and Teaching*, Pergamon, 1967.

W. Schramm, J. Lyle, and E. Parker, *Television in the Lives of our Children*, OUP, 1961.

David Self, 'Audio or visual? Some thoughts on the motivation of children's writing', *English and education*, vol. 3, no. 3, OUP for NATE, Autumn 1969.

J. M. Trenaman, *Communication and Comprehension*, Longman, 1967.

N. Tucker, *Understanding the Mass Media*, Routledge, 1964.

B. R. Wilkie, *The technique of special effects in television*, Focal Press, 1971.

Raymond Williams, *Communications*, Chatto & Windus, 1966; Penguin, 1968.

Schools Council Publications:

Working Paper No. 2, *A programme for research and development in English teaching*, HMSO, 1965.

Humanities and the Young School Leaver– An approach through English, HMSO, 1968.

ROSLA Working Paper No. 2, HMSO, 1968.

Society and the Young School Leaver, HMSO, 1967.

A. Hancock, *Planning for ETV. A handbook of ETV*, Longman, 1972. (Very much an administrator's point of view.)

Closed circuit television at Avery Hill College of Education, 1963–7. *Booklet No. 1*, ILEA.

ILEA Mobile video tape recording unit, *Booklet No. 2*, ILEA.

Useful addresses

Society for Education in Film and Television
63 Old Compton Street, W1V 5PN

BBC Television Enterprises Film Hire
25 The Burroughs, Hendon, NW4

BBC Television
Villiers House, Haven Green, Ealing, London W5
Teachers and students wishing to see the studios in operation are advised to book up (six weeks or so in advance) for a show being recorded during the day. Apply to the Ticket Unit, BBC, Broadcasting House, London W1

Thames Television (Schools)
306–16 Euston Road, London NW1 3BB
There are no trips around the studios. The Television Gallery is a very worthwhile permanent exhibition showing the history, development and production of television.

ILEA Television Centre, Tennyson Street, London SW8

13　The milieu and the method

ALBERT ROWE

The sharp polarisation that has recently taken place in organising secondary education is summed up by such labels as bi-partite *v* comprehensive, selective *v* non-selective, traditional *v* progressive. Unfortunately they contain just enough truth to mislead the uninformed and to be successfully used by the bigoted to achieve sectarian ends.

Such labels can be as crudely applied to English teaching: traditional *v* progressive, formal *v* informal, grammatical *v* non-grammatical, structured *v* unstructured, syllabus-bound *v* project-free, class-taught *v* individual-taught, competence *v* creativity.

Behind such arbitrary dichotomies lie equally arbitrary attitudes and assumptions. These are at root personal and political. Translated, they become elitist *v* non-elitist, minority *v* majority, and right-wing *v* left-wing. Around them their adherents gather other supposed dichotomies in support, the labels (as with those above) being used as terms of praise or opprobrium according to which side they're on: authoritarian *v* non-authoritarian, controlled *v* permissive, subject-centred *v* student-centred, knowledge-orientated *v* feeling-orientated, intellect-based *v* emotion-based.

A plague on both their houses! Such windmill tilting hinders progress, not helps it.

The power of such factions can be seen in the current concern of teachers of teachers of English on both sides of the Atlantic to prove that their subject is not a soft option but the prime instrument in the development of the intellect. Thus 'English teaching' as a concept takes a back seat and the new one of 'learning through language' is substituted. Put bluntly, what they're saying is that English teachers have always believed that the mother tongue is the tool of all learning as well as the most important means of developing each student's personal qualities, but they've forgotten or played down its primary role in the development of the intellect.

A very necessary statement in the present climate of opinion, perhaps, but I've much sympathy with the English teacher who can't see what all the fuss is about, or feels he's being put in M. Jourdain's position – *Par ma foi! il y a plus de quarante ans que je dis de la prose sans que j'en susse rien*, or wants to know exactly how all the new theorising will help him do his job more competently.

We're all familiar with the Janus-face of English: it has no subject matter and its subject matter is life itself. With the truth also that in a very special sense the most important method of teaching English is the teacher himself, his philosophy, attitudes and assumptions, conscious and unconscious, and his personal qualities. This is not to underestimate the importance of knowledge and professional expertise; it is simply to put the emphasis first where it should be – on the teacher as a person living and working among younger persons.

It follows that there will be as many methods of teaching English as there are teachers. Also that any teacher worth his salt will be eclectic, choosing what will best help him from wherever he can find it, whatever the labels. There are still no certainties, certainties belong to pathology, not to English teaching. Yet this does not mean that teachers, and young teachers in particular, need drift rudderless on a sea of subjectivism. It does mean that they should constantly be doing three things: assessing themselves as they change and mature – their strengths and weaknesses – for it is first themselves they teach; weighing up the experience of others to judge what, if anything, they can use successfully; choosing from this what will work best in the particular school they find themselves in at a particular time and with a particular group of students.

If you believe, as I do, that English is the keystone of the curriculum, then its general aims and those of the school should coincide if either is to be fully effective.

I see these as being first, to ensure that a student gains experience of as high as possible a quality of life so that he is in a position later, if he chooses, to go on pursuing it; second, to create a milieu in which he can develop social sensitivity and awareness, and a complementary non-party political consciousness; third, to lay the foundations upon which he can later build to earn his daily bread.

The dilemma of English teachers who accept these or similar aims and who find themselves working in authoritarian, divided and divisive schools, which make it impossible to achieve them, was thrown into sharp relief at the 1971 York NATE–NCTE Conference. There, Commission 7 was formed to look at the way schools were organised, at their procedures, systems of rewards and punishments, and learning–teaching patterns, for unless the school milieu was democratic and humane all attempts by an English department to achieve its proper aims would be hamstrung.

Similarly, English teachers should also look hard at the statement about 'learning through language' quoted earlier and challenge its truth, for never was it more imperative to take Dr Johnson's advice and clear one's mind of cant: hokum is hokum is hokum, no matter from what altitudinous heights it's dropped upon us.

For instance, is language the most important means of fostering each student's personal and intellectual growth? Among the most important means, yes. But in school it is the way of life, the total experience and the total nexus of relationships, which must be made *humane* if the student is to develop as we would wish him to, 'proceeding at his own best pace towards his own fulfilment'. In this development the experience of literature can play an important part, but only a part.

Because, though, the experience of literature has such potency it is, from the point of view of the closed authoritarian school, counterproductive, helping to turn students into disgruntled protesters, to deepen their alienation. From the point of view of English teachers it helps to turn students into the kind of compassionate, sensitive, caring human beings society so urgently needs. But this happens only when the school community the students find themselves in lives by these and similar virtues. Little wonder that, caught in the impasse of their schools offering one set of values and their subject another, the young teachers at York demanded that Commission 7 be set up. Any teacher of English worth his salt has to be as concerned with the sort of community his school is as with his own subject.

At the heart of a student's total experience in school will be the linguistic behaviour he is constantly exposed to, an important part of which is embodied in 'English'. The actual form of words we use is important, but so equally is the tone of voice, the looks, the whole face-and-body language (the kinesics). No one knows better than a student when we say one thing and mean another. How can students have any chance of developing their potential in school if they're cabined, cribbed and confined by the kind of total linguistic environment we're all familiar with – 'I've got 3 D now, the dopies!; Wrong again, you'll never get it right!; Mary's got nine out of ten, you've only got three, why can't you be like her?; Go away, can't you see I'm busy?; Stop asking questions all the time!; If you try harder, you may get a prize next year; I'll put your poem on the wall, it's very good for a D child.' Such permanent shrouds cripple personal growth and development.

Consider also the ludicrous claim made in the preface to the Schools Council Humanities Project: 'The ultimate purpose of those who teach the humanities is to shape minds and satisfy souls. . . .' Tell that to a youngster whose father has been out of work for years. And if the project then takes place in a closed, divided and divisive school in which the values embodied in the day-to-day living are the antithesis of those the project offers, what chance is there of anything worthwhile being achieved, let alone the cosmic purpose quoted?

There is much to be said for packages and integrated studies. The danger for English teaching should, however, be noted. It might be that English would cease to be the keystone, around which all else is built, and would move to the periphery, taking in everyone else's dirty washing.

What then happens can be seen in more and more schools. English becomes bastardised Social Studies, and even – as in one school I know – lays claim to the domain of sociology, the concern of which is society in man, whereas that of English is man in society.

In such a package, 'literature' is chosen because of its factual connexion, however tenuous, with the subject matter being handled. This is the opposite of an English department choosing themes because of their relevance to the students' personal concerns, and finding prose and verse of high quality and suitable level to illuminate each theme.

An English syllabus should be relevant, everyone would agree. The test of true relevance is this. There exist for any individual at a particular stage in his growth towards self-realisation matters of fact and matters of importance. Matters of fact belong merely to the periphery of his being: matters of importance are matters he feels to be vital and central to his proprium, to his very being, and to what he is striving to become. These are matters of true relevance, matters which fortunately English by definition should be handling and which it is best equipped to handle.

Don't think that I'm suggesting that matters of importance are necessarily either solemn or should always be treated in a solemn way. One can be deadly serious without being the least bit solemn. Humour and fun are great unlockers of doors and a teacher who can use them with a class is well on the way to success. A sense of humour brings in its train a sense of perspective, enabling him also to laugh with others and at himself, very necessary if a teacher is to survive for long in the classroom.

The danger of an approach using humour and fun will be patent to all but the most naïve. It is that the clowns in the class will use their not inconsiderable influence to turn everything into a circus. But the danger can be avoided, and humour and fun are as potent ways as any of bringing them into the fold. The disaffected also.

A mother teaches her child about roundness by ensuring that he sees and handles round objects: 'Yes, this is round and that's round, but no, that's not round, that's oval', referring the word back to the quality it stands for. Similarly a teacher, as one way of meaningfully building the language of disadvantaged students, will bring into class curious and fascinating objects. Together they and he will find the language to describe, say, the scimitar: 'Yes, that's silver, touch it. The pattern, see, has been engraved on it, cut into it with a sharp tool. The special word for this kind of engraving is "chased", I'll put it on the board. What? Yes, the handle – what's another word for the handle of this scimitar, of all swords? "Hilt", right. Hold the hilt. Careful. How does it feel? . . . What's its job? . . . Does it do it well?'

By such means at this simple level does the teacher ensure that verbalisation has meaning so that his students can make for themselves the magic circle – objects, experience, meanings and thoughts acting and reacting in an indissoluble alliance, and in the process the two latter growing in power and complexity.

Artefacts and *objets trouvés* too – flints, pebbles, shells, bones, feathers, driftwood, roots of trees – are in addition potent starting points for imaginative work in exactly the same way as Henry Moore's 'the Warrior' had its genesis in a pebble which reminded him of the stump of a leg.

This is by now too well known to need mention. All that I wish to draw your attention to is the neurophysical evidence that a conscious experience is obtained only through specific brain activity. Thus to feed and use the twenty senses to the full in one's teaching is an important way of ensuring that the brain is active. Intellectual growth and development, which should be one of the most important aims of a school, is for all students best encouraged when this truth about the senses and experience is recognised and acted upon.

Experimental work on sensory deprivation vividly brings this truth home. The boredom, apathy and fear of those who took part in the experiments sprang from the sameness of their environment, the lack of stimuli, and the fact that they were deprived of the company of their fellows.

Many of our students come from grim urban environments in which for long periods they are virtually alone, which provide no pleasure for the eye, the hand, the ear, the nose, and in which life is only tolerable if the senses wither.

Not only should we create an accepting and compassionate school community for their sakes and because it is the essential condition which enables them to share in the learning experience, but also we should create a milieu which is sensuously rich and varied, and in which life-enhancing sights and sounds and experiences can be shared companionably among themselves and us.

Every English room – to use the current catchphrase – should be a workshop. True. Equally, each should be as sensuously stimulating as a good art and craft studio, music workshop, or biology laboratory.

Nor should the English teacher forget that working elsewhere than in the classroom – indoors or out-of-doors – often provides welcome and stimulating change. In such a situation the aim of the work should be clear, the control effective, the purpose, through careful briefing, genuinely shared by the students, if educational profit isn't to go by the board for the sake of having a good time. The kind of good time we want them to have is the one that comes through trying to do a specific job seriously and well.

You are doubtless as tired as I am of the kind of cant which postulates that we should be paragons of all the virtues, personal and professional, to teach successfully. The truth is, we have to do what we can and make the best of what talents we've got.

For this reason I dare to suggest here, as well as cultivating and using your sense of humour, only two further things. First, read what you yourself love to your students. Use to the full the short story, a neglected but most powerful resource. Stories about or involving young people (but not written for them) are winners. Prepare thoroughly what you're going to read and rehearse it adequately. If you can't read well, then learn how to – listen to yourself on tape and find out how to use your voice effectively. Despite the McLuhan world we now live in there is no substitute for the immediacy of the teacher face to face with his students, and for the power for good (and bad!) this can have.

Secondly, write with them. To sit down and write with one's students, to have the courage to share in this revealing but rewarding enterprise, drafting and re-drafting, teaching them to do the same, should be an essential part of your armoury (cf. the art teacher). This is teaching by example at its best.

The process of writing is the same – and this should be emphasised – as the one a student engages in when he is in the art and craft rooms. Its exploratory nature, its value in getting to know oneself, makes it truly a matter of importance. The natural extension of this is to found a writers' club. Those that I know have been successful and well attended.

Teachers of English admit that they themselves should read as much as possible. I believe they should also write – not only with the class, but alone, for themselves. How else can they with the necessary personal authority set out to teach it? The paradox is that many of those who most ardently preach 'creative' writing take up their pen only to fill in their pools forms.

Thinking, listening, speaking, reading, writing, role-playing: these are the activities that an English teacher should be concerned with in his programme. I've put 'thinking' first because it's usually never mentioned. If we link imagining and fantasising with it, then its importance as a conscious and specific aim of our teaching becomes clearer.

There is the inner and the outer, the private and the public, the individual and the social, aspects of our lives. The test of education has been well stated as what a man does with his solitariness. Let's see through the mystifying cloud of claptrap we're surrounded with, e.g. that the education of the disadvantaged should be solely social and political and concentrated on their environment and the real [*sic*] world. Let's give priority to helping our students enrich their inner life, develop their inner resources and individual life style, treasure the life of the imagination. It is the individual that matters.

To read to your students has another advantage – it encourages them to listen. The modern world grows more cacophonous: even the poets are beginning to shout. But listening is only profitable when there's something worth listening to. Part of our job is to help a student develop his own guide-lines.

In M. Jourdain's spirit we need also to think hard about the nature and purpose of the speaking that goes on in the classroom. A young teacher in a secondary school who uncritically accepts the dogma of the primacy of speech falls into a pit. His students know, even if he doesn't, that anything's better than work and, given the chance, will turn the classroom into a Tower of Babel. But, like Caliban, they derive precious little profit from such hubbub.

Speaking should for the most part be about the work. A good teacher will see that it is purposeful and self-controlled. There are many 'registers' to become acquainted with, many modes of civilised discourse, many ways of discussing, debating and arguing honestly and without rancour, many sharings of thoughts and experiences and longings.

There is also a time for silence. Listening demands it. So does the internalised speech which most thinking and imagining involves, though it would be a hindrance to discourage the less able from mouthing this speech. Much writing also requires it.

For English teachers to talk of creativity without making clear that they are equally concerned with competence is to destroy their credibility in the eyes of colleagues and parents alike. English skills do matter and should be carefully and systematically taught – unlike the common cold many of them can't be easily caught.

Within a school one of the most important tasks for an English department is to make sure that its aims and methods are understood by colleagues. The other subjects have their subject matter and so their rationale is clear. The only rationale English has in their eyes is as the tool-subject; it should produce the skills a student must have to make the best progress in their subject.

Their case is the same as that of parents, employers and the general public. It is right, or partly right. An English department should heed it and do its best to answer it. If it does not, it is preventing itself from getting the support and understanding necessary for it to fulfil its more important aims: the development of the individual's imagination, creativity, etc.

However unpalatable, and whatever one's personal view of the future obsolescence of reading, it is essential that here and now every teacher of English should see himself first as a teacher of reading. He should arm himself with some of the specialised skills useful to cope with near non-readers, and with the equally specialised ones necessary to teach the complex art of expert reading with understanding at all levels.

Just as far too few teachers have ever taken seriously George Sampson's dictum that every teacher should be a teacher of English, so far too few English teachers have helped to shoulder the onerous burden of teaching reading, preferring to leave the most handicapped to the ministrations of the so-called remedial teacher, and with the abler waiting until the examination demands of what goes under the name of comprehension can no longer be denied.

Increasing competence and creativity can and must go hand in hand. Writing should as often as possible be purposeful. Both focus and audience are needed: focus because we write best when we keep our eye closely on the ball; audience because we write to communicate, sometimes with ourselves, sometimes with others.

The value of the thematic area-of-experience approach is that, provided the themes are relevant, all activities can be grouped around the theme and motivated by it. Discussions, voluntary readings, current wall-displays of writing and the like ensure that there is some communication. Writing that is self-communing and self-exploratory should also be encouraged and left to develop in its proper place – strictly in private.

Role-playing, I believe, is a most important part of the activities that English should be concerned with. It's best kept as part of the English lesson because it arises naturally as an integral part of the work in progress. Its place is the classroom, but it will at times lap over into any more ample space available. It has nothing to do with that dubious member of the (larger) English department, the drama specialist, whose work in creative drama only too often develops into one long and noisy all-in wrestling match, nearly always on the floor.

Its great virtue, especially with older students, is that it gives them, and particularly the inarticulate and the disadvantaged, opportunities to work out their problems under guise of acting out someone else's and, through talking about them, to understand and come to some sort of terms with them.

It is an error to suppose that all thinking is verbal. Intelligence is as directly exhibited in our actions as in our speaking and thinking. We have real mastery of a piece of knowledge only when we know how to use it to solve practical as well as theoretical problems. It is very important for English teachers to remember and act on this. It provides the firm ground for their belief that the affect-laden democratic values and attitudes that a student may be led to develop through the right kind of English programme, though often by him unable to be clearly and convincingly put into words (if into words at all), may issue in democratic action and a democratic way of life.

Consequently, they will note a student's actions as well as his words and will assess the success of their programme by this in addition to the usual oral and written work. Nor will they overhastily conclude that a student is not thinking, or trying to think, if he is dumb, hesitant or unable to express himself adequately.

An English programme should be coherent, structured and progressive. The syllabus and its accompanying schemes of work should embody these concepts: they should be sufficiently detailed to be a real guide to the course, while not becoming a strait-jacket. The spiral approach, where themes which are abiding matters of importance can be returned to but treated in greater depth and detail, has much to recommend it. Only the teachers in the English department, through on-going debate and consultation, can decide what balance to strike between the various activities – they know their students and their situation better than anyone else.

The themes (or areas of life and experience) make it possible for all the necessary kinds of English activity to be linked to them and so to be given significance, purpose, momentum and direction. They also enable language and literature to be treated as complementary parts of the one whole, as they should be.

And literature – the chosen words in the chosen order – comes here into its own. Here is the opportunity to add that other dimension to the student's experience. Here, invoking inspiration and good fortune, comes the chance to make more humane the student's whole consciousness, to bring him to reject the facts as they are *for him* in favour of the facts as they *are*, to make it possible for him to become many men and yet remain himself, to enable him to transcend himself and yet be never more himself than when he does.

Yes, but the chance will be slender indeed if the teacher is working in an inhumane school environment. Literature, or the humanities, alone won't do it. As Auden wryly remarks:

> and my day turned out torturers
> who read *Rilke* in their rest periods.

The world today needs people with 'feeling intellects', with emotional as well as intellectual knowledge. Provided that the school community is right, an English teacher has as important a part as any to play in helping a student to become this kind of a person.

Poets

The Teacher and the
Postmistress

JOHN MOLE

In a radio interview recorded shortly before his death C. Day Lewis
contrasted most attractively the mind of the novelist and that of the
poet:

A novelist's mind is like a perfectly run chain-store where everyone
knows what shelf everything is on: so they simply go to the store and
they take out a tin of blacking, a bicycle pump, a pair of gym shoes.
My mind, and the minds of a good many poets that I know, is like a
village shop where you have tins of Brasso, kippers, stamps, gym shoes
and a few other things all mixed up in a great jumble. The postmistress
knows where everything is, so if you ask her for a threepenny stamp
she knows where to go, but nobody else does.[1]

What, for any teacher, this warns against, I think – and the tempta-
tions to ignore it are considerable – is the imposing of any method in
the presentation of poetry to children which attempts to do much more
than ask the postmistress for such-and-such or so-and-so. This is not to
suggest that every child is a natural poet (a sentimental fallacy) but
that when considering poetry with children one should always be
aware of the mind in its 'village shop' aspect and, if only provisionally,
value its random and private arrangements above one's own sense of
order. How the postmistress chooses to come and go between her
supplies may fascinate, bewilder or irritate you as you stand there
at her counter but it is not a pattern for you to control: as customer
you could go to another shop, as teacher it is your concern to stay
where you are. If she takes a long time fetching you the kippers it
would be mean to tell her so or to suggest that she might keep them in
a fridge. If you point out to her that the obvious place to keep her threepenny stamps is here, in a tidy box right beneath your nose, you are
probably ignoring the pleasure she gets from bustling off into a back
room and returning with the album, left to her by her father, contain-

ing a penny black in mint condition. Of course, as a customer, you are bound to have a sense of rightness – that a penny (even of such value) is not threepence, that you asked to buy not to be shown, and that you haven't got all day – but wait . . . she turns a page and there it is, tucked in like a book mark, a strip of the stamps you wanted – as many as you need and more. Suddenly you are delighted by the whole performance. Only she could have done it *that* way. Suddenly, too, you have all the time in the world; you ask for a tin of Brasso – how will she come up with that?

My excuse for this rather bizarre development of Day Lewis's analogy is that it corresponds to my experience on first becoming a teacher and experimenting with 'ways of doing' poetry. Although I persuaded myself that I was on the side of *creativity*, I knew only too well what I wanted and that what I wanted was beneficial to the children. My mind was laid out like a comprehension exercise and 'what does the poet mean?' (meaning 'understand in the name of education') ought to have been carved on every desk top and used in evidence against me, I asked it so often and under so many disguises. I seized on similes and metaphors with a fearful rapacity – the more a poem had the better, they were good fuel for discussion. 'Do you think that's an effective comparison?' (not even 'Do you like it?') and 'why does the poet use *that* word, *do you think*?' soon bore fruit with several of the children who, when they wrote 'their own' poems packed them, sure enough, with neat comparisons and clever words. And the trouble was that I could see that this was happening and could do nothing about it. I had bullied the postmistress and she was putting it on as a girl at the pay-counter, swift and efficient, clocking it up on the adding machine, but *in spite of herself*. More and more I felt myself to be part of a conspiracy and that, despite my nicely formulated principles concerning poetry and life ('What does the poet *feel*?'), we were all involved in some kind of hoax. Where was the poetry? What was the point?

So, gradually, I tried to loosen up, to get rid of some of the solemnity and literary earnestness which was weighing me down. I remained rather conscious of the fact that I was trying out ways of making a lesson 'go' (I think this is still the case more often than I should care to admit) but I soon began to sense that my classes could be on the verge of some kind of freedom. In the upper school (mainly A level English courses) I continued for much of the time, uneasily, with standard procedures of critical analysis but with younger children I started to experiment. In what follows I shall try to describe one of the ways I have directed attention, when we have been reading poetry, to how a poem is made, and to outline a few of my attempts to create classroom conditions under which the children may enjoy writing their own poems. I shall finish with an account of an elective course I have recently begun running for sixth formers. If the emphasis is on language and technique rather than measurable substance (i.e. the poem's prose meaning) this is because my concern has become, increasingly, to arouse interest in how a poem works as what W. H. Auden calls a 'contraption', to nourish an appetite for words. What anyone takes away from a poem looked at in class will depend on how he has lived inside it: inside a house is inside bricks and mortar, inside a poem is inside a skin of words stretching this way or that. Or, not to shift from the house metaphor, inside poem is inside a room (the meaning of the word 'stanza') and, as a teacher, I should like to help a reader to recognise the room he is moving in. How he should behave there is not for me, but for the poem, to teach.

First, then, one of the strategies I sometimes use when looking at a poem with a class. I have never thought of naming it but perhaps it could be called 'versions'. What I do is play about with ways of adapting passages from the anthologies we are using and place the adaptations alongside the originals. Here are three I have tried with brief indications of the kind of discussion which arose from them.

I knew, for a start, that there were two versions of the first line of Tennyson's 'The Eagle', one referring to the eagle's 'crooked hands' and the other to his 'hooked hands' (good, and recommended in several books on the teaching of poetry, for the direct question 'which do you like best?') but why isolate that line as containing a difference even if it was the only one which had the poet's official stamp on it? Why not make some further alterations? So the last three lines

> The wrinkled sea beneath him crawls,
> He watches from his mountain walls
> And like a thunderbolt he falls.

became

> The patient sea beneath him crawls,
> He looks down from his craggy walls
> And like a shooting-star he falls.

Thus, in the guise of irreverently 'mucking about' with a famous poem, it was possible to open up a discussion in which the visual content of the first line, the tense poise of the eagle in the second and the force of his descent in the third was explored: how 'patient' throws 'a kind of mist over the sea. You can't see the wrinkles', how 'watches' is alert while 'looks down' is comparatively casual and doesn't *sound* like concentration, how 'mountain walls' is noble like 'castle walls' whereas 'craggy' suggests a wrong kind of wildness and doesn't fit the mood, and how a 'shooting-star' would be more appropriate to Guy Fawkes Night. My role was that of provocateur. I defended my changes, giving way gradually as the case was put for the original or listening with modest approval to support of the alternatives. To end with, the poem was read aloud by several members of the class, coming to rest on the poet's choice.

Encouraged by the diversity of response, I tried this idea at different levels and in different ways. For slightly older children one of the poems I took was Gerard Manley Hopkins' 'Hailstorm in May':

> Strike, churl; hurl, cheerless wind, then; heltering hail
> May's beauty massacre and wisped wild clouds grow
> Out on the giant air; tell Summer No,
> Bid joy back, have at the harvest, keep Hope pale.

Then, like a model exam candidate, I wrote out some kind of equivalent in prose:

Lash out and blow wildly, wind; let the disorderly hail destroy the beauty of May and rain clouds appear in the sky. Stop summer happening, don't let there be any joy, attack the harvest and don't let there be any hope either.

With little need for pointers, attention was drawn to the vigour and originality of Hopkins' language, beginning with the impact of the two first monosyllables replaced by my wan phrasing. Notice was taken of the inversions, the unifying image of invasion and rape, the realisation of the 'churl' as a recognisable enemy out of adventure books – 'have at thee!' –: how the whole noise of the poem, gone from my muffle, is achieved, its thrust, its recoils and bursts of phrasing. I had only to provide at suitable moments the appropriate technical terms – alliteration, personification, etc. – giving a name to aspects of the writer's craft which the children were discovering for themselves. Elements of poetic composition could be learned, and brought to knowledge, by heart and not by rote. I should, perhaps, point out that I tried not to miss any opportunity of naming a technique: I still believe very strongly that a good acquaintance with prosody is essential to the full enjoyment of a poem (not least of a poem in free verse for, as T. S. Eliot says, no verse is free for the poet who wishes to use it well). Those who complain that it's 'murder to dissect' are usually those who have been forced into the operating theatre.

Eventually, this approach found its way into my teaching of Shakespeare at exam level. Anyone who has taught *Macbeth* will recognise the origin of the next passage and the obvious inadequacy of it. Act 1, Scene 6: an emasculated Banquo speaks:

> What a perfect, peaceful place:
> A certain sign of heaven's grace
> Is that the martlet, gentle bird,
> Has nested here – for I have heard
> And noted for myself that he
> When setting up his mansionry
> Will always build and settle where
> A nimbleness is in the air.

With this in front of us, notice was taken of style, weight, the craft of poetry (the length of the lines, their levity, the pat use of rhyme, the regular metre as set against the slow and deliberate emphasis of the blank verse). My version was quickly seen and heard to omit or simplify much that served, in the original speech, to create the drama of the situation. Effective images and lines were seized upon and shown to be missing: 'No one would *speak* like that' – to which, of course, my reply was 'Would you have expected a man of action like Banquo to describe a bird's-nest as a 'pendant bed and procreant cradle'? All obvious enough, no doubt, but I found that what emerged was an awareness that Shakespearean blank verse is, in all its elaboration and rhetoric, a real and vital language. My effort could be consigned elsewhere as certainly having little to do with actual speech. So various discoveries were made by individual readers, and the amount of leading questions I had to ask were very few.

I have continued to play about with versions like these and have found increasingly that they can provide a meeting point between

G

my own fascination for language, my compulsion to fiddle with it, and the children's own resources of invention combined with their endless readiness to argue with a teacher to the last syllable if encouraged to do so. There is no *right* answer, there is only the poem and the version shaken together into a jumble out of which emerges a sense of language and its use. Nor, I suspect, is there anything very original about looking at poetry in this way (it was Aldous Huxley who changed Tennyson's 'And after many a summer dies the swan' to 'And after many a summer dies the duck'*) but it has led to my collaborating with a class and opening up a poem instead of wrapping it up. I have also found, as might be expected, that on the majority of occasions (with a class which has explored poems in this way) when I don't fiddle but simply present a poem for discussion, the language gets looked at directly as a register of the poem's 'meaning' and not, as I have experienced as happening so often, a deliberate puzzle to be unravelled in order to get at the (infamous) *'hidden* meaning'.

I am aware that it may seem unfashionable to lay such stress on poetic technique, that I could be accused of encouraging attention to surfaces – playing games and ignoring the depths – but I am fairly confident that this is not the case. I remember a teacher of mine, when I was beginning seriously to write poetry myself, commenting that 'the young man has everything to say but can't find the words to say it; the older man has the words but no longer finds it important'. Looking back, I'd call the second part of that remark a cynical attempt to impress me, but the first part probably contains the reason why I teach at all. And because I value poetry as a unique way of seeing and saying things, I have always been dissatisfied with teaching it as anything but itself. I should be the first to acknowledge the uses a poem can be put to, fitting into a mosaic of theme work, providing material for discussions on 'old age', 'loneliness', 'life in cities', etc.; this is undoubtedly

---

* Robert Graves, too, has made his own a mischievous habit of rewriting well-known poems in order to demonstrate the weakness he finds in them. There are good examples of this in 'Technique in Poetry' (*Mammon and the Black Goddess*, Cassell, 1965) and 'Legitimate Criticism of Poetry' (*Steps*, 1958). I have found Graves's mock-pedantic demolition of anthology pieces such as Blake's 'The Tyger' and Wordsworth's 'The Solitary Reaper' a good source for stimulating argument amongst older children, some of whom have already come to take these poems for granted: the schoolmasterly tone tends to alienate ('who does he think he is?') and send them to the defence of the poet, yet at the same time the relentlessness of Graves's detail demands that they examine their own responses at all turns.

of educational importance. When it comes to encouraging children
to write, I'm all for the use of every possible stimulus – music, pictures,
the handing round of objects, all attempts to kindle and merge the
senses.* This poem, for example, has continued to haunt me ever
since it emerged from a poetry lesson where I took a box of stones
into a first-year class, gave one to each boy and asked him to make
the dumb speak:

The Dreams of a Stone

Here I stand in solitude,
As oval as an egg,
Waiting for my solid body to change,
Every day a boring nothing.

My shadow forms from nothing
Till the long, black streak appears,
Then dissolves again to nothing,
Always nothing.

The night shrouds in
Till the moon and stars
Give a boring change from nothing,
A silvery change, though not what I want and need.

But there is still hope.
In a thousand, maybe a million years of nothing
It will happen,
I will change at last from a nothing life
To some part of something, great and glorious,
Some part of a volcano.

---

* I have, at the same time, to confess to an uneasiness about the number of
recent course books which include stark black-and-white photographs (often
sensational and intrusive on private grief) showing deprivation, suffering and
human wastage. It is rather tempting for the teacher to put these in front of a
child with the *implicit* command to emote, and to value the result as indicators of
the child's awakened sensitivity to the world around him. Many anthologies of
children's poems are full of such responses, and they are certainly flattering to the
liberal conscience, but, as Roy Fuller has written somewhere, 'mere feeling is too
easy'. I think it is the teacher's responsibility not to use poetry lessons as a means
of encouraging children to become what a far from reactionary friend of mine
calls 'sensitive young socialists' but rather to stimulate the complexity of response
out of which all *real* political commitment of lasting value (revolutionary or

Why a volcano, with its fiery funnel?
Why not a mountain
With its shadows cast by small
Insignificant flowers on the bleak graveyard sides?

It could be a mountain,
So why do I want a volcano?
Is it because the hollow funnel
Is the front door to my home town?

Or is it because if I journey there,
Some day I will actually be larger,
Maybe a lot larger.
Perhaps I will even grow to a desolate mountain.

This, clearly, has a beautiful, intuitive sense of form – the more remarkable for coming from a boy who kept insisting that he 'couldn't imagine things' (I have found that highly imaginative children often, and in complete sincerity, make this claim). However, I think that it is important if one is teaching poetry to spend a good deal of time introducing pattern and design and trying to make it a principal starting point. It is easy to be nervous about this, to feel that one is in league with the old schoolmasters who insisted on carbon copies of the Shakespearean sonnet or Masefield's metre at its most chugging, but why, really? Most children enjoy puzzles – making things fit, trying to get something to come out right. Absorption in a puzzle is a full engagement of the imagination in which the placing of pieces is a series of steps in a growing excitement. I think there is a similar excitement to be found in the making of a poem, and that, far from having an inhibiting effect, to present children with a variety of forms to experiment with involves them in a kind of adventure which stimulates the imagination and, as it were, fascinates them into the discovery that they are actually *saying* something too. They are discovering what to say and how to say it at the same time, and, as with puzzles, there are forms to suit all stages of capability and accomplishment.

In short, I have discovered that the way of encouraging the writing of poetry which I find most rewarding is *formal*, in the best sense of

---

otherwise) may emerge. And for this to happen it is vital to grasp that poetry is not fundamentally propagandist, not even in the cause of human decency and compassion.

the word, and that the classroom seldom seems more relaxed and humming with invention than when there are rules. I try to pass around as many possibilities as I can – demonstrating and suggesting until everyone has something for private use. If I were to list the variety, here, I should merely be doing what is done much better by a good poetry handbook[2]; but some suggestions may perhaps be mentioned.

A very simple kind of beginning, which is hardly a form at all, is one which I have borrowed from an account by the American poet Kenneth Koch of his experiences teaching in a New York public school.[3] It involves the presenting of basic thought-skeletons to be fleshed out, for example 'Once I was . . . now I am', 'I wish . . . but', 'He says . . . I say', etc. Into these, anything goes and comes out with a controlling rhythm which can work repetitively or cumulatively. Two illustrations must serve – one, a lyrical exploration and the other a knotty, humourous piece which delighted the class when read aloud:

Once I Was

Once I was water, a mere droplet
Trickling from beneath the stones,
Cold, icy, mountainous.

Now I am a brook, a burn
Hurrying over rocky beds,
Clear, fresh, sweet-smelling.

Once I was a deepening stream
Cascading through arching trees,
Shaded, flowing, life-bearing.

Now I am a stately river
Travelling past the country-side,
Majestic, quiet, solemn.

Once I was an estuary
Sweeping into the ocean,
Deep and wide, expansive.

Now I am the open sea
Encircling all the continents.
The mighty power of God's world.

I Wish

I wish I could
But I can't.
Why can't I?
I wish I knew.

I could do this,
And I could do that.
But I can't do this,
Oh, no! Not that.

I finally found something
I could do.
How I found it?
I wish I knew.

Then there are the many small units based on syllable counts, such as the familiar Japanese Haiku (seventeen) and Tanka (thirty-one: five lines with a 5 7 5 7 7 count) or the cinquain, originated by the American Adelaide Crapsey, which is also a five-liner but with a count of 2 4 6 8 2. These can provide the shapes for individual poems of any amount of combinations: I might suggest to one child that he write a poem in three sections, opening with a Haiku, putting a Tanka in the middle and closing with a second Haiku, or to another that he might use the cinquain pattern over several stanzas or alternate the cinquain and the Tanka. Once the poem gets going, my answer to the frequent question 'Does it matter if I have more than seven syllables in one line?' is 'No, not if a longer line seems to go right' just as when I'm asked 'Does my poem have to rhyme?' the reply is 'Not unless you want it to'. The rules are there to initiate, and I think it is as important that any of them may be broken at any time as it is for the writer to recognise that something is happening when he breaks them.

Of the more complex forms, I have found the villanelle and the sestina particularly popular. The former often works as a means of coaxing music from the logically minded who have convinced themselves that they cannot write poetry, in as much as the alternation and coming together at the end of even the most prosaic statements tends to transform them into *effect*. Here is one by a sixth former, a science specialist whose enthusiasm for chess was matched by his mistrust of poetry. When he had completed it (and he did so very quickly) he told me that it should prove that he could not write a poem. When I persuaded him to read it aloud and hear how it sounded, most of the class disagreed with his assessment:

The Black Queen

The black queen begins her long flight,
The players ply their subtle art,
And on the chess-board starts the fight.

Certain goals which one must expedite,
Use the deadly knight as a dart,
The black queen begins her long flight.

Pawns jump into the box so white,
Black rooks leave as if in a cart
And on the chess-board starts the fight.

One player sees the mating light,
If only that queen would depart.
The black queen begins her long flight.

Pawns move like bites from a small mite –
Is chess a real game of the heart? –
And on the chess-board starts the fight.

Bishops caught in corners so tight,
But now the final venomous dart,
The black queen moves on her long flight,
And on the chess-board ends the fight.

The metre is uncertain, there is a lot of awkwardness, but there is for all that the *drama* of form. And when he 'cheats' at the end, he knows exactly what he wants to achieve.

The sestina consists of six stanzas of six lines each, and a concluding tercet. The end words of the first stanza are all repeated in the succeeding stanzas (including the tercet) and in a precise order which varies with each stanza. The pattern can be worked out from the following example by a fourteen-year-old who, again, showed no particular enthusiasm for poetry, preferring whenever possible to write discursive essays. I believe that in this case the word game, the puzzle, liberated his imagination – producing a poem which is quaint but genuinely felt:

Stacks of Happiness

They stood there, smiling, by the window,
The bride and groom feeling
Fresh and new like a rich green pasture
And around them the relations, and friends at the
    edge,
All in their correct and proper place,
In symmetrical rows like chimney stacks.

And around the room, in stacks,
Stood the presents, with a few neatly placed by the
    other french window,
As well as cake plates and forks all over the place.
The champagne was all gone except for the strange
    feeling
In the Page Boy's stomach, putting him rather on
    edge –
Still, 'Slip out and take a breather in that pasture'.

Out in the pasture
The boy saw the hay-stacks,
One with its top nearly falling over its edge;
He ran back to the window
And rushed in, without feeling
Any respect for the place.

Inside, he returned to his youngest-in-the-family
    place,
Forgetting about what he saw in the pasture
But remembering, with a horrible feeling,
The weekend homework he had left in stacks
On his desk in his room (by his net-curtained
    window)
Next to the desklight which was close to the table's
    edge.

'Darling, darling, come here by the edge,
You must be in the photo, because it's your right
    place.'

His mother said, as a little red robin flew from under
   the window
To its nest in a tree by the pasture,
While behind it rose the black, dirty smoke from the
   stacks
Of the factory, belching their pollution without any
   feeling.

The bride's mother had got one of the presents, and
   had started feeling
What was inside, when the wrapping paper split all
   along the edge
And the sellotape she used to restick it with was
   stacks
Too much, and bits got stuck on the carpet all over
   the place,
But then a black cloud burst all over the pasture
And rain started leaking in through the crack in the
   window.

The hay stack in the pasture toppled over its edge
And the rain leaked in on the presents and all over
   the place, but let's not have a hard feeling
For the bride and groom's wedding has opened a
   window for them through which life, happiness and
   blessing is mounted up in stacks.

Of course, this is all only an *emphasis* in my teaching, based on my belief – to use Richard Wilbur's image – that 'the strength of the genii comes of his being confined in a bottle'. Very often I encourage 'free' writing both on an individual basis and as part of group poetry projects, but descriptions of creative ideas abound in books on the teaching of English and I think it would be more worthwhile for me to limit this chapter to the study of form. At worst, I can be dismissed as a curiosity.

What I should like to mention, though, is the 'writers' workshop' which I have started to run for sixth formers who are interested in imaginative writing but who have little opportunity to develop this interest during school hours.[4] It is in no way a revolutionary course and, in so far as it is voluntary, it really only makes any impact on those who already feel the need for it. My decision to offer it arose out of an awareness that there is a tendency in myself, and in other English teachers I know, to place a different emphasis on imaginative work when teaching older children. Because there is little scope for it in the current O level syllabus and none at all at A level (which is dominated by the concept of university Eng Lit discipline – which in turn made me the kind of poetry teacher I began as) we tend to value the writing of poems and stories as a leavening, a kind of going to church on Sundays for those who have got out of the habit of praying. We acknowledge its importance but are prevented by the syllabus from presenting it wholeheartedly as an essential activity. If we are stubborn and do so, we are asked – often by the very students who enjoy it most – what it is contributing to their chances of getting a good A level grade. We may have some nice, woolly answer but the fact that the question has to be asked at all is widely incriminating and it can still make one feel very nervous. The ultimate irony, of course, is that a book like Housman's *The Name and Nature of Poetry*[5] can be studied by sixth formers for its assessment of the metaphysicals or the Augustans, and its highly individual judgements can be related to the texts which the class happens to be preparing for the exam, but when Housman begins to speak of poetry being 'more physical than intellectual' the reader, who was last encouraged to write a poem in the fourth form three years ago, may be missing what could have been the opportunity to prove this definition on his own pulse. Thus the real originality of Housman's book remains as much a part of academic discussion as the peripheral uses it can be put to.

When I was given the chance of organising a general studies course, the purpose of which was to take arts and science students outside their immediate areas of specialisation, I decided to see what interest there might be in a 'writers' workshop' among those who had gone underground with their imaginative writing since the middle school and those who wanted to pick up old habits. For the scientists it would clearly be something different and for the English specialist, too, it would be new ground on which exposition of the objective correlative or the pathetic fallacy would be taboo unless forced to our attention by the problems encountered by a particular member of the group in writing a particular piece. So the course was offered and fifteen volunteers started to meet with me twice a week for two double periods of one and a half hours each. The ground rules were simple: for the course to develop there would have to be a steady supply of finished work or work-in-progress, all of which I would duplicate and hand round. As a general studies teacher I was to be allowed £10 a term for books; no books, then (we would plunder the English department), but the money to be spent on travelling expenses for the practising writers we would invite to join us. Attention would be paid to craft, to the satisfaction or difficulties of saying something particular in a particular way. We would be joined in a common bond based on a high percentage rate of failure, learning together that – as Graves says – 'the writer's best friend is the wastepaper basket' and that no academic smokescreen can hide this fact from him. My role would be that of mediator and repository of some skills, nor would I be exempt from the obligation to circulate work of my own with which I was having difficulty. We should become, I hoped, a society of apprentices. Where we might go from there would depend. . . .

So far things have come on well. I ought to explain why, but it is hard to define an atmosphere. We have, for a start, been lucky in our guests and the enthusiasm they have generated. In some cases we have been favoured by coincidence; for example, one of the group was friendly with a girl whose father – he gathered – was a writer, and who turned out to be a well-known American poet temporarily in this country. Generally, though, I have been tremendously encouraged by the readiness of people to come simply if asked straight. Magazine editors, often themselves poets, have shown great interest and discussed members' poems as if they were submissions. Several important magazines, in fact, directly encourage school contributions and this has added the impetus of possible 'outside' publication. The *Critical Quarterly* for some years has been running a poetry competition for poets under the age of nineteen and publishing commended poems as well as the prizewinners in the *Critical Survey*. Also, the poetry magazine *Workshop*[6] has recently given over a page of each issue to poems chosen from those sent in from schools, printing them with no special indication that they are by schoolchildren. Some newspapers, too, promote competitions for the short story and though I would be the first to admit the dangers of the competitive spirit where writing is concerned, I'd be very reluctant to dismiss the incentive it gives to young writers. Such external contact is good for the kind of group I am concerned with, and it is not hard to establish. It is well known that writers often teach to supplement their income and that many teachers are also practising writers. Several of my friends who have written and published poems, stories or novels have welcomed the opportunity of visiting the school to read and discuss their own work; they tell me that it has been a worthwhile experience for them and it has certainly given the class a sense of the urgency of constructive criticism. Here is a writer, sometimes of distinction, who can be moved more than Shakespeare by what is said about his work. To worry away at a phrase or word becomes a real dialogue and the enthusiasm with which members of the group have taken to this kind of active (as distinct from deskbound) criticism keeps in my mind the fact that it is possible even for an English specialist to go through school without ever meeting a contemporary writer for whom the imagination is a way of life. To arrange such meetings is, I think, to make Shakespeare, Milton, Yeats, etc. *different*.

Looking back on this account, I'm really not sure what points have been made. I suppose I don't have any systematic approach to the teaching of poetry, only a sense of certain importances and a kind of blind trust in what I enjoy doing. What I hope I may have been able to trace is a move away from teaching poetry as *content* to an involvement in the process of writing which is bound up with the exploration of craft. I believe that to enjoy words is to find that you have something to say, and that an atmosphere in class somewhat like that of a good art room in which the materials, colours, shapes, etc. abound is infinitely more likely to bring about an 'understanding' of poetry than one which arises from talk and discussion about the poet's 'purpose', his 'use of' metaphor and simile and so on, or even what he 'feels about' love, war or death. And the understanding, rather than 'comprehension', of a poem is the peculiar shade of human understanding that poetry in itself, and not as the appendage to prose which it has become in so many recent school anthologies, can offer. This is what I have arrived at for myself, anyway, and it is really all I find I can offer for debate. The rest is up to the postmistress in each of us.

References

1 *The Listener*, 27 July 1972.
2 The best I know is Babette Deutsch, *Poetry Handbook*, Cape, 1970, an invaluable, alphabetically ordered volume of method and example.
3 Kenneth Koch, *Wishes, Lies and Dreams*, Random House, 1970.
4 A tape transcript of a discussion between members of this group, and a selection of their poems, appears in *Understanding Children Writing*, Penguin, 1973.
5 A. E. Housman, *The Name and Nature of Poetry*, CUP, 1933.
6 Edited by Norman Hidden, 2 Culham Court, Granville Road, London N4 4JB.

Further Reading

The following are a few books which I have found useful sources of invention and ideas:

W. H. Auden, *The Dyer's Hand*, Faber, 1963.
T. Blackburn (ed.), *Presenting Poetry*, Methuen, 1966.
Ted Hughes, *Poetry in the Making*, Faber, 1967.
A. MacLeish, *Poetry and Experience*, Peregrine, 1965.
P. Orr (ed.), *The Poet Speaks*, Routledge, 1966.
J. Press, *The Fire and the Fountain*, Methuen, 1966.
J. Reeves, *Understanding Poetry*, Heinemann, 1965; Pan, 1967.
J. Scully (ed.), *Modern Poets on Modern Poetry*, Fontana, 1970.
L. Simpson, *An Introduction to Poetry*, Macmillan, 1968.

15 How can I tell what I think till I see what I say?

W. H. AUDEN

There is only one trait that is common to all poets without exception, a passionate love for their native tongue. This means that the phrase *Poets are born, not made* must be false, for babies are born speechless. What psychological conditions encourage such a love is anybody's guess. Perhaps, such phrases as 'my mother tongue' and 'the milk of the word' are significant.

*　　*　　*

I may be generalising too much from my own experience, but I suspect that, for children who may later decide to become poets, the kind of verse that will appeal to them most will be comic or nonsense verse, not 'serious' poetry. In my own case, my early favourites were Hoffman's *Shock-Headed Peter*, Belloc's *Cautionary Tales*, Harry Graham's *Ruthless Rhymes for Heartless Homes* and, of course, Edward Lear and Lewis Carroll.

In comic verse the role of language is so much more obvious. It seems as if it is the language, its rhymes and metrics which has the power to create the event, not, as in serious poetry, the event in the poet's mind which looks for its fit linguistic expression. Eor example:

> In the drinking well
> which the plumber built her,
> Aunt Maria fell:
> We must buy a filter.

*　　*　　*

When he first begins to write verses, the surest sign that poet-to-be has real talent is that he is more interested in playing with words than in saying anything original. Originality, if he ever achieves it, will come later.

★   ★   ★

There have been times and places, in the Wales of the Middle Ages, for example, when would-be poets received a professional education like lawyers and doctors. Today they have to educate themselves, and the results are not always satisfactory. If I had to take a class in 'writing poetry', I would entirely ignore all questions of critical judgement and taste, and devote the time to questions of fact, that is, to prosodic analysis, rhetoric and philology, the history of the language. Every poet (and every critic of poetry, too) should know the difference between a bacchic and a choriamb, and be able instantaneously to spot the use of epanorthosis or chiasmus. Alas, all too few of them do or can.

★   ★   ★

Whatever else it may be, the making of a work of art is a form of play, that is to say, not something which the maker must do, like eating or sleeping, but something which he finds it fun to make. That is why formal poetry is the norm. Everyone knows that one cannot play a game without rules. One can make the rules what one likes, but one's whole fun and freedom comes from obeying them. There have been poets, Whitman and D. H. Lawrence, for example, who convince one that they had to write in free verse, but they are the exceptions. To succeed in writing free verse, a poet must have an infallible sense for line endings. All too often one feels that the line endings are purely arbitrary and that the whole thing should have been written out as a prose poem.

★   ★   ★

In most cases though not, perhaps, in all, the initial impulse to write a serious poem comes, I believe, from the sense of awe and wonder aroused in the poet's imagination by beings or events that he finds sacred or numinous. This response is involuntary: it cannot be willed. Some of these beings have seemed sacred to all imaginations at all times, for example the Moon, the four elements, and those beings which can only be defined in terms of non-being, darkness, silence, nothing, death. Others, like kings, are only felt to be numinous in certain cultures.

It is rare for a poem, even a love poem, to be based on a single such encounter. In the poet's memory there are usually a number of such experiences, apparently unrelated to each other, that is to say, a crowd. This crowd the poet attempts to transform into a community by embodying it in a verbal society where, if he is successful, the feelings all become members of the same community, loving each other and it. A poem may fail in two ways. It may exclude too much and so be banal, or it may attempt to embody more than one community at the same time, and so be chaotic.

*   *   *

Speaking for myself, at any given time my mind is preoccupied with two interests, one thematic, the other formal or linguistic, matters of metre, diction, etc. The theme searches for the form which can most adequately embody it; the formal concern looks for those aspects of a theme with which it can deal most adequately. When the two finally come to an agreement, I am able to write a poem.

*   *   *

Not only in youth but at all stages in their writing careers, most poets are conscious of a model, some predecessor who can help them to find their own true path. In finding such models other people can seldom help. Occasionally, an older person, because he has read more, may be able to make a fruitful suggestion to a young poet, but only on condition that he knows the latter, his sensibility and interests, very well.

*   *   *

In choosing one's models, it is possible to make mistakes. My first models, Thomas Hardy, Edward Thomas and Robert Frost, were, I think, wholly beneficial, but I have come to the conclusion that Yeats and Rilke, both, of course, great poets, were, for me, bad influences, the former by tempting me into an over-inflated rhetoric, the latter by making some of my poems too *schöngeistig*, too much

Poetry with a capital P. Needless to say, the fault was entirely mine, not theirs.

★   ★   ★

In writing poetry, men and women, it seems to me, have quite different problems. A woman finds it hard to detach herself sufficiently from her experience, to make her poems conform to Wordsworth's definition 'emotion recollected in tranquility'. A man, on the other hand, can all too easily become an aesthete, that is to say, make statements, not because he believes them to be true, but because he thinks they sound poetically effective.

★   ★   ★

The difference between a major and a minor poet is not one of poetic quality. Indeed, a major poet is likely, in the course of his career, to write more bad poems than a minor one. The difference between them is this. In the case of a minor poet, if one takes two poems of his, both equally good but written at different times, it is impossible, on the evidence of the text alone, to say which was written first. In the case of a major poet, on the other hand, one can always trace his development in time; he writes differently in youth, in middle age and when old.

★   ★   ★

Poets themselves have little interest in why or how they started to write poetry. Their primary concern is with what they should write next. In an age, like ours, of rapid social and technological change, this has its dangers. To ask 'What sort of poetry should I write at the age of sixty-five' is a sensible question, but to ask 'What should I write in the year 1972?' is sheer folly. It can only result in a submission to the fashion of the moment, a desperate attempt to be 'with it'. Plato tried to model political life on artistic fabrication: this, as we know, can only lead to political tyranny. The error made by all too many artists today is the exact opposite: they try to model artistic fabrication on political action so that, instead of trying to make an artistic object of permanent value, they surrender to the tyranny of the immediate moment and produce meaningless 'happenings'.

Political and artistic history are quite different. The only alternative
to a political act is another one. In the case of a work of art there are
two alternatives, another work of art or no work of art.

* * *

Achilles could only kill Hector once, and in Troy, but the Iliad can
always be re-read and translated into other tongues.

* * *

Again, while the history of science exhibits progress, the history
of art does not. No work of art can supersede another. In time every
successful new work of art takes its permanent place in the tradition.

* * *

Poems are primarily personal utterances, addressed to other persons.
What a poem means is the outcome of a dialogue between the words
on the page and the person who happens to be reading it, that is to
say, its meaning varies from person to person. Personal utterance,
however, is not to be confused with self-expression. The experience
a poet attempts to embody in a poem is that of a reality common to
us all. It is only *his* in that it is perceived from a perspective which nobody but himself can occupy. From the poet's point of view, the ideal
reaction of a reader to something he has written is: 'My God, I really
knew that all the time, but I never realised it before.'

* * *

Whatever useful functions it may perform, nothing could be less
like a work of art than a dream.

* * *

Since he is a human being, every poet is, of course, an individual as
well as a person. He is born into a particular society at a particular
moment in historical time, and, however unique the perspective from
which he views it, the world he sees and most of the ideas by which he
interprets it are necessarily those of his society and his age. Here again
he must practise critical detachment lest he allow conventional re-

sponses to falsify his vision. But he must accept his society and his age as facts with which he has to deal. This does not mean that he must swim with contemporary fashion: he can and should reject much that others accept. But he must know clearly what he is rejecting and why. If he tries to think of himself as a disembodied angel, free from all limitations, all relations to his contemporary neighbours, what he makes will be false.

*   *   *

Because its maker is an individual, every genuine work of art exhibits the quality of *nowness*, which enables an art historian to given an approximate date and place for its making. Because he is a person, it also exhibits the quality of *permanence*: it continues to be relevant long after its maker and society of which he was a member have passed away.

*   *   *

The arts cannot change the course of history. The political and social history of Europe would have been what it has been if Dante, Shakespeare, Goethe, Titian, Michaelangelo, Mozart, Beethoven, etc., had never existed.

*   *   *

'The sole aim of writing', said Dr Johnson, 'is to enable readers a little better to enjoy life or a little better to endure it.' To this I would only add that works of art are our chief means of breaking bread with the dead, and without communication with the dead a fully human life, I believe, is not possible.

*   *   *

Let me finish, as I began, with language. Whatever his duties as a citizen, a poet, *qua* poet, has only one political duty. Everything he writes must be a model example of the correct and subtle use of his mother tongue, which is always in danger of being corrupted by journalism and the mass media. I call this political because, when words lose their meaning, physical force takes over.

Examinations

16   What are we trying to test?

W. A. MURRAY

In this chapter I am going to put forward some personal views about the nature of English as a subject and the problems of examining it. Before I try to define what I see as the substance of my subject, I wish to make it clear where I stand in relation to some of the educational controversies that involve teachers of English along with the rest of the profession. I have little sympathy with those who take polarised attitudes about the nature and maintenance of academic standards in English. Black Paper type notions about the growing illiteracy of the university candidate or the college of education student have a sound basis only if one accepts the rather rigid conventions on which such estimates of illiteracy rest. Natural languages change with time, and societies change. What is correct today is not necessarily so for ever. Even the value attached to correctness itself alters, which is why I myself prefer to use terms like acceptability or efficiency of function. On the other hand, some modern teaching certainly overemphasises emotional spontaneity as a principle of merit in the use of language. Both acceptability and precision of use are more important for most purposes. Much that is of real value in language as it is used results from training and discipline. Much is also measurable, quite objectively, given a sufficiently sophisticated approach. Without such measurements neither assertions of declining standards nor assertions about the value of new educational practices can be judged, nor should they be permitted to alter the basis of our teaching. Neither am I persuaded by those who maintain that any examination of individual attainment imposes unbearable stresses. What imposes the stress is the social use of the results of examinations, and the social values attached to them.

Traditional forms of examination are currently being scrutinised very critically, and often profoundly altered in technique. The social applications of the system are changing too, but not for the better. As more and more pupils stay on after the age of sixteen social pressure increases for the provision of a certificate at the end of almost any kind of course. The tendency is clearly to try to meet this kind of demand, which has nothing to do with rigorous measurement of attainment. We are thus developing a market currency of certificates in response to social forces, to the disadvantage of our real knowledge of the skills and the natures of the young people who must run the society they will inherit from us, and for whom effective language is a vital necessity.

English, as a subject in our educational system, is always under two kinds of pressure. It is required to achieve high performance in its pupils, and it is taken for granted as something they can acquire from their environment almost without effort, which therefore requires less academic time and less well-qualified staff. (As the phrase goes, every teacher is a teacher of English.) These conflicting forces are inherent in mother-tongue situations in which the essential feature is a natural language, the medium of one's thoughts and a primary element in one's consciousness.

Our mother tongue is, for all of us, the most intimate feature of our personal mental world. Indeed much of our mental world consists of our language, stored in our memories, or realised in unspoken forms. As the anti-grammar-in-examinations lobby never tires of reminding us, every child who learns to speak knows the grammar of its mother tongue. The catch word here is clearly 'knows'. Children acquire or assimilate or develop the famous 'intuition of the native speaker', but they may well begin with something more fundamental – whatever it is in the structure of the human mind that leads to its possession of what Noam Chomsky terms the deep structures of language, those unknowable antecedents to the conscious forms of language. As so many modern linguists agree, 'linguistic competence' (in the sense in which they use the term) is a property of our mental structure, at least in the broadly normal personality. What can be measured individually is performance, the ways and the extent of realisation of the possibilities which competence grants us. I consider therefore that a large part of the measurement of skills in the mother tongue is concerned with various sorts of linguistic performance.

Looking at English as a 'subject' from that point of view how can we define it? First perhaps rather simply as a series of skills: speech, reading, writing and an activity I describe for the moment as 'criticism'. In speech we need to know about the performer as listener, how his performance compares with some 'norm' (which we can select) in aural memory, the speed of understanding various sorts of meanings or concepts. It is also useful to know something about his capacity to distinguish varieties of speech appropriate to different situations, something of his powers of analysis of pattern in language. All these capacities have a direct bearing on the efficiency of learning processes in all other subjects and also on personal development and adjustments within the social group. We also need to know active as well as passive powers in speech. We need to measure their development and to diagnose causes of inefficiency. We should not concern ourselves necessarily with teaching native speakers to use a particular social variety of their mother tongue, however much parents may feel that the English teacher is there to make their children 'speak nicely'. We should be concerned primarily with effectiveness of communication, range of active vocabulary, sophistication of command of structure, and with speech reactions to complex situations and varied stimuli. In short, with speech as the speaker's contact with living experience; his means of intellectual and emotional growth and adjustment. Speech is both a means and the measure of growth and it precedes and underlies the written word. We have already developed some techniques for measuring performance in it but we need a great deal more research and ingenuity, much more knowledge of the norms of our community, much more concern with remedial work for speech-handicapped children, and many more teachers with the right professional skills in this difficult area, especially in primary schools. In a culture fully interpenetrated by radio and by television, both speech media, we have the opportunity and the need for new methods and new educational thought. The basis of both must be accurate and sophisticated measurement, an unobtrusive but universal concern with the levels of individual skills. Of course much has already been done with the media in education, often brilliantly, but the effects are thinly or unevenly spread. So too, it is still far from automatic that speech defects should be diagnosed, let alone remedied, and we are very far from being able to pass from one level of our educational system to another the kind of data about individuals as speakers and listeners which would give us the means of ensuring better continuity of personal development.

The skills we require in reading and writing parallel those in listening and speaking in obvious ways, like range of active and passive vocabulary (words we use and words we merely recognise). But there are other important features of the written system which we must teach and test as part of the mother-tongue discipline. The written language still has the advantage over the spoken in speed, in the possibility of repeated assimilations of identical material, in the use of more elaborate patterns, in considered precision of meaning, in its power to incorporate diagrams, and a wide variety of signs and symbols which would be far too clumsy in spoken language.

In recent enquiries about teacher training it has been noted that teaching methods for reading are often neglected. There is also a fair amount of evidence from higher education that many students read slowly and inefficiently in their mother tongue. The causes, of course, are complex. Poor reading skills are unlikely to result simply from too much television combined with the bad effects of illustrated comics. Undoubtedly there are results from changing social habits, but until we can describe the changes accurately perhaps we had better be cautious about their consequences. Here, certainly, is an area of mother-tongue teaching where far more frequent and careful measurement of skill is needed – more examination, if you like to call it that. If you doubt this, try asking a well-qualified university entrant to read a complicated piece of English prose or verse at sight, without warning, and then compare the result with the unscripted speech of the same student in a bar or common room. English, the mother tongue, includes both registers, but the average student's levels of attainment are widely different in each. What is true of reading aloud is equally true of the silent and much swifter process which makes up most of our reading for study or for pleasure. Yet, after primary school, how many of our young people are trained, tested, compared, in these central skills?

When we consider written English, an interestingly different situation is evident. A very great deal of dedicated effort has gone into introducing many children to imaginative or 'creative' writing, regarded by many of its advocates both as psychologically valuable in personal development and as a means of intellectual training. Those who have to evaluate this type of work often talk in terms of 'sincerity', 'freshness', 'originality', 'sensitivity', 'accuracy of observation', 'emotional spontaneity', and so on. Valid as such qualities may well be in writing, judgements about them are necessarily subjective and often seem, to me at least, ill-founded and even naïve. There is certainly little agreement on the principles of judgement among the judges, as I discovered when conducting a conference of examiners in creative writing; they failed to suggest any criteria except the individual critical judgements of the examiners. It was agreed that multiple critical judgements were better than single ones, a point to which I will return, after a cautionary tale or two.

A colleague of mine who went, imbued with strong liberal anti-examination feelings, to teach English in an Indian state, set her class the theme 'examinations'. Almost the first essay began thus: 'In an examination I sit in a room I vomit all that I learned on to the paper'. She awarded the delighted candidate a high mark for freshness of language and spontaneity of emotion. Within the next week or so, however, she encountered the verb 'vomit' used habitually in the English language newspaper of the district purely in its literal sense, without any of its physical meaning in English English. In the local variety of English the original sentence was trite, conventional and dull, something which any teacher trained in linguistics would at least have suspected.

Many, perhaps most, children have the capacity for acquiring the kinds of language they need. Anyone who has brought up children, or observed them in bi-lingual or multi-lingual environments, will have been struck by their adaptive skill. The same is true of variations in the mother tongue. If we want children to learn literary tricks of style they will do so if the reward is sufficient to generate a motive. The enthusiastic teacher often contrives to produce quite remarkable results in creative writing from his pupils, but we need to exercise a deal of caution in interpreting those results.

A year or two ago a seminar of teachers, inspectors of schools and others involved in evaluating creative writing was asked to place a series of pieces by children in order of merit. In the ensuing discussion the presenter of the topic, a distinguished exponent of creative writing, whose pupils had produced the material, concentrated his praise on one piece of prose which in his view represented the value of sincerity. The piece was on a given theme, 'A death in the family', and the example he rated first was about the death of the child's father. When asked for my opinion, I said that, provided the piece was supported by a copy of the death certificate, I would rate it very highly as a sincere personal account, otherwise unremarkable in style or imaginative content. This was held to be an insensitive comment, as the piece was supposed to exhibit an intrinsic sincerity which made any comment on its rather obvious tear-jerking style rude and inappropriate. This case is a good example of the serious dangers behind much creative writing. If the subject dealt with an actual situation it ought not, in my view, to have been set for that child as part of a mass exercise. If it did not, it could certainly not be sincere in the manner claimed for it. As a linguistic exercise it was banal and rudimentary. After all, how many tear-jerkers does the average ten-year-old encounter on the media? As I have already said, children acquire registers of the mother tongue with even greater facility than they acquire foreign languages.

Perhaps even more dangerous than insincere 'sincerity' is spurious freshness and false precision of description. The same occasion produced perfect examples of these. The theme this time was 'A Pebble' and the form, verse. We were assured that there were slim, cool, smooth pebbles; lumpy, bumpy, gnarled pebbles, and hot, exotic pebbles, and of course our individual pet, special pebble. I suppose that, in this case, a pebble had been handed round to encourage the search for descriptions of visual and tactile responses. There was obviously a model for this style somewhere in the background, probably Gerard Manley Hopkins. The principle is in a way sound enough – finding more precise language for one's sensory responses is obviously valuable. The example chosen, however, lent itself to ridicule by the simple substitution of the word 'girl' for pebble (the adjectives fitted 'girl' rather better), and the poems became quite funny rather than precious or mannered. The trouble, I suspect, lay in the very literary sensibility of the teacher, which inevitably moved the pupil towards 'literariness' of response. If we are to avoid creating a new, rather sterile fashionable rhetoric of creative writing, we shall have to develop better techniques of evaluation and a more critical attitude to our assumptions about appropriate methods of teaching.

It might be salutary to regard creative writing simply as a limited, though important, part of language teaching, in which we stand to gain in aesthetic development and certain kinds of imaginative growth. Creative writing can be used to bring together experiences which cross subject boundaries or extend beyond school into the wider world. In evaluating such writing, however, we should look carefully at modern stylistics, and we should be much more sceptical of our own subjective assessments, especially of the psychological aspects of children's style.

I come now to the last of my list of skills in the mother tongue: 'criticism'. By 'criticism' I mean a much wider process than 'literary criticism'. If language can be regarded as a kind of symbolic model of our experience which we retain, use and develop in step with our lives, it is necessarily a continuously self-adjusting model. By criticism I mean here the mental activity of adjustment between model and experience. I therefore include analyses of meaning and of linguistic form, along with an awareness of the broader relations of experience with its retention in memory and its verbal or written expression.

The mother-tongue discipline is responsible for training and measuring the necessary linguistic skills in all subjects; thus it has to be designed to develop analytical self-awareness in the user of language. Of course, this is to claim a central importance for mother-tongue education which few systems concede in theory, though they have to strive towards it in practice. A beginning has already been made in Great Britain in experiments aimed at assessing the use of the English language in other subjects as an alternative to formal examination in English. In such attempts, almost at once difficulties arise between the English teachers' ideas about language and the subject specialists' demands or linguistic views.

Clearly, we need much more breadth of training on both sides. Teachers of English must try to understand the language of their scientific colleagues and of the technologists, and, in return, we need less naïveté and perhaps less conservative rigidity from our colleagues together with agreement about how and what we should measure in their students' performance.

If I have stressed the function of English in other subjects, I have not done so to deny or minimise its aims in more traditional directions. The English teacher is a kind of custodian of meanings. A major part of his role is to transmit the ability to understand our past: not, I would maintain, just our inheritance of literary classics; he must also transmit enough of the context of past literature to enable it to be seen in its setting and for its relevance to be judged.

Many teachers of English approach the teaching of English literature and, regrettably, its examination, as though it were their principal function to create standards of literary value – a kind of hierarchy of chosen works and authors, or even, sometimes, chosen works of chosen authors. This attitude, common, I suspect, to reformers and traditionalists, is very damaging to the development of individuals and very narrowing to the subject. A generation ago anyone who had read Dickens in adolescence would have read *Pickwick Papers* as well as *Bleak House, Nicholas Nickleby* and *Hard Times.* Now one can expect *Hard Times,* and a hard line on it as well. Literary criticism is an activity involving the whole personality – analytical power, memory, experience, imagination, judgement, both aesthetic, and social or moral. It is a slow and rare growth in individuals. I do not believe it to be a matter of absolute standards at all. It does not seem to me to be teach-able as any kind of learned skill, system or dogma. The rote-learned product of the opposite view is everywhere visible in the standard critical essays of our examination system, which prove only that our students can master the current critical register and are therefore passably good at language.

Of course the teacher of English can, and inevitably will, greatly influence the development of individual taste and enthusiasm. It is at once a precious and a dangerous power. If his efforts were directed more at the understanding of meaning and of significance in the social pattern than at evaluations, or revaluations, in the terms of up-to-the-minute literary criticism, I think that the literary part of English would be freed from a great deal of sterile cant, and the sensibilities of our students allowed to develop in a less stereotyped way. Perhaps, also the continuity and relevance of many sorts of liter-ary experience might more deeply influence the present.

Having looked at English as a range of skills centrally important to the processes of education and development, I turn now to how we assess the attainments of individuals in these, and how we might do so if it were possible to have a free hand in changing the present system.

First of all I must declare myself in favour of many aspects of our public examination system – its impartiality, its administrative effi-ciency and, within certain limits, its present willingness to experiment and to innovate on the results of experiment. There is a price to be paid, of course, in the rigidity of a large system, its relative predict-ability, and the limitations it may impose on the construction of sylla-buses or on experimental teaching. It is sometimes claimed that we could rely for much evaluation of performance on the professional judgement of teachers. I am not convinced that this is sound. As long as we use our examination system to organise entry into employment or higher education we shall have to have a system which allows com-parability of results from different regions and different backgrounds. I cannot see that a school-based system would ensure this, although the professional judgement of teachers is an extremely valuable part of the business of assessment. I should like to see the growth of a form of organisation which could incorporate both principles and make them mutually supporting. Why should we not have a system of assessment in which part of the responsibility is carried alternatively by schools and by examining boards? We could, for example, within any particular region, examine the use of English at sixth-form level in one year by a school-based, externally moderated examination, and in the next year by a public examination through the normal machinery of an examining board. Comparison year to year and throughout the region would ensure a controllable standard. With modern computer techniques, complex correlations and investigations are relatively easy, and can be used to guide such a system.

It is also important to correct the neglect of the assessment of language after the age of sixteen, which is a major anomaly in our system. If we are to look coherently at language skills as I have described them, we shall have to devise an assessment pattern which includes measuring capacity in spoken and written language over a wide range of activities. Part of this can be achieved indirectly and unobtrusively by investigating language use in other subjects. Part calls for the invention of new ways of measuring as well as efforts to extract more information from our present methods.

It is a major defect of examinations as we have them that the form of presentation of the results often suppresses valuable information about the candidate's performance. Whenever we average several questions as a grade or overall percentage, we tend to equate the uneven with the even performer, and to suppress the significant profile. There is scope here for very useful research into profile-marking systems. The present techniques of multiple 'subjective marking', which I mentioned earlier, although helpful in many cases, incline towards averaging the disagreements rather than solving them. The results of this tendency appear in many statistical investigations of examination results in English, in which the distribution curves may show virtually no one in the top or bottom ranges of the mark scale, a pattern quite different from that found in science or mathematics. There would be another advantage, too, in a profile system. We could develop in our computer memories idealised profiles for various purposes. They could represent norms of achievement at various ages, or norms fo requirement for various applications; and the computer could easily compare the individual example with the pattern. Instead of using the terms pass, re-sit, fail, the stop, caution, go, of the examination traffic light, we could begin to advise our students more precisely about their performance, and we might come to regard our measurements of attainment as a diagnosis leading to greater systematic knowledge of the individual candidate and thus to more satisfactory direction of his studies.

If we can once begin to disentangle in the public mind the business of measuring skills from the social uses for which we choose to employ our measurements, we can, perhaps, begin to remedy some of the bad effects of our present examination system, and to take a more rational view on what is involved in the maintenance of standards in the mother tongue.

As I write this, news of the provision of free nursery education for the under-fives has just been announced, beginning with those in disadvantaged areas. The opportunity thus opened up for radical improvement in English language skills at the pre-school stage must be fully realised and used by the profession. Modern English language training must obviously become a more important part of the education of teachers of all subjects, and especially of nursery and primary school teachers.

Training in English skills for teachers should include training in modern methods of assessment, and should demonstrate the areas in which judgement is possible, as well as exploring areas of doubt and experiment. If we do this systematically for assessment at all stages, we may, eventually, be able to begin to cure some of the worst effects of our examination system, without sacrificing two of its central purposes, impartial judgement of candidates and the maintenance of reasonable levels of effectiveness in the mother tongue.

Further reading

The Teaching of English Studies, Communication 3, Secker & Warburg, 1959, especially chap. 1.

H. J. Muller (ed.), *The Uses of English. Guidelines for the teaching of English from the Anglo-American Conference at Dartmouth College*, Holt, Rinehart & Winston 1967.

C. Butler and A. Fowler, *Topics in Criticism*, Longman, 1971.

J. Pearce and A. Wilkinson (eds.), *English in Education*, vol. 2, no. 3, *English at Sixteen Plus*, Bodley Head, 1968.

17 A consumer report

SU FELTON

If you have travelled around the country far enough to hear a cockney complaining about his 'trouble and strife', or 'skin and blister', or the equally incomprehensible Geordie who ends every sentence with 'weyaye hinny', it does indeed seem a good idea to teach the English, English. However, having taken the English language examination, I am convinced that there must be better ways of doing it.

There is something wrong with the examination system as a whole when, after spending two years accumulating irrelevancies, one is only allowed two hours in which to express them, and two weeks later they have been forgotten completely. The English language paper is particularly irrelevant to almost anything that one may do afterwards, and does not even have interest as a point in its favour.

It is difficult to say exactly what the purpose of this examination is. Obviously, as those of us who take it can already speak the language quite adequately, its function does not lie there. It cannot attempt to teach people to write creatively. Presumably then, it is to give us a better understanding, and a more fluent and correct use of the language in its literary form. Few of us will ever need this, but should we be called upon to do so, we are 'qualified' to write.

The examination itself lasts for three hours. In the first hour one is expected to write an imaginative composition. Unfortunately, I fail to find much imagination in such titles as 'a speech after a dinner party'. If the examiners set such titles deliberately to see how we cope with the problem, this is acceptable, but one suspects that it is because they are incapable of thinking of anything more interesting. If inspiration is not found immediately in the subject, it certainly will not be drawn from blank walls, rows of desks or the prevailing silence of examination rooms, which can only lead to an extremely dull essay.

Although the question states 'interesting' writing, this is not a factor essential to passing. One has to 'take care with grammar, spelling and punctuation' and, if sufficient care is taken, a pass is quite possible on these merits alone. This must be wrong in principle, as punctuation

H

and grammatical rules are becoming less and less important in modern literature. Had James Joyce written *Ulysses* with its unpunctuated passages, for the O level examination, he would undoubtedly have failed!

As important as inspiration in writing creatively is time. One hour is totally inadequate, and considering that many of the greatest authors have spent a lifetime writing one book, so severe a time limit is nonsensical. My own experience of trying to write four hundred and fifty 'interesting' words was particularly trying. Owing to my English teacher's usual inefficiency and capacity for confusing times, I arrived a quarter of an hour late for the examination. After I had filled in the form, read the questions and decided on a subject, just over half of the allotted time remained to write the essay, which of course did not allow for fidgeting, pen sucking or trying to get rid of the inevitable writer's cramp.

The first part of paper two is a précis which is equally difficult to justify in terms of practical usage. Although it is useful to be able to select the most important points, one never has to confine them to a specific number of words. A précis is therefore no more than the art of writing notes in complete sentences, which rather defeats the object. An editor is the only person I can think of who may have to condense a passage, but as he would omit sections rather than rewrite them, the only use for précis is in the O level examination. However, preparing for this part of the examination was not a complete waste of time, as we learnt a considerable amount from the passages about black and white rhinos and the problems of dustmen in a block of flats.

The comprehension question has more to offer as it is relevant to literature and general reading. Defining the meanings of words, though often they do not make a lot of sense when taken out of context, is a useful exercise in discovering more obscure parts of the language. The fault in this section of the paper is that many of the questions are a matter of interpretation where there is no definite wrong or right answer. This type of answer needs to be qualified but it is often impossible to justify an argument within a limit of thirty words.

From the point of view of relevance to the A level examination, the comprehension is the only useful part. It would have been beneficial if in addition to prose appreciation, poetry had been included, though obviously on a simpler level. Going straight from an ordinary level language to advanced level literature, one of the biggest problems is how to tackle poetry appreciation, as it comes as something completely new.

In spite of the fact that the comprehension question is the most useful part of the paper, in modernising the paper the London University Examining Board decided to leave it out. It has been replaced by a multiple-choice question, again on a prose passage. The answers to choose from are either so obviously right or wrong as to be ridiculous; or else no answer is exactly correct without being qualified, which there is no opportunity to do. A multiple-choice paper is quite reasonable in mathematics or chemistry where answers are short and definite, but English is concerned with the expression of the writer, and when a candidate is asked to put a tick by someone else's ideas instead of expressing his own, he cannot be making full use of the language.

Perhaps the biggest disadvantage of the paper as a whole is that it gives students a false impression of English and often misleads them in their choice of advanced level subjects. Having done very little work over the course, yet still managing to get a grade A pass without much difficulty, English presents itself to some as a tempting 'easy option' to continue for a further two years. After following the language course where the syllabus is anything but difficult and there are no facts to remember, beginning the advanced literature course one is amazed at the amount of work and the vast difference in the type of work.

Our school, being one of the 'more progressive' with a wider range of subjects, does not offer the English literature course at ordinary level even if specifically requested by a group of enthusiastic students. I cannot, therefore, speak from experience about this, but the literature course is reputed to be one of the easiest examinations and, for some reason, particularly so for female students. Admittedly, this was one reason for the demand for it, but the main reason was interest. Studying texts, to however low a standard, must be more interesting to anyone than learning rules of grammar. Contrary to what one might expect, those in other schools who have done the literature course say that it has no relevance and very little resemblance to the advanced level, so at least I have not missed anything of vital importance. But since the study of literature can only concern itself with the study of literature, one wonders how the papers can be so different.

Though the literature examination is more interesting than the language, neither seem to serve much practical purpose and the examiner's time could perhaps be better spent devising questions a little more useful to life after the examinations. Throughout courses in all subjects, we were constantly being told to treat the examiner as an idiot. This assumption is taking things too far, but certainly these intelligent people are not putting their wisdom to its greatest effect in such examinations.

In classes to prepare for the language paper the staff are faced with the problem of trying to make a thoroughly uninteresting syllabus interesting. It is all very well to say that everyone was left to work at their own pace, but in fact to work at all was practically impossible in such a crowded and noisy classroom. This happened because there is very little in this subject that a class can learn as a group.

Boring as it may be, and elementary to most of us, the basic grammar work has to be dealt with. Considering how much grammar there is in a language, it is strange that we were limited to the function and position of the apostrophe. Once this art has been mastered it seems that everything has been learnt and the teacher can proceed, with a clear conscience, to introduce more interesting diversions to the lessons.

At the beginning of the course almost all the lessons were devoted to 'the hoard'. This was a cardboard box full of books, some of which suggested projects and 'things to do'. As no one was quite sure what they were expected to do, and certainly not enthusiastic enough to find out, these lessons were little more than a chat. Any written work which did arise was eagerly marked with scrawled comments and encouragements, but to little effect.

Fortunately, English lessons changed completely with the arrival of a new teacher, and 'the hoard' was abandoned but always remembered as one of the less successful parts of my education. Our new teacher managed to keep control comparatively well if only by the pleading way he said, 'Cool it, folks, settle down' every five minutes. He made the best of a bad syllabus, if only by ignoring it to concentrate on the more interesting side of life. Written work became more regular even if it was only once a month and it was returned at equally well-spaced intervals with the innumerable spelling mistakes always pointed out but never corrected. Considering the importance placed on correct spelling it really should have been taught, for now, only months away from advanced level, my spelling is more erratic than ever.

Towards the time of the examination, the amount of written work increased, and included the excitement of past papers. Needless to say, the amount of work submitted for marking did not increase at quite the same rate, in fact it did not increase at all, for we were of the opinion, whether through careful consideration or sheer laziness, that English was a subject that either came naturally or not at all, and any amount of effort and practice could not change it.

To digress from the set course we tried all sorts of ideas, one of the most popular of which was reading plays. Though of all the plays started in class the only one I remember finishing was Peter Terson's *The Apprentices*, and its success was due rather to the coarse jokes than the quality of the play.

One of the more interesting parts of the course was that during a double period, though unfortunately the attention is not at its peak first thing on a Monday morning, films were shown once a fortnight. Or rather half a film was shown due to the lack of time, which was to say the least, frustrating. The films were usually of a high standard, including *The Importance of Being Earnest*, *A Taste of Honey* and *All Quiet on the Western Front* which we saw no less than three times, declining the offer the fourth time round. As films could be one of the most enjoyable parts of the syllabus, true to form the examining board include them neither in the language nor the literature.

Strangely enough, although language is essentially spoken, the oral examination is ignored by the English department in our school. Personally, this is no great hardship, for I would find talking to a complete stranger an unnatural and terrifying experience. But I am in a minority, and a great number of people would benefit from an oral, being able to express themselves better orally than on paper. This assumption is based on experience in a set where the noise of people expressing themselves was at times intolerable.

Being rather dissatisfied with the language paper, I feel I ought to make some constructive suggestions. English is not a subject where facts can be regurgitated but should be based on continuous assessment. The essay question should be given to candidates in advance of the examination so that they can write when they feel like writing and without being restricted by time. The précis and multiple choice question paper should be replaced by an appreciation paper more like that given at advanced level, though obviously of a simpler nature. In cases where literature is not taken as a separate subject it would be a good idea to include a general paper on books, plays and films.

In view of the quality of the examination, the importance given to it by places of further education seems absurd. If you are one of those people who attach a lot of importance to certificates, it does look impressive on the bedroom wall, but this is its only advantage as I have now forgotten where the apostrophe goes!

18 How not to make specialists literate

LEWIS STEDMAN JONES

Every secondary school is judged by its sixth form. The sixth former, after all, is its end product, its brand image. The two-year course to A level nurtures – brings carefully to blossom and final flowering – the choicest plants of its teaching. The years before the sixth have been but a preparation for it; and O level has eliminated the last of those weaklier comrades fit only to become hewers of wood and drawers of water. Now, in the sixth form begins that metamorphosis by which the child becomes the man; the pupil becomes the student. The days of spoon feeding and learning by rote are over and the days of critical analysis and independent thought begin as part of a process that will turn out well-integrated, *compleat* young men and women.

Such a view of the sixth form and sixth formers is common among those not actually breathing in the daily chalk dust of experience. Not that schoolmasters do not have their own pictures of the ideal sixth former, but it is one tempered by conditions as they exist. My own is both a simple and a modest one. He or she is a young man or woman who is socially, culturally and politically aware; a person who can distinguish between the good and the meretricious; who thinks it worthwhile to queue for hours for gallery seats at the National Theatre or the Festival Hall; who cares about and becomes involved in the issues of his time and his environment.

However, this not too impossible she or he emerges from our schools too often not as a result of the sixth form training but in spite of it. Everybody agrees that one of the most pressing educational problems of our time is the provision of an adequate general education for our specialists. Our dilemma in the second half of the twentieth century is that the pace of discovery, scientific and technological, is such that specialisation is forced upon us to a degree never known before, monopolising the time of our specialists and shutting them off from each other in their separate disciplines. C. P. Snow in his now famous lecture on 'The Two Cultures and the Scientific Revolution' in 1959 sounded the alarm.

Snow stressed the need for a new definition of literacy. Those 'literary gents' who raise their brows and curl their lips in scorn at those scientists who have never read a major English novel are just as illiterate, just as much prisoners of their own specialisations as the scientists are of theirs. Ignorance of the second law of thermodynamics is just as much the mark of the philistine as is ignorance of *Hamlet* or *King Lear*. The scientific equivalent of being able to read is the ability of define 'mass' or 'acceleration' but rarely had he met anybody among the traditionally educated who had the first glimmering understanding of either. So 'the great edifice of modern physics' is going up to remain forever closed to the great mass of the 'cultured' because of their abysmal ignorance of basic scientific concepts. Obviously mass illiteracy in either culture is fraught with dangers for our future and there is something seriously wrong with an educational system that has failed so signally to cope with the scientific revolution and allowed such a position to arise.

Snow's lecture was to trigger off a controversy that was to reverberate down the corridors of educational power for a very long time. The correspondence columns of *The Times* (both the daily and the *Literary Supplement*), the quality Sundays and the weeklies were peppered with criticisms and anecdotes illustrative of the illiteracy of our scientists. There was less illustration of the ignorance of science by the specialists in our traditional culture. Thus it was that schools became alerted to the need for general studies in the sixth form and technical colleges for departments of liberal studies. Thus it was, too, that by 1964 Oxford and Cambridge and some other universities – by no means all – required candidates for admission to pass a 'Use of English' paper. The purpose of the new examination presumably was to provide a bridge between the two cultures. But it was something of a one-way bridge for traffic from the new scientific to the old traditional culture, for it was implicit both in the syllabuses and in the question papers that boys and girls blinkered by science A levels had been neglecting the skills in the mother tongue that they had painfully acquired up to O level and were reverting to the barbarism of outer darkness. Thus the 'Use of English' paper was designed to test the students' ability both to understand prose of some difficulty and to express themselves competently if not elegantly. There were to be no set books, no set subject matter. The best possible way to prepare for the examination was to read widely and practise writing regularly. The question papers, then, probe candidates' skills in essay writing and in the comprehension of a passage of some length. There is a third question which seems to doff the hat in the direction of the new culture since it involves the elucidation of statistical data.

This vagueness in the syllabus is splendid in that it presupposes that teachers would prefer the maximum of freedom in the way they prepare their students for the examination. But it also presupposes that students have unlimited time for wide general reading, and this is questionable for a variety of reasons.

The image of the sixth form in the minds of most people has its origin in the calm unhurried days before 1939 when it was a small elite group whose nearest approach to general studies came in the Head's weekly religious education period when he gave a romp to his own particular cultural or religious hobby-horse. Such a picture ceased to be true after the 1944 Education Act and the reorganisation of the external examination brought into being a new type of sixth former.

The predecessor of the GCE O and A levels were the Senior School and higher school certificates. The 'School Cert' was a group examination at which all candidates had to offer English, maths, a foreign language, a science and a fifth from a large group of alternative subjects. Failure in any one of the compulsory subjects meant failure in the whole examination and all subjects had to be offered again in any subsequent attempt. Performances in each subject were graded as pass, credit or distinction and candidates who gained credits in all the compulsory subjects and in a fifth optional one gained exemption from matriculation. This was the entrance examination to the university and it was also the qualification necessary for entry into the sixth form. There were no upper or lower age restrictions for entry to School Certificate and bright pupils could and often did matriculate at a tender age so that it was quite common to find boys and girls of fourteen in the sixth form. There were murmurs of protest against such premature abandonment of general education at the time, and with the reorganisation of the examination, entry to O level was prohibited before the age of sixteen.

But the fundamental reform introduced into the new General Certificate of Education was the substitution of a single subject for a group subject structure. This in itself was enough to effect changes in the sixth form, but, when taken in conjunction with the new impetus

given to education by the war, the scientific revolution and the raising of the school age, its whole character was radically altered.

The size of the sixth form increased enormously, not only because
of the greater numbers staying on in school but because the new single
subject structure of GCE O level admitted those whom the old examination would have barred. School Certificate at least had the virtue of
administrative tidiness in ensuring an equality of qualification in the
sixth form. Many of the new sixth formers embark on A level courses
with a backlog of O level subjects still to be obtained if they are to
satisfy the entry conditions to their chosen careers. A levels make greater
demands on these pupils not only because they have to reserve part of
their energies for O levels but also because the scientific revolution
continually expands and makes more difficult the syllabuses of their
specialist subjects.

There was another innovation in the new GCE structure germane
to this topic and indefensibly bad. A false dichotomy was introduced
into English studies at O level. English was made into two subjects –
English language and English literature – and university and professional entry conditions left pupils in no doubt which they considered the more important. Whatever the limitations of the old
School Certificate, every candidate at that examination had at least
read and made some sort of study of one Shakespearian play, one novel
of accepted quality and one anthology of verse. GCE makes it possible
for pupils to avoid even a nodding acquaintance with literature after
the age of fifteen on their entry into the O level year. Thus English
was to become for thousands and thousands of boys and girls nothing
but a series of dreary titles for drearier essays; a mere ragbag of passages on which to practise their skills of précis writing, punctuation
and clause analysis. What schoolmaster does not wince at hearing the
expression 'the two Englishes' being bandied about our schools?

This then was the state of a large element of our sixth formers
when C. P. Snow alerted the nation to the perils of the growing gulf
between our two cultures. The architects of 'Use of English' were not
altogether correct in assuming that sixth formers had unlimited time
for the wide general reading they claimed was the ideal preparation
for their examination. For reasons which are understandable these
sixth formers resented this commandeering of their free study periods.
They needed all their time to make sure of success in A levels and if
any time could be spared from that pursuit they felt they should be
devoting it to the O levels they still needed. 'Use of English' might

have been accepted and taken seriously had a satisfactory performance at its examination been made an entry condition for all universities but only Oxford and Cambridge continue to make this demand although they, the northern universities (the Joint Matriculation Board) the southern universities and the Associated Examining Board still offer the paper at their examinations.

Even unencumbered sixth formers feel that 'Use of English' is a bore. The two periods of minority time they are called upon to devote to it are in their minds a waste of time and their excuses for dodging them are as ingenious as they are numerous. All reflect a resentment that the English teacher sensitive to the justification for his students' criticisms finds it difficult, if not impossible, to rebut. Only the Oxford and Cambridge candidates and the more conscientious guarantee a viable weekly attendance. The following random selection of sixth-form opinions of 'Use of English' is revealing of the examination's limitations:

'I do not understand the object of the statistical data which have to be interpreted in some questions.'

'I dislike the fact that the course is geared to an examination.'

'I do not understand what the course is aiming to do.'

'The course is aimless.'

'The examination at the end of the course seems an inadequate one to me. During the course we are not meant to have studied anything, but to have developed some qualities in ourselves which will make us more discriminating, while at the same time being open-minded. It is all too vague.'

'The main reason for taking "Use of English" seems to be that it is required by certain universities and this tends to produce a feeling of antipathy among the pupils . . . the problem may be increased by the course's lack of apparent purpose.'

'The course seems to have no aim other than its end examination. As far as I'm concerned I am studying my A level subjects but merely "doing" "Use of English" for the exam. . . . It is not demanding enough.'

'At least it gives an opportunity for expressing opinions on current topics and events.'

The trouble with 'Use of English' is not its intention but its syllabus. Its very brevity and the freedom allowed in the methods of preparation pose heavy problems for the teacher. He can devise a meaningful scheme of work embracing the wide reading recommended by the examiners but this will require resources in the way of reading matter which the school, after satisfying the set-book demands of other English examinations, simply cannot supply. What then is the hard-pressed English teacher to do with students already fully stretched by A levels and other commitments? He draws up bibliographies of good reading and refers his students to the public libraries or to the purses of their parents and there the matters ends; for if he attempts follow-up homework he is met with howls of honest protest about lack of time. He can urge them to buy and bring to class in equal numbers the *Observer* and the *Sunday Times* and read and discuss the review sections with them. A depressingly small number continues to do so after a few weeks and yet another experiment falls flat on its face. Lecturettes? They go well for a time and then a scheduled speaker goes absent or cuts class or forgets his script until we are back once more limping from one improvisation to another. At last he is forced to fall back on the crutches offered him by one of the many textbooks that were rushed on the market to fill the need created by 'Use of English'. Such books consist of extracts designed to train and test precision, clear thought, comprehension, faulty English, appreciation and statistical data. Excellent as such books can be if the guide lines laid down in their prefaces are adhered to and they are used merely to stimulate the student to further and fuller reading, they frequently form the only preparation for the examination. Thus we are returned to square one and 'Use of English' becomes nothing more than an A level version of the O level English language paper – a hotchpotch of disjointed, disconnected passages for précis writing and comprehension. How weary, stale, flat and unprofitable!

The truth is that the school curriculum, hounded as it is by the external examination system, has no time to pay more than lip-service to 'Use of English' or general studies as a whole, and in writing this I am not unmindful that the Joint Matriculation Board now offers an A level course in general studies. Secondary education, for all our efforts, is still basically vocational; our sixth forms are little more than conveyor belts to the universities. Certainly they are too little concerned with the quality of life for which they are equipping their charges. There is a tragic irony about this, for the scientific revolution whose pace is making it impossible for its specialists to devote significant time to general education is at the same time introducing an age of leisure which makes it vital that we allow more and more time to traditional culture if we are to enjoy our new freedom. The age of the computer and automation in which man will find himself with less and less to do and more and more time in which to do it is dawning. Meaningful leisure, therefore, is fast becoming the greatest and most urgent problem facing the developed countries of the west. Children now in school will in their lifetime work a three-day week, a prospect exciting or shattering according to the care with which we prepare them for it. We cannot claim to have been taken by surprise for the trend towards a shorter working week and a rising weekly wage has been with us since the first half of the nineteenth century; it is only the sudden increased tempo of the trend that has jolted us into a consciousness of the dangers ahead. Increased means and increased leisure, said Disraeli in a speech in Manchester in 1872, are the two civilisers of mankind. But only, he might have added, if we know how to use both wisely. Unoccupied or badly used leisure leads to boredom and boredom in its turn is a temptation to anti-social behaviour. It would be interesting to know just what effect the increased affluence and leisure already in our society has had on the increase in crime and drug taking. This may seem an extreme statement of the case against the neglect of general studies, but an education system that permits such a neglect is, perhaps, contributing to the production of a delinquent at one end of the scale as everybody agrees it does to that of an illiterate specialist at the other.

Teachers, of course, are aware of these issues and the Schools Council has been toying with suggested modifications of the existing examination system for some time. But it would appear that a greater sense of urgency is required and time is of the essence.

It is right that specialisation should begin in the sixth but it should never have been allowed to monopolise sixth formers in the way it is doing. A level syllabuses must be modified; the pressure on sixth formers eased. Catch up on the specialist time lost by lengthening the degree course in the university if you like, but let us use the time gained in the sixth form to make of general studies something that will permanently enrich the lives of our students. Relieved of some A level pressure sixth-form teachers could design a syllabus that would do much more than test the skills that 'Use of English' exists to examine. The Mode III as used at present in CSE could be employed and the syllabus, having been built by the school, would be submitted to the external examining board for approval. Thereafter the examination would be set, administered and marked by the school staff again with external moderation to ensure the maintenance of standards. Such a two-year course in general studies would become a condition of entry to all universities.

Subjects in the course would be approached laterally and not vertically as at present. That is, students would study the whole field of human endeavour and achievement in a particular period – a century, perhaps. Thus within the century chosen they would be expected to show some knowledge of the social and political history, the art, the science, the religion, the philosophy and the music and the literature of the time. Depth of knowledge would not be called for but an appreciation that each period has a common idiom of inspiration that informs all its activities and makes them fit together like the pieces of a jigsaw puzzle; to appreciate, for example the common texture uniting the music of Bach, the poetry of Pope, the architecture of Bath and the painting of Canaletto to make a harmonious tapestry that could only be called the eighteenth century. One need hardly add that such an approach to any century offers perhaps the best method of understanding our own.

The choice of such courses is as numerous as the teachers devising the syllabuses. But no matter how imaginative and stimulating the syllabus devised might be, it must be made examinable and success at such an examination must be made a condition of entry at all, I repeat, all universities. Only thus will we enhance the status of general studies in the eyes of sixth formers. The Joint Matriculation Board has pioneered an A level course in general studies but it makes but little impact because of its optional nature. Our society is so geared to work and our education system is so fundamentally vocational that unless we give general studies a visible market value any attempt to establish it nationally will fail. But if we do give such a value to the work, sixth formers will devote themselves to general studies with the same wholehearted determination with which they now approach A level in their specialist studies.

Nor should we think of general studies as a course consisting entirely of textbooks and wide reading. An exciting facet of the scientific and technological upheaval in which we are living is the revolution in resources and methods of teaching. If we are to utilise these fully we must begin to think less in terms of books and more in terms of the audio-visual aids that are now at our disposal. Schools now should possess not only science but also language laboratories, not only laboratory technicians but media resource officers. The duties of such technical assistants would not be confined to the maintenance of equipment; primarily their duty would be at the behest of the teaching staff to tape any sound broadcast or television transmission for use in the classroom. Thus the sound and videotape recorders make it possible for all programmes, both radio and television, to be available to the teacher, and timetable restrictions on their use are a thing of the past. With the co-operation of the BBC and commercial television to provide programmes complementing the preparational and follow-up work of the classroom the most comprehensive of courses in general studies is possible.

We are now less than thirty years away from AD 2000. Life patterns are changing with a bewildering rapidity. Teachers have no task more urgent than that of helping their students to orientate themselves for life in a very different world.

Further reading

W. A. Reid, *The Universities and the Sixth Form Curriculum*, Schools Council Research Studies, Macmillan, 1972.

C. P. Snow, *The Two Cultures and the Scientific Revolution*, CUP, 1959; expanded edition, 1964.

The syllabuses of the Associated Examining Board, Southern Universities, and the Joint Matriculation Board for the Use of English examination.

19 'Young people' under examination

W. D. EMRYS EVANS

What is it all for? This seems to be the basic question, and I think we are obliged to review it in considering the neglected age-group of sixteen to nineteen. Work in English (and, no doubt, in other subjects too) in the sixth form and in colleges of further education has for a long time been dominated by the demands of A level. Now, there is an increasing number of young people for whom A level is not a suitable goal, and teachers and examiners are beginning to wonder whether indeed A level just as it stands is very suitable for anyone. Is the study of literature alone sufficient content for the English curriculum at this stage? Where do our boundaries lie? What frontiers are really needed? Lower down the school, subject boundaries are falling rapidly. Humanities, social sciences, combined arts and combined science courses are making the timetables of many secondary schools below the sixth form look quite unlike anything we knew ten or fifteen years ago. And yet the old subject divisions reassert themselves as the public examinations approach. Is this mere expediency, or is there some real reason why they should do so?

I called it a neglected age goup. I know that many teachers and others will not accept this view. Traditionally, the British sixth form is one of the most cherished groups of students of comparable age in the world. Work of high academic standard conducted in small groups by highly qualified teachers has given it an international reputation. And yet in a real sense it has been neglected. Higher education has undergone radical changes in the last few years. In many cases this has led to the questioning, and often the redrawing or abandoning, of old subject boundaries here too. English studies can be found in schools of languages, literature and humanities. The introduction of greater attention to the study of language has quite properly complicated the issue. Drama – especially perhaps in the colleges of education, but also in some universities – appears as a subject in its own right. Meanwhile, lower down the schools, talk, improvisation, creative writing, the making of tapes, the study of society directly and through literature, film and television, and associations with art, music, dance, local studies and many other kinds of work have transformed the face of subject 'English'. And yet most sixth formers, and many students preparing for A level in colleges of further education, are still narrowly confined to the study of a relatively few texts from English literature. This *might* still be right, but it would need very clear justification.

I want to look at some of the viewpoints I hear presented by teachers about what work is needed. Because I teach at a college of education, I do not at present have much to do directly with sixteen- to nineteen-year-olds, though I did work with them for eleven years. What I see from day to day are the nineteen- to twenty-two-year-olds (and over) whom these young people have become. I have some direct evidence to offer from them, but my case rests mainly on what I hear from the sixth form and further education teachers, and the A level examiners, whom I meet at conferences and in the course of my work, or whose arguments I read. But before turning to this, I want to look at the pupils or students we are talking about. To know what they need or would like, we need to know more about them. This is what I think they are like.

They have no clear name. Some adults may choose still to think of them as 'boys and girls', while they themselves often find 'young men and women' a bit pretentious. Those who are still at school are still called pupils, but some are already employees; those who are at colleges are students, while in the age group there will already be some fathers and mothers, many aunts and uncles, and a few with considerable responsibilities for other people of whatever age. They are engaged on some of the most crowded years of their lives. School has ended or will soon end, but before that it can either seem to justify itself in the sixth form as a climax, or tail miserably away and be gladly left behind. Jobs begin; so does college or university – or, for some unlucky ones, a first period of unemployment. They begin travelling on their own, at home or abroad. There are strong loves and strong hates, discovering of oneself and other people. At eighteen, now, comes the vote, to be received either apathetically or with political commitments strong enough to lead to jail or political office or both. Whether we like it or not, many will drink, smoke tobacco or pot, and spend enormously on clothes, entertainment, records, motorcycles, cars. And relationships will change, often alarmingly, with family, with friends, with teachers and institutions, even with the various selves one may seem to oneself at different times to be.

Some teachers who still see their sixteen- to nineteen-year-olds neatly dressed in school uniform and at their sixth-form desks may think this picture of diversity overdrawn. Statistics will not necessarily convince them of its closeness to life, though I mean to quote some figures. But, for instance, Dorothea Brooke is 'under twenty' when she marries Casaubon, Elizabeth-Jane eighteen at the effective opening of *The Mayor of Casterbridge*, Stephen Dedalus in his late teens in much of *Portrait of the Artist as a Young Man*, and Fanny Price is still only eighteen or nineteen even when Edmund finally declares his love for her. The hopes and fears and loves and pains of many of the central figures of the books we read with our students are those of their own age group.

Some figures (taken from the Schools Council's Working Paper 45) may also help to support my insistence on the diversity of this age group. I have had to simplify the statistics a good deal to get them in to this chapter without intolerable length or a resort to tables, but I do not think this entirely vitiates them for most people, and they can be checked in the original publication. Between 1962 and 1970 the number of school pupils in England and Wales in their first year of A level increased from 78,722 to 133,597. The number who got two or more A level passes increased between 1961 and 1968 from 6.5 per cent to 10.5 per cent of the whole age group. In further education colleges, A level candidates increased at a rate of roughly 1,500 a year from 1962 till 1968–9, when the increase was 2,000 and in 1969–70 it was over 2,500. (Of those sixteen- to nineteen-year-olds who are in schools or colleges at present, probably one in four is in a college, not a school.)

Meanwhile, about 12,500 of the pupils who began A level courses in 1968–9 are estimated to have left within the first year without taking any A level exams; about 13,000 failed all their A levels and more than 21,000 passed only one. Together, these add up to around forty per cent of those who embarked on the A level course – although seventy-five per cent were originally aiming for three or more A levels. If we consider these figures along with those (for whom, as far as I know, no figures are available) who are not taking A level in the sixth form at all in the first place, it could reasonably be suggested that over half of a typical sixth form intake find A level not a suitable course for their needs. The drop-out rate for arts subjects is higher than for the sciences, so it may be that the proportion of those doing A level English without its being the course best suited to their needs is actually over a half.

The figures relate to the exam because this is where the counting has been done. But it seems to me that such arid figures, applied to this quantifiable group, still bear out the impressionistic sketch of diversity that I drew earlier, and make absolutely essential a review of our purposes and our principles. I want to look at some of the suggestions now in the air for reforming the work, because that, I think, is all one can do at this stage. What is really needed is a full and honest reappraisal of what we are doing, why we are doing it, whether it is what we should be doing, and, if not, what is. Opportunities are being offered for such a reappraisal at present, by individual schools, by examining boards and by professional bodies. The real reform must come out of these discussions: this chapter has no panacea to offer, only a few reminders of things that should be on their agenda. But, in passing, there seems to have been very little research, so far, into the needs of this age group, or the practice of schools and colleges in providing for it. This may be partly due to the fact that the Schools Council's funds are strictly reserved for schools, whereas the work needs to take into account both schools and colleges of further education. It is important that systematic studies should be made, to give us sounder information, and I hope funds and staff for such projects will be made available soon.

Among teachers, I have found several important attitudes to the basic question. First, there are those who want to keep the study of literature as the sole component of their curriculum. Secondly, there are those who argue the need to study language other than literary, including speech as well as written texts. Thirdly, there are the advocates of drama, both for its own sake and as a method of learning and teaching. Fourthly, there is a large number of teachers who would like to see students' own imaginative or creative writing given a place – perhaps a place of honour – in their work. And, concurrently with all these, the question arises; 'What is the model we offer ourselves and our students for our work?'

It might be as well to take the last question first. At the 1971 York Conference of English teachers from Great Britain, Canada and the United States, the commission concerned with 'English for the Young Adult' reported the need to 'question the applicability of the frequent practice of presenting the specialist as the model for . . . students to emulate'. Where sixth-form teachers in grammar schools have thought they could justifiably assume that most of their pupils would be going on to university to read an English course which was primarily or solely concerned with literary criticism, it has, understandably, been the professional academic literary critic whose approach to literature, whose style and whose manner has been the preferred model. As a result, reports the Canadian periodical, *English Quarterly*, reviewing the York Conference, 'students . . . feel obligated to fulfil what they conceive to be the expectations of the school, the teacher, the examiner; the result is half personal, half formal, often without clear aim, coherence or consistency'. In response to this, Professor Barbara Hardy is quoted, in the same source, as saying, 'Should not the key questions be, "How do you feel? What is happening?" Students are doing so many expected things, they are not exploring the humanity of the story.'

The use of this model may well be already dying a natural death. For most teachers the easiest, perhaps the only, model one can offer a student is the model one builds for oneself. For years many teachers have seen themselves primarily as scholars and critics – on a small scale, perhaps, but scholars, academics, for all that. I think it is perhaps fortunate that fewer teachers now going into the schools choose this model. Today's young English teachers are at least as likely to have thought of themselves as perhaps becoming artists, journalists or social workers, than as becoming scholars. Hence these are the models that they are more likely, perhaps unconsciously, to pass on to their students. And for the majority of the sixteen- to nineteen-year-olds we are concerned with, I think these will be better models, as well as more likely to lead to the sort of questions Barbara Hardy suggests.

This change of interests on the part of teachers may well have something to do with the fact that, when reform of sixth-form curriculum or A level syllabus is being discussed at present, the new component most frequently pressed for seems to be a 'creative writing' component (under whatever name). Yet in spite of at least one attempt to do so – by the Scottish Certificate of Education Board – most people agree that this is not likely to be best done by setting a timed paper with suggested topics. It is more likely to be a matter of offering constant opportunities for this kind of work throughout the course, and collecting a part of what has been done for assessment as course work. The feeling that a place must be found for it in the sixth form and the colleges is very soundly based. Imaginative writing – 'poetic' or 'spectator-role' writing – has become increasingly important in the earlier years of education, from five to fifteen; what sense can there possibly be in suddenly dropping it just at that stage of adolescent self-doubt and self-discovery when it could be most valuable to the writer? Some traditional (and generally, I think, relatively small) schools may think they can afford to do without it in the formal curriculum because school magazines and other voluntary activities provide enough incentive for it to be carried on. But I have seen and heard a good deal about school magazine editors – staff or pupils – scrounging around desperately for material from the very few who are prepared, under pressure, to provide it. This is not good enough. If the practice of looking at the world, especially the world of human emotions and affections, through the relative coolness of words – of organising and contemplating experience through the imposition of form – is of real value to anyone, the opportunity, and even the expectation (though certainly not the compulsion) to try it should be there for everyone. And, as things are, that means it has to be 'on the syllabus', in some form or other.

Drama, I am convinced, is equally important. The case may not be quite as easy to make or as apparently obvious, but there can at any rate be no doubt of young people's own wish to engage in dramatic experiences. Street theatre, the fringe, theatre in education, and the use of dramatic techniques in simulation exercises are all popular, and their value, though it may not yet be fully documented or objectively established, is very highly estimated by many people. The involvement of the whole personality, mind and body, its commitment to a role and its realisation of alternatives through the direct experience offered by drama is immensely enriching and exciting, and again it may well never be more so than for young people in our age group. And drama must involve language; it demands the intuitive, sensitive pursuit of the *right* words in the right tone for effective improvisation, as well as the studied reflection on carefully chosen language needed to realise a playwright's text.

Improvised drama may well be one of the best techniques for introducing the consideration of language which is not literary. To try to take a role very – or even slightly – different from one's own personality is to require an awareness of how other people speak, and how their language interacts with and affects their behaviour. Literature helps with this too, of course, but, as George Steiner writes, 'Literature is language in a condition of special use . . . language freed from a predominant responsibility to information . . . [and] in some degree outside ordinary time'. These very qualities which raise literature in some sense above 'ordinary' language can also disable it as a vehicle for learning that sensitivity to ordinary language – 'transactional' and 'expressive' language – which we all need. This is where the use of the specialist student of literature as a model comes most into question. How much clear evidence there can ever be that years of studying literature necessarily, or even usually, increases a person's sensitivity to the many signs of human thought and emotion conveyed by language every day, I do not know. But my own experience suggests that one can divorce the two considerations all too easily; that one can talk and write fluently and convincingly about Shakespeare and Tolstoy and Yeats and Lawrence, and still be very often an utter fool in one's understanding of and sympathy for the people one meets and talks with and listens to at home or at work or in the street. Material such as the Schools Council's *Language in Use* project – still a pioneer in its field – and especially the degree of success it seems to have had in engaging the attention of students in approved schools and colleges of further education (since A level may well have been instrumental in reducing the opportunities to try it in sixth forms) suggests that the place for the study of non-literary language is at present underestimated.

If any teacher of the first group I referred to, whose faith is firmly placed in the study of literature as quite, or nearly, sufficient a basis for his work, has managed to read as far as this, he might well suppose that now I must intend to make a misguided attempt to pour scorn on his belief. In fact, I do not mean to do so. I do not think that I can or should. The real difficulty, I still think, comes from accepting arguments that have been put forward with reference to English departments at universities, and their uncritical adoption for our – however slightly – younger and very different students. In *Nor Shall My Sword*, F. R. Leavis continues his plea for the existence of the university English (i.e. English literature) school as a collaborative community of students and teachers, and for its place as a 'vital', 'generative' centre in the university, which should itself play the same role in the community at large. At the same time, however, he insists that 'no one should be admitted to read English at any university who isn't of university quality and hasn't a positive bent for literary study'. He is critical of the demand made on the undergraduate, the 'assumption regarding the amount of reading and learning he can reasonably be asked to get done in his two or three years'.

I do not agree with all Leavis's proposals even where university English is concerned. I believe undergraduates too would profit from some attention to the language of everyday life; their study of literature as well as their living would be enriched by it. Leavis himself points out how some of T. S. Eliot's effects 'depend upon his appealing to the reader's sense of how things go naturally in the living spoken language and the speaking voice' – a sense not to be acquired by many years' exclusive attention to literary idioms. But there is sound sense and long experience behind his hope of community, and his insistence on criteria for selection and admission. In sixth forms and further education, we have not the same powers of exclusion and have no right to ask for them. It is, I believe, the case that, even of those who now take A level English *and* go on to college or university, only about ten per cent specialise in English when they get there. Ideally, perhaps, that ten per cent would be those Leavis would admit, and then (or even a little later) they might properly go on to the kind of attention to literature he both recommends and exemplifies. But they must have had a chance to find their 'bent for literary study', and they are not more likely to have done so because they have *had* to study texts exclusively for the previous two or three years. Some opportunity to act and improvise, to write their own poems and stories and plays, to consider how people talk, argue, persuade and aim to mislead, is quite as likely to help them all. Those who do want to go on to university are likely to arrive there fresher, more ready and with more experience in life and language to bring to their reading; those who do not, or who do not choose (or are not chosen) to specialise in literature, will also be less jaded and readier to respond to its worth when they meet it outside the classroom.

Even given a curriculum in which literary studies are largely predominant, there is still the vital question of how they are approached. The academic specialist remains a bad model: pastiche and parody, wide reading as well as detailed study, acting plays as well as writing about them, will not only make the time more enjoyable but will send on a richer individual to whatever work, leisure or study follows school or college. This is where my own students come in briefly. Nothing took me aback more, when I moved from school to college teaching, than the discovery that so many students come on from one to the other with their A levels, but with practically no sense at all that literature is supposed to give pleasure. A first-year student's file I have in front of me at this moment comments – not uncritically – on the work we have done together in the first three or four weeks of the academic year, but says that the writer finds our sessions (involving the writing of some poems, the playing of some games, and wide-ranging discussion as well as critical writing) 'a refreshing change from the rather dogmatic and traditional approach that one experiences at O and A level'. It is not all like that, of course: many teachers who work on these syllabuses give their pupils a full and engaging experience. But it *should* not be like this for *anyone*, and I think greater diversity of study and greater attention to the varying needs of young people should make such a remark a good deal rarer, and the sense of pleasure both more frequent and deeper.

One major problem is by now all too clear. We cannot do everything with everybody. Selection of material there must be, but it should be selection on argued and rational grounds. So far, I believe, there has been a conspiracy to pretend that a consensus exists about what it is proper to teach and learn in English during the ages between sixteen and nineteen, while in fact there is no such consensus, only an increasingly tired and questionable tradition. This fact people are beginning to realize. Now a new trap threatens us. It seems sometimes to be accepted as axiomatic that if the old, unreal consensus must go, another consensus must necessarily replace it. I can think of few worse possibilities than a curriculum which replaced exclusive concern with literature by a rigorous regime of, say, one quarter literature, one quarter 'linguistics' (a word which has very little place in studies of language at this level at all), one quarter drama and one quarter 'creative writing'. Whoever ultimately comes to have the overview of this age group's curricula needs to provide, first, choice, and secondly, a rationale on which the choice can be made. I have suggested some of the elements that need to be included in the range of choice. My suggestions are not intended to be exclusive, though I think all the elements I have mentioned do need to be available. The patterns offered will depend a good deal on the controlling authorities; still more, I hope, on individual schools and colleges. At present, the authorities are the examination boards, with their representation from schools, universities and colleges. In some ways, I think these are good authorities – probably better than any central body such as the Schools Council or the Department of Education and Science, whose capacities should remain advisory. They allow – indeed they often encourage – a fair degree of autonomy in the schools. Their main disadvantage is their preoccupation with assessment, with the quantification of what it is often impossible to reduce fairly or meaningfully to grades and percentages. How best to assess the achievement of an eighteen-year-old in English so that we can say to an interviewer – whether for a place in higher education or for a job – that he is good, bad or indifferent, is a question I have shelved in this chapter, not because I don't think it's important – it is, and will almost certainly remain, vitally important – but because I think it has tended to dominate discussion too long to the exclusion of the consideration of students themselves and their wishes and needs. It might perhaps be possible to have parallel authorities at work, one operating from the necessary standpoint of the assessor, the other from that of the curriculum designer and teacher who suggests what is wanted first (and why), and how to grade it only afterwards. Such bodies should consist of teachers from all levels, but I think students, pupils and non-specialists should have a place there too. If the Boards take increasing responsibility for curriculum, they could well run both bodies, one advisory, one executive (and I have heard of some such experiments being tried); if not, here is a place for the teachers' unions, the students' representative bodies, the Schools Council or the DES to offer facilities I believe we need.

Finally, to revert to my first and most radical suggestion, laid aside (you may have noticed) since paragraph one. Is subject 'English' to continue at this level as a separate entity at all? I think this is a real question, and, as I have said, one which has been given the answer 'no' already in some schools and colleges. The arbitrary nature of the boundaries we draw already makes some important areas of human experience slip through our fingers as educators. Is song literature or music? Who discusses film and television in school? How, above all, is young people's own direct experience of life to be related to their more academic studies? If anyone is dealing with these problems at present, it is individual schools and colleges and their various departments, trying to realise their responsibility, as complex collaborative communities, to the students who make up the majority of their members. Such reconsideration and reconstruction deserves informed and critical support: authority and precedent should not set out to make it difficult. In ten years' time sixteen- to nineteen-year-olds may be experiencing working days quite different from those we know now. Change is the norm, not the exception, in our world; with an attentive eye to the past, we should be able to move more confidently into the future without suffering from either cramp or over-elation.

Further reading

As I have remarked above, this does seem to me to be a neglected field. I know of no recent full-length study of English for students at this age level. However, several writers who cover a wider field give it some attention, including:

J. Britton, *Language and Learning*, Penguin, 1972, especially chap. 6.

F. D. Flower, *Language and Education*, Longman, 1966, especially with reference to further education.

There are many reports and papers about examinations. Most are merely products of the *status quo*, and do not raise fundamental questions, but a recent report which I refer to above is:

Schools Council Working Paper 45, *16–19: Growth and Response, 1, Curricular Bases*, Evans/Methuen Educational, 1972.

On the special place of language study at this level, the following are of interest:

Patricia Creek, 'Language study for the sixth form', *Talking and Writing* (ed.) J. Britton, Methuen, 1967.

J. McH. Sinclair, 'The integration of language and literature in the English curriculum', *The Context of Language*, *Educational Review*, University of Birmingham, 1971.

P. Doughty, J. Pearce and G. Thornton, *Language in Use* (units to be selected by the reader), Edward Arnold, 1971.

Notes on Contributors

Notes on Contributors

G. C. Allen is Professor of Education at the University of Sussex. He studied English at Oxford and was subsequently at Hamburg, and in the USA with a Harkness Fellowship. He has previously been an HMI (Staff Inspector in English) and, for a period in the 1950s, Cultural Advisor in Germany.

Roger K. Applebee is Associate Professor of English at the College of Liberal Arts and Sciences, University of Illinois. From 1963–6 he was Associate Director of the National Study of High School English Programs (USA) and in 1967 co-directed a parallel study of secondary school programmes in the United Kingdom with Professor James R. Squire. He was for eleven years a secondary teacher of English in Rochester, New York.

W. H. Auden, as well as having held various university appointments in England and America including the Chair of Poetry at Oxford, has also taught in schools. From 1930–2 he was at Larchfield Academy, Helensburgh, Scotland, and from 1932–5 at the Downs School near Malvern. The last book of his poetry to be published was *Epistle to a Godson*.

Nicholas Bagnall is education correspondent of the *Sunday Telegraph*. He was formerly editor of the *Teacher*.

Myra Barrs has taught for ten years in schools and further education and is now Head of English at a comprehensive school in Kilburn. She has edited a volume, *Identity*, in the third stage of the Penguin English Project.

Edward Blishen taught for fifteen years, ten of them in an Islington secondary modern school. He is the author of *Roaring Boys* and *This Right Soft Lot* and now works as a freelance writer, broadcaster and lecturer.

Garth Boomer taught for six years in secondary schools in South Australia and then served as consultant in English from 1968 to 1971. He is now lecturer at the Raywood Residential In-Service Education Centre and for the academic year 1972–3 was given study leave to the University of London Institute of Education. His publications include *Themes and Images*, *Sandals in One Hand*, and *The Runaway Sun*.

James Britton is Goldsmiths' Professor of Education in the University of London. From 1971 to 1973 he was Chairman of the National Association for the Teaching of English and has also been Director of the Schools Council Research Project on the Development of Writing Abilities, 11 to 18, and distinguished Lecturer for the National Council of Teachers of English (USA). His publications include *Language, the learner and the school* (with Barnes and Rosen) and *Language and Learning*.

Anthony Burgess taught English in secondary schools for six years and was subsequently a Research Officer for the Schools Council Project on 'the Development of Writing Abilities 11 to 18'. He is at present a lecturer in the English Department of the London Institute of Education.

Emrys Evans has taught English to secondary school pupils in Gloucester, London and New York. Since 1966 he has been a member of the English Department at Coventry College of Education. He is Council and Executive member of the National Association for the Teaching of English and a member of the Schools Council English subject committee.

Su Felton was born in 1955 and is at present at a comprehensive school where she is studying for her A levels with English literature as her main interest.

Noël Hardy was Head of English and Drama at Sir Philip Magnus School, Kings Cross, London, until he came to the Inner London Education Authority Television Centre where he is now directing a humanities series. He was a contributor to Commission 2 at the York International Conference on Teaching and Learning English in 1971. He has edited *The Modern Experience* to be published in the Penguin English Project.

Lewis Stedman Jones is at present researching programmes for Educational Television. He was formerly Head of the English Department and also Deputy Headmaster of Holland Park School.

Andrew Macalpine is Head of the English Department at Thomas Calton School in Peckham, South London. He was previously Head of the Department for English as a second language at a boys' secondary school in Camden Town and before that was in educational publishing. He has written a number of articles for *The Times Educational Supplement*, mostly on English as a second language.

Michael Marland is Headmaster of Woodberry Down Comprehensive School in North London. He is on the committee of the York/

Nuffield enquiry into the preparation of teachers for working with socially deprived children, the Independent Television Authority's Schools' Committee and the Bullock Committee on the Teaching of Reading and the Uses of English. He is the author of a number of books including *Head of Department* and *Pastoral Care*.

John Mole is a poet whose work has appeared in a number of periodicals as well as on the BBC. A collection of his poems, *The Love Horse*, was published in 1973. He has taught at the Haberdashers' Aske's School, Elstree and is now head of the English Department at St. Albans Grammar School.

W. A. Murray is Professor of English and Head of Department in the University of Lancaster. He has also been a lecturer in English in the University of Sheffield and Professor of English in the University of Khartoum.

Albert Rowe has taught in a variety of schools and in a college of education. He resigned as Head of David Lister Comprehensive School to write full time. He broadcasts and lectures extensively in Britain and overseas, and contributes regularly to educational journals. He is the author of *The Education of the Average Child* and *The School as a Guidance Community*, co-author of *English Through Experience* and compiler of *Active Anthologies*.

Frank Whitehead is Reader in English and Education at the University of Sheffield. He is also Editor of *The Use of English* and Director of the Schools Council Programme of Research into Children's Reading Habits. He is a former chairman of the National Association for the Teaching of English and was Associated Director of the Dartmouth Seminar in 1966, an Anglo-American seminar on the teaching of English. His books include *The Disappearing Dais: A Study of the Principles and Practice of English Teaching* and *Creative Experiment: Writing and the Teacher*.

Ken Worpole left school at sixteen and went into the civil engineering industry for four years before deciding to become a teacher. He now teaches in the English Department at Hackney Downs School, a boys' comprehensive school in East London.